THE FABULOUS FIOR

OVER 100 YEARS IN AN ITALIAN KITCHEN

The History of San Francisco's Fior d'Italia
America's Oldest Italian Restaurant,
Established 1886

THE FABULOUS FIOR
Over 100 Years in Italian Kitchen

by Francine Brevetti

Copyright © 2004 by
San Francisco Bay Books
13966 Beitler Road
Nevada City, CA 95959

www.fabulousfior.com

ISBN 0-9753351-0-3
Printed in South Korea

To my mother Tecla Brevetti,

my grandparents,
Alberto Puccetti,
who worked at the Fior d'Italia over 100 years ago,
and his wife, Gemma Lenci Puccetti

and Chef Gianfranco Audieri

TABLE OF CONTENTS

The Fior d'Italia is in the heart of the Italian district of San Francisco and I should not hesitate to say that it is more Italian than Alfredo's in Rome. But it is also as authentically San Franciscan and American as the Crocker National Bank. The men who gave it its character will soon be gone – most of them have already gone. In another fifty years its patrons – the Pardinis, the Grazinis, the Martinis, the Gianninis – will be five and six generations removed from the immigrants who first ate there. Men as immigrants will have long since passed away from North Beach. But not their sons and daughters nor *minestrone* nor *vino da pasto* nor *scaloppine*. These will endure as an added grace to the America of tomorrow – these and something of the matrix whence they derive: the magnificent sanity and durability of the Italian people and their will to live and bear life's burdens gracefully.

Americans by Choice
Angelo M. Pellegrini, 1956

Foreword

I've been writing crime novels set in San Francisco now for the better part of two decades, and in that time many of the bar/restaurant venues in the City have nearly taken on the roles of living characters. John's Grill on Ellis, The Little Shamrock at 9th and Lincoln, and my own fictional Lou the Greek's on the very real Bryant Street all seek to capture some elements of the City's personality and spirit, and hopefully help to infuse the books with a sensibility that is unique to San Francisco. But when I sat down to write *Guilt*, I felt that I needed to set my opening scene at a restaurant that all by itself encapsulated not just a few elements, but so much of the City's *essence* that its mention alone would conjure up for my readers an immediate identification with San Francisco. There was no question that only one restaurant in this town of great restaurants could fit this bill -- the Fior d'Italia.

Let's start with the location. Or location, location, location as the real estate folks would have it. Could there be a more felicitous spot in the City for a great restaurant? You're in North Beach, after all, and the smell of roasting coffee beans infuses the air. Washington Square, with its *tai chi* classes and frisbee games, is just across the street, beneath the twin towers and Sts. Peter and Paul Church. You're sitting at the bar of the Fior d'Italia, maybe sipping a negroni, an early afternoon martini, or a perfect espresso. Outside there's a light breeze and the sun is shining and in five minutes you'll be ordering veal or calamari from a waiter who's been here forever and knows exactly what he's doing. When the food arrives, you may be surprised at how beautifully it's prepared, how flawlessly it's served, how delicious it tastes. After all, the Fior has been here for over a century; it's the oldest Italian restaurant in the country. It's a tourist place, right?

Well, yes and no. Tourists come here, to be sure, and who can blame them? But it wouldn't be a destination for long if it didn't deliver the goods, the goods in this case being authentic, carefully-prepared, fantastic tasting Italian food. A restaurant can boast of all the tradition in the world, but in the Mecca of *haute cuisine* that is San Francisco today, if the kitchen doesn't hold up its end of the quality spectrum, nobody's going to go there to eat. But look around you. The Fior d'Italia is packed today. It's packed every day. Why? Because it's a great place with terrific food. That's what it's always been, and what it remains today.

I've been eating regularly at the Fior since my very first trip to San Francisco. It's where my dad took me for the first dinner I ever ate out in the City. Back in the late 1960s, when I was a student at the University of San Francisco and later at the University of California, Berkeley, for me it became the ultimate place for a super-fancy dinner date. Although the waiters were never anything but perfectly professional, I remember as a college student being a little terrified by the gentlemen in tuxedoes, the Italian language all over the menu, the simple sophistication of the adult dining experience. I didn't suspect back then that one day the formal, traditional, somewhat intimidating Fior d'Italia of my youth would become a comfort spot for me and my friends, that thiry-five years or so after my first dining experience here, I would reserve the Tony Bennett room for my fiftieth birthday party.

The restaurant didn't change. I did. But through all the ages of my life, the Fior d'Italia has retained its ambience, its glamour, and its magic. That's why I feel so privileged to be a small part of *The Fabulous Fior – Over 100 Years In An Italian Kitchen*. This is a wonderful book with a great story to tell. Sit down with it and enjoy a well-told tale of one of the City's true treasures. Then sit back, order another glass of Pinot Grigio, and raise a glass to the next hundred years of San Francisco's premier Italian restaurant, the Fior d'Italia.

John T. Lescroart

Introduction

At Oakland, California's train station in the mid-19th century, frightened Italian immigrants jump tentatively from the boxcars that had carried them from the East Coast after they made the cruel passage across the Atlantic. Nervously, their eyes dart about for any loved ones who have come to meet them. There are many arriving for whom no one waits. They all seek an end to poverty.

Meanwhile in San Francisco, more weathered groups of Italians alight from large sailing ships from South America. These men had already sought their fortunes in Argentina, Brazil, Colombia and Peru. Disappointed or intrigued by the possibility of further success, they now turn their sights on North America and California's goldmines. Or, if they've given up on quick riches, they look to California's kitchens.

The opportunity to take on the story of Italian immigrants to San Francisco and the cooking they brought with them was too compelling for me to resist. Since I am the descendant – on both sides of my family – of Italians and a native of San Francisco, when the owners of the Fior d'Italia told me they wanted the restaurant's history told, the path for me was clear.

I'd grown up hearing the travails of immigrants making the journey across the ocean and the continent. My maternal grandmother was one of the lucky ones who had relatives waiting for her at the train station. My maternal grandfather, on the other hand, was among those Italians who alit at the Port of San Francisco from after a stint of several years in Sao Paulo. They were both natives of Lucca in Tuscany.

The same maternal grandfather, Alberto Puccetti, was a waiter and part-owner of the Fior 100 years ago. He served Enrico Caruso, April 17, 1906 – the night before the big quake when Caruso fled the city, vowing never to return. *Nonno* stands in his tux with six other Fior waiters and the founder, Angelo Del Monte, in a photograph near the restaurant's entrance.

While our connection to the Fior ended when he sold his interest, the memory of his association with it lives on in my family.

In the late 19th century and the early 20th century, the Fior d'Italia was a beacon of elegance in a rough-and-tumble time in the city's history. It was a meeting place of the literati and artists. It attracted European dignitaries including Guglielmo Marconi, Enrico Caruso, and American celebrities, such as Rudolf Valentino and Mary Pickford, to name a few.

So what journalist wouldn't jump at the chance? Especially one whose grandfather's mustachioed image hangs near the front door.

The result is an inside view of the families who headed the Fior for its first century and how they met the passing decades. But this is more than an en famille account. My working title for the manuscript was "The World through Our Kitchen." This was important to me as a guide because I wanted to convey the flux of history as it stole through the restaurant and as it stained the lives of those connected with it.

The oldest continuously running Italian restaurant in the United States, San Francisco's Ristorante Fior d'Italia survived the Great Fire and Earthquake of 1906, Prohibition and the Great Depression. It has maintained its character despite the Beat Generation, which bloomed around it, and the gentrification of North Beach. It still draws illustrious patrons, such as Joe Montana, Luciano Pavarotti and Tommy Lasorda. The restaurant has recently attracted a great deal of attention for challenge to the Internal Revenue Service in that U.S. Supreme Court on the calculation of gratuities. The story that follows traces the restaurant and its owners through the permutations of time, politics, economic difficulties, failures and successes.

F.B.

September 2004

Acknowledgements

This offering is the product of the love of many people. Every person quoted in this book and many who were not cited were committed to seeing this tale told.

This history could not have been written without the vision and support of Bob and Jinx Larive, the Fior's principal owners. It just wouldn't have happened without them. They cheered me on when I despaired of ever finishing this project.

"Remember when you thought you'd finish this in a year or so?" Bob still likes to tease me.

Special thanks to the relatives of the Fior's founders who recreated their parents' and grandparents' stories for me. Who patiently corrected me, added detail and clarification without reservation. These are the family of Angelo Del Monte, especially his granddaughters, Janette Biagini Barrocca and Mary Del Monte Nowicki.

Among the Marianetti family, Paul Mantee who shared family history with brio, generosity and affection, painting a world I could never have touched without him. And Rick Marianetti for his understanding of the workings of the restaurant at a time when the old world was receding.

Andrew Canepa, whose scholarly mind and personal library put resources my way I could never have discovered.

Tom Vano, who has devotedly taken the photographs of the Fior d'Italia for 50 years and preserved them for this book.

Chef Gianni Audieri, who suffered several interviews sabotaged by a faulty tape recorder, only to repeat them without complaint. Whose knowledge of Italian cuisine and whose consummate skills in the kitchen gave the food portion of this book richness that rivals his exquisite sauces.

Each member of the staff of the Fior d'Italia was generous in sharing his and her time, stories and passion for the restaurant. They always welcomed me as a friend.

Thanks also to my editor, Linda S. Kleinschmidt, and book designer Milan Hájek, whose exacting standards kept me on my toes and who were committed to creating a worthy testimonial.

To Tina Salter for her immense knowledge of cuisine and for her skill in testing the recipes.

To Bonnie Engel for proofreading, for moral support and holding my hand during the final edit of the book.

And never least, to Tecla Brevetti, my mother, whose recollections of North Beach's early life and her father's work at the Fior, brought a palpable life and humor no one else could have supplied.

Without the work of the worthy Peter Anderson and Dianne Levy, the input of Frank Marianetti would have been lost. They recorded Frank's detailed and fearless recollections, making the modern era of the restaurant comprehensible, making it breathe.

How does one thank the deceased?

Rose Scherini, who added her considerable scholarship about the internment of Italian-Americans during World War II.

Victorine Alibertini, who depicted the color, energy and contributions of visiting European performers among the Fior's clientele before World War II.

And waiter Rudy Velarde, whose bouncy good will and happiness in contributing to this manuscript make it doubly sad that he cannot share in reading it.

CHAPTER I: The Gold Rush to 1900

On the walls of Ristorante Fior d'Italia in San Francisco's North Beach hangs a pen and ink caricature – humorous yet dignified – of a gentleman sporting a huge handlebar moustache under a slick pate. He wields a fork around which a springy clump of spaghetti is coiled.

The cartoon depicts Angelo Del Monte, born in 1861, and the founder of the oldest, continuously operating Italian restaurant in the United States, the Fior d'Italia, the flower of Italy.

A culinary institution in San Francisco, the Fior d'Italia carries inside its doors the history of Italian cuisine, Italian immigrants and their lives in North Beach to the present day. While Del Monte opened the doors of the restaurant in 1886, the establishment's origins really must be considered to have started from a much earlier date --1848 -- with the discovery of gold at Sutter's Mill in Coloma, California on the banks of the American Fork River.

That singular event would change America, Europe and Asia. The Gold Rush would spur the greatest voluntary migration the world had ever known. Perhaps no other historical event had a stronger impact on the State of California. Without the Gold Rush, San Francisco might have grown quite modestly as a port but might never have seen its full potential. Without gold, there may have been no Fior.

Between 1849 – the first year that lured humanity to California's hills -- and a mere three years later when the tumult slackened -- the population of California rocketed to 220,000 from 90,000.

Quite coincidentally (one must always wonder about "coincidences"), the year gold was discovered in California marked a turning point in decades of war on the Italian peninsula. At this moment in time, Italian patriots were trying to unify Italy and claim it back after decades of dismemberment under the rule of the French and the Austrians. In 1848, the same year thousands were flocking to California looking for wealth, Giuseppe Mazzini established a republic, an event that eventually united the Italian city-states into a single nation.

The years of strife that Italy had endured since the Napoleonic wars had ravaged and impoverished the peasantry who were scraping out desperate existences as sharecroppers. Their plight was pitiful enough to spur them to leave their beloved *Italia*. By the early 1850s, the news of gold's discovery in North America penetrated even the remotest villages of Europe.

"They had been told that for the price of passage to California, a man could pick out gold from the crevices of rocks with only his bare

The original pen & ink caricature of Angelo Del Monte from 1912

hands and his knife," wrote Dr. Deanna Paoli Gumina in *The Italians of San Francisco 1850-1930.* [1]

Little wonder that Italian men were among the multitudes that risked their lives in a pell-mell, headlong dash for the ore, braving oceans, wilderness and alienation from their families and homes to seek a better life.

Gold in California was the "pull" for these immigrants. But their poverty at home was the "push" that motivated them even more.

In the late 1880s, "A man could work a 12-hour day in the quarries in the Bay Area and make $1.25; in Italy he would only earn 25 cents for the same labor. So most of the peasants who emigrated did so to make enough money to return to Italy, buy land and live well." [2]

When they arrived, many felt that the climate and geography of California – its blue waters and the deep gashes of the Coastal Mountains -- reminded them of home. Some even called the state, "our Italy." No wonder North Beach eventually became known as "Little Italy."

However, few immigrants stayed in the gold fields where life was brutal and success infrequent. Many reverted to the life they knew best, taking up fishing, crafts and small retail businesses. The vastness and fertility of the soil in the surrounding areas were also a draw for immigrants who took up agriculture.

Into this historical picture appeared nineteen-year old Angelo Del Monte. He was from the Province of Liguria whose major city is the port of Genoa. Angelo was born in 1861 in the seaside town of Le-

vanto. When he was about ten, his family moved to another Riviera city, La Spezia. Here he spent his childhood helping his father who ran a boarding house for the workers of Genoa's shipyards.

In 1869, when Angelo was a tot of eight, the Transcontinental Railway was being completed. The connection of the Central Pacific to the Union Pacific Railways reduced the four-month trek from sea to sea to six days -- far away in America. Angelo could not know then that this very event would eventually help him get his start in a new country.

We know little of Angelo's state of mind when he left at nineteen, barely a man. But we do know that his brothers, Francesco, Giacomo and Ferdinando had already left the old country and settled in the Bay Area. A family-held account of Angelo's life reads: "He left Italy on the *Rubattino* of the Florio Rubattino Line on August 6, 1880. After 17 days of rough, stormy weather, he disembarked in Boston."

These notes do not explain why the Italian consul in that city took an interest in the immigrants on that vessel and saw that they were housed – although miserably so – in a barn. The consul also arranged for their transcontinental passage in hay-strewn boxcars that arrived a week later in California.

Angelo headed north to Calaveras County to try his luck prospecting for gold. Like countless others, he intended to make his fortune by mining. But soon he found the life of the camps intolerable enough to abandon his goal.

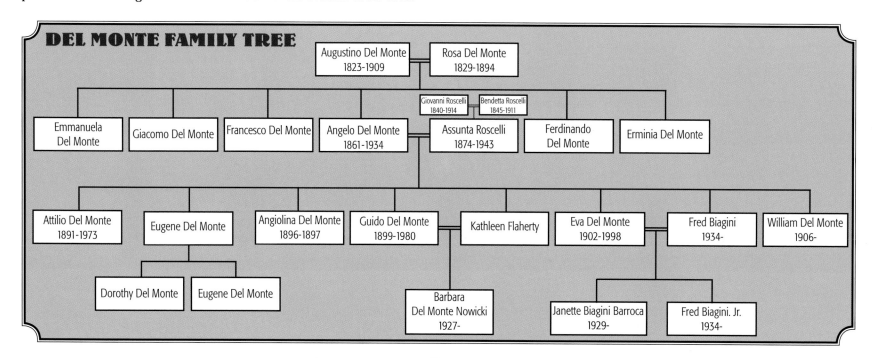

DEL MONTE FAMILY TREE

Augustino Del Monte 1823-1909 — Rosa Del Monte 1829-1894

Emmanuela Del Monte | Giacomo Del Monte | Francesco Del Monte | Angelo Del Monte 1861-1934 — Assunta Roscelli 1874-1943 | Ferdinando Del Monte | Erminia Del Monte

Giovanni Roscelli 1840-1914 — Bendetta Roscelli 1845-1911

Attilio Del Monte 1891-1973 | Eugene Del Monte | Angiolina Del Monte 1896-1897 | Guido Del Monte 1899-1980 — Kathleen Flaherty | Eva Del Monte 1902-1998 — Fred Biagini 1934- | William Del Monte 1906-

Dorothy Del Monte | Eugene Del Monte

Barbara Del Monte Nowicki 1927-

Janette Biagini Barroca 1929- | Fred Biagini. Jr. 1934-

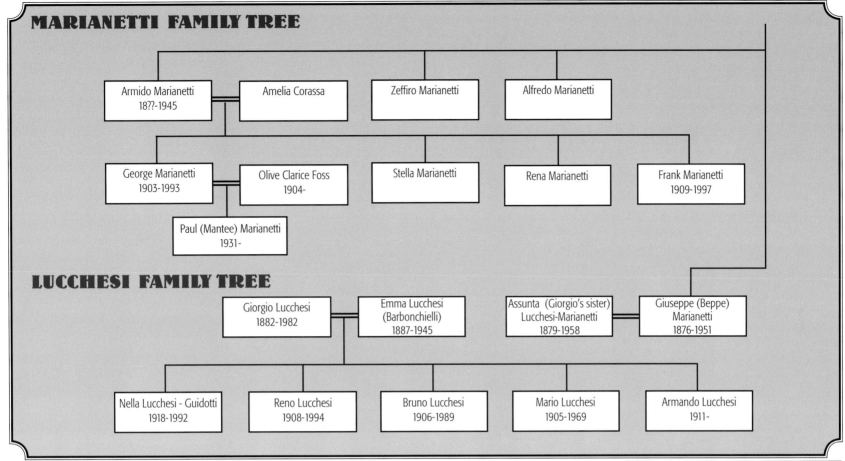

MARIANETTI FAMILY TREE

| Armido Marianetti 18??-1945 | Amelia Corassa | Zeffiro Marianetti | Alfredo Marianetti |

| George Marianetti 1903-1993 | Olive Clarice Foss 1904- | Stella Marianetti | Rena Marianetti | Frank Marianetti 1909-1997 |

Paul (Mantee) Marianetti 1931-

LUCCHESI FAMILY TREE

| Giorgio Lucchesi 1882-1982 | Emma Lucchesi (Barbonchielli) 1887-1945 | Assunta (Giorgio's sister) Lucchesi-Marianetti 1879-1958 | Giuseppe (Beppe) Marianetti 1876-1951 |

| Nella Lucchesi - Guidotti 1918-1992 | Reno Lucchesi 1908-1994 | Bruno Lucchesi 1906-1989 | Mario Lucchesi 1905-1969 | Armando Lucchesi 1911- |

It wasn't long before he landed back in San Francisco, where he worked as a busboy at a restaurant named Bazzurro's for $1.50 a day. He went on to become a waiter and a bartender.

Obviously enterprising, Angelo succeeded in amassing some capital and he left Bazzurro's after five years of employment there. The following year, in 1886, he purchased his own modest eatery at the age of twenty-five.

It was not uncommon among Italian immigrants of that era to desert the gold fields and resume a trade in San Francisco and its environs they knew from the old country. Angelo Del Monte was one who made good with this fall-back strategy. Although he had left the gold camps in disgust, he learned something there that he put to use in San Francisco.

According to his granddaughter, Janette Biagini Barroca, Angelo saw that miners and fortune hunters in the camps were paying exorbitant prices for food. He also noticed that when they came to San Francisco for supplies they spent a lot of money on the luxuries and commodities they could not enjoy in the gold fields. He realized that "people wanted good food at reasonable prices," Barroca said. Having been raised in an Italian boarding house, he also had first-hand experience of what it took to satisfy the working class appetite and the palate of his countrymen.

The restaurant's original site was 432 Broadway but a photograph was later mistakenly altered to read 492.

go to the wholesale market before 8 A.M. and choose the best fruits and vegetables. A box of peaches was 75 cents and a box of tomatoes, 35 cents.

Angelo wasn't the chef himself. Rather, he depended on the skill of cooks and waiters he hired to carry his business's reputation. Tradition has it that he often found himself trying to mediate and smooth over frequent disputes among the cooks and waiters. One night the restaurant was full and the cooks in the kitchen were having a row. It escalated. Somebody threw a meat cleaver and the staff stormed out.

"Those who stayed with the businesses of feeding, housing, and supplying miners with goods often fared far better than the dreamers," Dianne Levy, a San Francisco writer and historian observed.

The restaurant Angelo acquired was originally a Mexican one at 432 Broadway. It served, among other customers, a bordello upstairs. This much is sure. What is disputed was its name. It was either the Flor de Mexico or Cinco de Mayo. Whichever the true name was, Angelo changed it to Fior d'Italia, the flower of Italy, and he enjoyed a brisk trade quite early.

According to family accounts, cooking was done on a coal stove and coal was reasonable at $7 a ton. Vegetables came into town from the Colma area on horse-drawn trucks, so anything picked at sundown came to market nice and fresh the next morning. Angelo would

Angelo, left with a restaurant full of people, went home (conveniently around the corner) and got his wife Assunta to come down and take control of the kitchen and cook the orders.

"My father told (the waiters) he couldn't cook but he promised he'd handle the money part. He told them if they stopped arguing and fighting, he'd make them all (nine) equal partners. And he did," said his daughter Eva Del Monte Biagini.

A certificate shows the transfer of 10 shares to an A. Vannucci in 1910, based on the restaurant's $9,000 in capital or 180 shares at $50 each. Making his staff partners promoted harmony but it also gave each partner the support he needed to become independent eventually. Angelo's eldest son, Attilio (b. 1891), eventually branched out on his own. Among the Fior contingent that later moved on to start their own restaurants in the Bay Area were names such as Lucchesi,

Lippi, Campaglia, Puccetti and Quattrin that were to remain in the San Francisco restaurant trade for decades.

While Angelo was striving to carve a life out for himself in San Francisco, two other very personal dramas were unfolding that would affect him and the Fior profoundly.

The Roscellis

In the mid-1870s, Giovanni Roscelli, also from Liguria, had left behind his wife Benedetta and their infant daughter Assunta (b. 1874) to try the new country. He planned to work until he could afford their passage and then send for them.

We don't know his trade, but we do know that he earned a meager sum even for that era. It wasn't until baby Assunta had grown to six or seven that he managed to save the $1,000 necessary to send two steamer tickets back to Benedetta.

"He was just getting ready to buy the tickets to send for his wife and child when the bank where he kept his money went under and he lost the $1,000," recounted Barroca, Angelo's granddaughter.

So Giovanni was forced to start his arduous task all over again. By the time Giovanni recouped his loss and sent for his family again, his daughter had passed her eleventh birthday. Although it had been well over 10 years since he'd seen his wife, they went on to have a second family with the eventual arrival of Frank (b. 1887-88?) and Mary (b. 1891).

"That has to be the greatest love story of all," Barroca remarked about their apparently harmonious reunion after so many years apart.

The daughter Assunta grew up in North Beach. She passed the Fior frequently in her daily travel and routine. Angelo, already proprietor of the restaurant, would see her walking down Broadway. According to family tradition, he fell in love with her before they were introduced. In 1890, when Assunta was sixteen, they married. She had her first child in July of 1891, six months after her mother had borne her third child, Mary.

In 1893, the first building that housed the Fior – the home of the original Mexican restaurant that had served the brothel upstairs -- burned down. We know nothing of how this event affected the Del Monte family or the restaurant's clientele and reputation. By the time it reopened across the street the same year, Angelo's brother, Giacomo, and his father-inlaw, Assunta's father, Giovanni Roscelli, had become partners with him.

The Marianettis

Another family's fortunes, also churning in fate's maelstrom, would soon intersect with the story of the Fior. In 1896, Angelo Del Monte took in another part-owner, Armido Marianetti. He hailed from Maggiano, a village between Lucca and Viareggio in Tuscany. Armido would become central to the Fior years down the road but his story started in Tuscany long before he met Angelo.

The Marianettis of Maggiano were barely surviving on their 50-acre farm raising cattle, poultry and vegetables. Armido's brothers Zeffiro (nicknamed in America "Cook-oh" for cook), Alfredo and Beppe (for Giuseppe) immigrated to San Francisco. Zeffiro (or Cook-oh) came in 1894 and landed a job at Lucchetti's restaurant where he prospered and eventually became a partner. Three years later he sent for Armido who was now fourteen but had never been out of his village.

Unlike Del Monte, who arrived before the immigration processing center was erected at Ellis Island and long before the Statue of Liberty was erected in 1886, Armido would have experienced both. He would have been one of the masses to queue at Ellis Island for permission to enter the country as well as one of those exhilarated by the sight of the great lady holding her torch.

Armido's son, Frank Marianetti, later recounted, "He had very little money so he went steerage from Lucca to France to take the ship to come to America. One of the greatest visions in his life was seeing the Statue of Liberty. He had tremendous feelings about America. People could go to school, learn to read and write, and make enough money in a week that took a month to make in Italy."

A. Vannucci, an employee, acquired 10 shares in the restaurant. Making employees part-owners was a means the founder established to keep peace among the staff.

He worked the first month without pay because he was on trial. He never forgot that he worked the whole month for no money. After that, he sent money back regularly to his family in Italy.

He was very ambitious and very smart, even with no schooling. He did his job very well because he liked working in the kitchen. He was one hell of a cook. He made ravioli by hand. He'd roll out the pasta, paper-thin and had a great table he worked on using a huge rolling pin. He became expert at rolling out the pasta and making the filling....That was only one of his jobs at Lucchetti's.

After passing through Ellis Island, speaking not one word of English, Armido boarded a train headed west.

"His brother was supposed to meet him when he got there, but there was a mix-up...so nobody was here to meet him. My father was stuck in the station alone. He fell asleep in the doorway, practically penniless and hungry. He had only a loaf of bread on the train for the whole trip," Frank recounted.

Finally, the older brothers arrived at the train station and spotted him "asleep in the doorway, a ninety-pound, skinny kid from Italy." They greeted each other with joy and tears. Thanks to Cook-oh's connection, the thin little newcomer took a job as a dishwasher at Lucchetti's, where they provided him with room and board. Frank described the scene:

Fifteen dollars a month was the pay with no days off. Seven days a week, every week. It was in the produce section of San Francisco. Early arrivals came for breakfast at five in the morning. The restaurant served until ten at night. My father ate well, which was a big thing, because he was practically starving and he worked hard.

Armido's talent with food was finally recognized, and he joined the Fior in 1890. Again from Frank: "Angelo (Del Monte) ran into my father at Lucchetti's, and he liked what he saw, so he offered my father a better job. "Come with me, Mario (Armido's nickname)," he told him, "and you get a day off." That was a big thing. My father didn't have a day off in three years. "And if you're as good as I think," Angelo said, "I'll make you a partner." He'd get a cut of whatever profit there was. A very good set-up. At one time, there were ten other partners as well."

Eventually all four Marianetti brothers came to work at the Fior with Alfredo becoming a cook. As many new immigrants who were coming from Italy, Zeffiro-Cook-oh, Alfredo, Armido and Beppe (Giuseppe) settled across the bay in Elmhurst, where they raised many of the fruits and vegetables served at the Fior. Armido's grandson, Paul Mantee recollected that Beppe would come to the restaurant in the morning driving a cart carrying the produce from his garden. By 1903, Armido Marianetti had become a full partner with Del Monte.

In 1893, there was a fire. We don't know if it destroyed only 432 Broadway or whether there was much wider damage. But the annals of San Francisco reveal that historians logged fires and earthquakes of some magnitude repeatedly throughout the 18th and 19th centuries.

The restaurant moved to 492 Broadway, near the northeast corner of Broadway and Kearney, where it was to stay for three decades. On the walls of the Fior hangs the photograph of the inside of the entrance of this building. Several staffers lined up by the bar stand before the storefront window with the name showing backwards: FIOR D'ITALIA.

The Fior's entrance from the inside looking out.

SCALOPPINE DI VITELLO (VEAL SCALOPPINE)

Using the veal loin, cut three slices of 4 ounces each per person. Cut across the grain so the muscle won't shrink or curl. This should be a generous $\frac{1}{4}$ inch thick slice, pounded to just under a $\frac{1}{4}$ inch thick.

3 tablespoons clarified butter (see page 76)

12 slices veal scaloppine (about 1 pound), pounded just under $\frac{1}{4}$ inch thick

Salt and freshly ground black pepper

All-purpose flour, for dusting

1 shallot, minced

6 ounces cremini mushrooms, thinly sliced

3/4 cup Marsala

1/2 cup chicken stock

1 tablespoon unsalted butter

Chopped fresh flat-leaf parsley, for garnish

Preheat the oven to 200 °F.

In a large sauté pan, heat 2 tablespoons of the clarified butter over medium-high heat. Season the veal generously with salt and pepper. Dust lightly with flour and shake gently to remove any excess. Arrange in a single layer in the hot pan and cook until lightly browned, about 2 minutes per side. Don't overcook! Transfer to a serving plate and keep warm in the low oven.

In the same pan, add the remaining 1 tablespoon clarified butter and the shallot and cook over medium-high heat until translucent, about 2 minutes. Add the mushrooms and cook until the liquid they release has evaporated. Add the Marsala and cook 2 minutes. Add the stock and season to taste with salt and pepper. Cook until slightly thickened, about 2 minutes. Add the unsalted butter and whisk until melted. Return the veal and any accumulated juices to the pan and baste with the sauce.

To serve: Arrange 3 slices of the veal on each of 4 warmed serving plates. Spoon the sauce over the veal, garnish with the parsley, and serve immediately.

Serves four

CHAPTER 2: The Fior Presents Its Cuisine

Most Italian immigrants to northern California in this era came from Liguria (Genoa's province), Tuscany (especially Lucca) and Sicily.

Initially, those who settled in the city congregated on Telegraph Hill, where the terrain reminded many of home and the rents were cheapest. As they became more numerous, the immigrants fanned out to the foothills of North Beach. The Latin Quarter, a neighborhood whose population overlapped that of North Beach, was composed mostly of French, Basque, Spanish, Mexicans, Portuguese and Italian immigrants. They also settled as often as possible near relatives and their neighbors from their villages back home and married among them as well. This tendency to reside among their own people preserved local traditions, dialects and cuisine and kept them distinct for some time.

As we've noted, Angelo Del Monte was from Liguria, and he would be called *genovese* (Genoese) among his fellow Italians after the foremost city of the province. Many of his partners were also Genoese but others were Tuscans like the Marianettis. The restaurant's fare was based on the cuisine of these two areas of northern Italy.

Most people who have no Italian heritage think of Italian food as pasta and pizza. In fact, pizza is a Neapolitan creation that until recently was unknown in northern Italy. It was certainly unknown to the founders of the Fior and no doubt their patrons as well. Pasta indeed appears throughout Italy, but its presentation and its sauces vary from region to region.

These distinctions among regions matter deeply to Italians. Each one's local cuisine is as sacred as his regional dialect. Before "Italian cooking" became homogenized in this country by its introduction to American mass culture, there was really no such thing as "Italian" cooking. There were rather Piemontese, Milanese, Tuscan, Bolognese, Neopolitan and Sicilian cuisines, among many others.

These cuisines differ markedly. For instance, while rice, spinach and veal are very prominent in northern Italy, these ingredients are not used in the dishes of southern Italy. Southern Italians were more likely to eat pork, that is, those who had meat to eat at all. And the southern provinces use olive oil while northerners prefer butter. As Gumina, an expert in Italian-American heritage, explained:

For decades the Italian diet was regarded as an amalgam of ethnic dishes basically consisting of pizza, macaroni and plates of spaghetti seasoned with a heavy red sauce when actually these

---

MAY 1, 1886

Fior d'Italia
RESTAURANT
SAN FRANCISCO

MENU

Veal Saute	.05	Tenderloin Steak	.30
Calfs Brains	.05	Veal Cutlets	.10
Risotto with Clams	.10	Porterhouse Steak for 2	.60
Veal Scaloppine	.15	Chicken Broiled	.20
Calfs Liver	.15	Chicken Saute	.25
Fritto Misto	.20	Squab Casserole	.40
Frog Legs	.40	Tortellini Bologna	.05

Special Dinner with Wine   35¢

NOTICE
Any inattention or overcharge please report to Manager.

The Original 1886 Menu

are the regional dishes of Naples that Americans associated with the whole of the Italian peninsula. Unless one was well-traveled or a gourmet, there was little regard for provincial distinctions (such) as foods cooked in butter, or the egg-enriched, flat, limp pastas (like) ravioli, lasagne and tagliatelle characteristic of the northern provinces.

The menus of the northern Italian craftsmen who founded the Fior reflected their origins. The earliest menu, dated on the day the restaurant opened its doors, May 1, 1886, listed only one pasta dish, the Tortellini Bolognese. And notice the prices!

The waiters pose for a formal portrait. On the right, the young man standing behind the seated gentleman with the white vest is Attilio Del Monte, the younger brother of founder Angelo. On the top row, Alberto Puccetti stands on the left.

The customers of the early Fior were working class. There was little pretense in the décor. A modestly sized bar stood just inside the storefront window. Cane chairs surrounded wooden tables that sat four. A white tablecloth covered each table and waiters wore tuxedos from the earliest days.

In the many photographs that hang in the Fior, you can see the kitchen help decked out in aprons, turbaned and mustachioed.

The World through Our Kitchen

The Fior did not exist in a vacuum. The bustle of the world outside resounded within its walls. North Beach, while an Italian enclave, was certainly not sealed off from the world either.

The world's most humble and the world's most celebrated dined at its tables as the Fior gained its reputation. While there were many Italian restaurants in the city and in Little Italy at the time, the Fior stood out among the most prominent. Gumina rated the five most celebrated as Bazzuro's, Campi's, Sanguinetti's, Coppa's and the Fior d'Italia.

Bazzuro's was the restaurant where Angelo Del Monte first found work when he settled in San Francisco. Its owner, Frank Bazzuro, introduced San Francisco to the Genoese fish stew, cioppin, now called cioppino (cho-PEEN-oh). Campi's Italian and Swiss cuisine was a family restaurant that nevertheless drew many professionals from the financial district during its heyday.

The combination of Southern Italian family-style cooking, copious beer and music lured the working class to Sanguinetti's. Meanwhile, Bohemians and artists flocked to Coppa's, the most popular Italian eatery before the 1906 earthquake.

Still "the fanciest Italian meals came from the Fior d'Italia," Gumina said. According to her, these five "provincial Italian restaurants laid the groundwork for a gastronomical industry that has contributed greatly to the economic structure of San Francisco. By 1900 when the influx of Italians increased, North Beach, the heart of the Italian settlement had become an eating paradise – at workers' prices. Italian restaurants stretched along Columbus Avenue from Montgomery Street to Francisco Street, along upper Grant Avenue, and on almost every side street between Chinatown and Fisherman's Wharf."

The Fior's history is studded with famous patrons. Among them were Guglielmo Marconi, inventor of the wireless radio, A. P. Giannini, the founder of the Bank of America, the incomparable tenor, Enrico Caruso, and artists, politicians, and royalty.

The histories of talented and successful Italians in San Francisco are deeply intertwined. In 1899, twelve year-old Louis Michael Martini came from Liguria to visit his father, Agostino, who was working in San Francisco in the seafood business. The day of Louis's arrival, Agostino took him promptly to dinner at the Fior. It wasn't until Louis returned to Italy to study the science of winemaking -- oenology -- that he was ready in later years to found and lead Louis M. Martini Wines back in California.

But one doesn't build a business solely on the reputation of the

The kitchen crew and waiters.

clientele. It was local businesses and their employees that supported the Fior's steady luncheon trade. Angelo's youngest son, William, still remembers that much of the clientele from the lunch trade came from the nearby American Biscuit Company at Broadway and Sansome Street.

"We used to buy a sack of broken cookies for 50 cents (from American Biscuit) and bring them home for the family," he said.

Damned Progress

In the late 19th century, even though San Francisco was growing apace, it was still not a large city. The area west of Van Ness Avenue was still country. The Marina was a lagoon. It wouldn't be filled in until the Panama-Pacific International Exposition of 1915.

During these early years when the Fior was gaining its sea legs, the restaurant was situated in one of the world's roughest neighborhoods, the Barbary Coast. The neighborhood drew its name from the northern coast of Africa that had for the previous 500 years been plagued by Berber pirates (hence Barbary). It was a risky neighborhood named after a murderous one.

With the rapid increase in population that the Gold Rush ushered in and the intense interest of capitalists in exploiting mining, railroads and other industries in the area, both the social turmoil and social stimulation were huge. No place more clearly exhibited this uproar than the Barbary Coast. The area encompassed by Montgomery, Broadway, Stockton and Washington Streets was the playground of sailors on leave, miners and farmhands. It was also home to all the entertainments they enjoyed.

In his book, *A La California. Sketch of Life in the Golden State*, Colonel Albert S. Evans described the scene on the Barbary Coast when he took a walk on the wild side with friends one night in 1871:

It is Saturday evening, in the middle of the raining season, when no work is doing upon the ranches and work in the placer mines is necessarily suspended, and the town fairly swarms with 'honest miners' and unemployed farm-hands, who have come down from the mountains and the 'the cow counties' to spend their money, and waste their time and health in 'doing' or 'seeing life' in San Francisco. The Barbary Coast is now alive with 'jay-hawkers,' 'short-card sharps,' 'rounders,' pickpockets, prostitutes and their assistants and victims. [1]

Evans went on to describe his explorations of the quarter's saloons, bordellos, gambling houses and opium dens, all of which made up what he called "the lower hell, the maelstrom of vice and iniquity... strewn from end to end with the wrecks of humanity."

It is amusing in hindsight that our Fior, which became known for its family-style cuisine and atmosphere, took root in such a tawdry spot. Indeed, the Fior's first customers may have been the habitués and employees of the brothel upstairs.

North Beach grew steadily northward toward the wharves where the fishing fleets were moored. As Italian immigrants became more numerous, they sent to Italy for their families to join them after taking their first steps in the new economy. As a result, the North Beach population grew and expanded.

The Del Monte family thrived as the Fior thrived. Eventually, Angelo and Assunta had six children: Attilio, Eugene, Angiolina, Guido, Eva (later Eva Biagini), and the youngest, William, born in January 1906. Angiolina, born in 1896, died the following year.

By the end of the 19th century, Italian Americans were gaining the prosperity they had sought, including chocolatier Domenico (later Domingo) Ghirardelli, who got his start selling confections in the mines at the foothills of the Sierras and went on to establish an industry in San Francisco. There was Andrea Sbarbaro, the visionary and vintner who founded Italian Swiss Colony Company, Marco Fontana of CalPak, and banker A. P. Giannini. All showed that the Italian colony was a force to be reckoned with.

The city as a whole was maturing from the rough-and-tumble aftermath of the discovery of gold and silver, the expansion of the fishing and fur trades and the completion of the Transcontinental Railway to a more sophisticated, financial center, with new banks opening.

Prussian immigrant, Adolph Sutro, who exploited the riches of Nevada's Comstock Lode, became San Francisco's mayor at the end of the 1800s. California's first Arbor Day, promoted by the quixotic poet Joaquin Miller, was celebrated on November 27, 1886, with ceremonies on Yerba Buena Island, the Presidio and Fort Mason. Mayor Sutro donated a consignment of trees for the event.

In May of 1898, the California First Regiment embarked for the Philippine theater of the Spanish-American War on the vessel, City of Peking. They shoved off from a dock on First and Brannan Streets. And just a year later, a movement grew strong to erect a monument to Admiral George Dewey, which now stands in Union Square. [2]

Throughout the 19th century, dozens of earthquakes – usually followed by conflagrations – struck Northern California and the San Francisco Bay Area. These assaults did not seem to concern the city, now grown so prosperous and vibrant. Neither its leaders nor its population could conceive of the catastrophe that lay ahead.

A typical night serving the regulars at the Fior.

Trading Names – Or Not?

Another habitué, Marco Fontana was the head of California Fruit Packing Corporation that eventually adopted the name, Del Monte Foods Corporation. In fact, Fontana had been Giacomo's (Angelo's brother) best friend in Genoa and they retained their friendship in the new country.

Angelo Del Monte's descendants assert that Fontana was apparently casting about for a new name for his company. He claimed not to like the name Fontana for his cannery and expressed his preference for the name, Del Monte. We don't know why.

Reputedly, Giacomo agreed and the Del Monte Foods Company got its name. Needless to say, such an agreement would hardly be possible today without money changing hands or lawyers scribbling pages and pages of agreements.

This charming tale could not be confirmed with the Del Monte Foods Company. In fact, the firm traces its name back to a coffee it packaged for the then Del Monte Hotel in Monterey, California.

But even if it isn't true, the fact that it could be conceived certainly reveals the close friendship that existed between the Del Montes and Fontana. There was no family relationship.

OSSO BUCO (BRAISED VEAL SHANKS WITH GRAMOLATA)

This is George Marianetti's recipe, which appeared in A Cook's Tour of San Francisco, by Doris Muscatine. This recipe is one that takes well to sitting in its own juices. It's a good dish to prepare early and reheat when you are ready. It tastes even better the second day. Degrease after refrigerating.

Serve with risotto alla milanese (See page 22) or polenta (See page 132)

1/2 cup olive oil
4 veal shank pieces with marrow (1 pound each), about 2 inches thick
Salt and freshly ground black pepper
All-purpose flour, for dusting
1 small yellow onion, chopped
1 stalk celery, chopped
1 small carrot, chopped
2 cloves garlic, minced
1 cup brown stock (page 30), plus more as needed
2 tablespoons tomato paste
1/2 teaspoon salt
1/4 teaspoon freshly ground black pepper

Risotto alla Milanese (page 22), for serving

GRAMOLATA

Chop each gramolata ingredient separately or it will turn to paste.
2 tablespoons minced fresh flat-leaf parsley
1 teaspoon grated lemon zest
1 anchovy fillet, minced
1 clove garlic, minced

To make the gramolata: Just before serving, combine the parsley, lemon zest, anchovy, and garlic in a small bowl; stir to combine.

Preheat the oven to 350°F.

In a large, heavy, ovenproof casserole, just large enough to hold the veal in a single layer, heat the olive oil over medium heat. Season the veal generously with salt and pepper. Dust lightly with flour and shake gently to remove any excess. Arrange the veal in a single layer in the pan and cook until well browned, 15 to 20 minutes in total. Using tongs, transfer the veal to a plate and keep warm.

In the same pan, combine the onion, celery, carrot, and garlic; cook, stirring occasionally, until the garlic is fragrant and the onions are translucent, about 3 minutes. Stir in the stock, tomato paste, salt, and pepper. Return the veal to the pan and bring to a boil. Cover and transfer to the oven. Cook for 45 minutes. Check that the liquid is still just covering the meat—if not, add a bit more hot brown stock. Continue cooking, covered, until very tender, another 45 to 60 minutes.

To serve: Arrange the veal shanks on 4 warmed serving plates and spoon the sauce over the top. Garnish with a sprinkling of the gremolata and serve immediately with the Risotto alla Milanese.

Serves four

RISOTTO ALLA MILANESE (RISOTTO WITH SAFFRON)

8 cups chicken stock, or 1 (49 and a 1/2-ounce) can chicken stock plus 1 3/4 cups water
1/4 teaspoon powdered saffron
2 tablespoons olive oil
1/2 cup minced yellow onion
1 1/2 cups Arborio rice
2 tablespoons unsalted butter
1 cup freshly grated Parmesan cheese, plus extra for garnish
Salt and ground white pepper

In a small bowl, combine 1/2 cup of the chicken stock with the saffron; set aside to steep. In a medium saucepan, bring the remaining 7 1/2 cups chicken stock to a boil. Lower the heat and maintain the stock at a simmer.

In a large sauté pan, heat the olive oil over medium-high heat. Add the onion and cook, stirring occasionally, until translucent, about 2 minutes. Add the rice and cook, stirring continuously, until well coated with the oil, about 2 minutes. Add 1 cup of the stock and cook, stirring continuously with a wooden spoon, until all of the stock has been absorbed, about 3 minutes. The rice should never be completely dry, but also never be totally submerged in the stock. Add another 1 cup of stock and cook, stirring continuously, until all of the stock has again been absorbed. Add the saffron mixture and then continue adding the stock, 1 cup at a time, until the rice is tender, but firm to the bite—this will take an additional 15 to 20 minutes. You may not need all of the stock. Remove from the heat. Add the butter and Parmesan and mix well. Season to taste with salt and white pepper.

To serve: Divide the risotto evenly among 4 warmed serving dishes. Serve immediately with extra Parmesan.

Serves four to eight

CHAPTER 3: Shaking in 1906

San Francisco's Italian colony was enjoying its own Italy-in-America culture at the opening of the 20th century. These relative newcomers, immigrants and their children had founded newspapers, theaters, mutual aid societies, schools, clubs, lodges, churches and -- most tellingly -- their own cemetery. This activity signaled that the dream of making a quick fortune in California and returning to Italy to retire was now less than the general expectation of most.

Underlining their growing stability and prosperity, Italians and Italian Americans established several banks, the Italian American Bank, Columbus Savings & Loan and Banca Popolare Operaia Italiana Fugazi. American-born A. P. Giannini, a frequent patron of the Fior, eventually left the board of Columbus Savings because he was the lone board member who wanted to lend to the working class.

Lending to the working class was a shocking idea at the time. Up until then, banking services had been available only to the wealthy and the Anglo-Saxon establishment. It was believed that lending to the working class was folly since these unfortunates would never repay. The working class, urban and rural alike, did not have bank accounts. But Giannini believed in "the little people" – the butchers, the barbers, the waiters and the truck farmers.

In 1904 Giannini started the Bank of Italy for the purpose of helping "working folks" start their own businesses, expand them, and buy property. Since Giannini was a genuinely altruistic and magnetic personality, it's easy to see why Angelo Del Monte, a member of the working class himself, supported his bank. He became a charter member, an investor in the Bank of Italy and held one of its original 28 accounts.

Giannini lunched frequently at Del Monte's Broadway restaurant and brought his staff along with him. He was "a regular," recalled William, son of the founder.

The Fior owners and staff were doing well. Despite their success, Armido Marianetti never forgot his origins. He had a big heart and he understood the patrons he entertained. Though prices at the Fior's infancy were comparatively low, Armido often gave the needy a break seeing them as loyal customers of the future.

"Take what you can spend and we'll feed you," he would say. "We want you to come here, not elsewhere."

His son, Frank Marianetti, remembered that when he was a child, the restaurant reserved a special table for 20 people that was always filled with recent arrivals from Italy.

"Three or four hours at night, those 20 chairs were taken. They turned out to be friends of my father or those who had come here and heard about my father being such a center for helping Italian immigrants. It really paid off well . It was a big part of our business," he recalled.

As Armido had been when he first arrived, many immigrants were unsure of their futures and had no clue how they would find homes or jobs. Often they were without funds. Armido developed a reputation for compassion, drawing together lost souls who knew they could find a friend who cared about their welfare. He would advise them wisely and even find them work. Often enough, Armido would simply put people to work in the kitchen, starting them out washing pots.

While the restaurant welcomed the poor, the Fior had also become an elegant place, the ne plus ultra of Italian restaurants. It attracted society, diplomats and artists.

"The rich people on Nob Hill would send their servants down to make reservations for them. Then they would follow in their horse-drawn carriages," recalled Tecla Brevetti, daughter of Alberto Puccetti, a Fior waiter and a part-owner.

Theaters and Tremors

Artists, actors, singers and musicians from Europe visited the Fior regularly. Italian theatrical and musical touring companies played often to enthusiastic audiences in North Beach.

The adored Neapolitan tenor, Enrico Caruso, made his San Francisco debut in *Lucia di Lammermoor* at the Tivoli Opera House in 1905. He probably made his first visit to the restaurant at this time. The next year he returned to San Francisco and ate there on the night of April 17 just before he left to sing *Carmen* at the Civic Auditorium.

At that time the custom was to eat quite late, well after 9 or 10 P.M. and the Fior didn't close until the wee hours of the morning.

Around 5 A.M. on April 18, 1906, after cleaning up, waiter Puccetti was closing the restaurant and decided to take a stroll outside for a breather. It had been an exciting night. Puccetti had been honored to be able to wait on the celebrated tenor once more. Maybe he was savoring this memory as he sat on a hydrant. As he did, a deep thundering noise erupted. Puzzled, he rose and looked around for its source. He had moved just in time. The hydrant exploded suddenly shooting geysers into the sky.

"Before his startled eyes, the pavements split, the front of houses disintegrated and people were tumbling into the streets," Tecla Brevetti wrote in her biography of her father. That was just the first flicker of the cataclysm that struck San Francisco, a cataclysm that was followed by days of tremors and fire.

The Great Earthquake had struck with a foreshock, a main jolt of almost 60 seconds. While the Richter scale of seismic activity wasn't developed until 1935, geologists' estimates put the 1906 cataclysm at no less than 7.8, a release of energy 16 times more powerful than the 1989 Loma Prieta earthquake in 1989. Over the next three days, what the quake had not pulverized, the fire incinerated. Twin catastrophes, these were what devastated the most modern large city in the country, if not in the world, at that time. An estimated 3,000 perished and 300,000 were left homeless.

The Fior's makeshift replacement after the Great Fire and Earthquake of April 16, 1906. The Fior was back in business after a week, serving soup to the homeless.

Mayor Eugene Schmitz, a man often accused of cronyism and corrupt relationships, finally asserted his leadership at this moment:

He ordered troops from the Presidio to patrol the burning districts and keep people away from the ruined and collapsing buildings. He sent a special detachment to guard the treasurer's office at City Hall, the vaults of which contained six million dollars. In his drive across town he had seen several instances of looting. This prompted his boldest order: that looters be shot dead on the spot. Lighted candles were forbidden in any building in the city. He also ordered that all saloons be closed immediately, and the sale of liquors banned. Any establishment caught selling liquor would have its stock spilled in the street. This liquor ban lasted about 10 weeks. [1]

During this catastrophe, the Fior was demolished. The owners and the staff dispersed to seek their own shelter. For the Fior families, as for many others caught up in the chaos, survival meant leaving town. Some went by carriage, others by cart or horseback south to San Mateo County. Droves headed for the Ferry Building to cross the bay to Oakland and its surrounding communities.

The magnitude of the destruction inspired stories that were passed on for generations. Every person who survived had his tale of what he was doing when the quake struck.. At 5:17 A.M. on April 18, it was mayhem in the Del Monte house. Angelo's wife Assunta, together with her five little ones, was scurrying about to assemble her family. She grabbed the baby, William, in one arm and in the other she snatched the tablecloth by all four corners, leaving much more valuable items behind in her panic and confusion.

Angelo put his family in a wagon and drove to the Ferry Building, heading for Oakland. His son, Guido, a tot of seven, later remembered riding in the wagon down Broadway as both sides of the street blazed around them.

Others were not so lucky. Kathleen Flaherty, who grew up to marry Guido Del Monte in 1923, was only four when the quake struck. Kathleen and her family lived in a house on Shannon Alley, not far from Union Square. The tremor consumed all they had. The Flaherty family was eventually put up in a tent in Golden Gate Park. Since the water mains had broken, there was no running water anywhere in the city. Kathleen remembered as a toddler having to help her family fetch water with her little pail while camping out in the park.

Down by Fisherman's Wharf at Palladini's Fish Company, Armido Marianetti's father-in-law, Giuseppe Corassa, was working when the earthquake first jolted. Pummeled with rocks and almost buried by them, Corassa miraculously crawled out from under the crush. Overwhelmed by his escape, he proclaimed it was a sign from God that he should work no more.

Meanwhile, dazed in front of the restaurant at the first impact, waiter Puccetti had struggled up Telegraph Hill to find his fiancée, Gemma Lenci, who lived near his sisters. The next day, Gemma and her family went to San Pedro Valley (now Pacifica) by horse and wagon to stay with relatives who operated a produce farm there. A few days later, Puccetti went to fetch her in his horse-drawn wagon. On the way back into the city, they married at Corpus Christi Church. They took a ferry to Oakland for their honeymoon where they bought a chicken to celebrate. It was important that life go on.

The army, the navy and the National Guard occupied the city. They guarded valuable buildings and kept order in Golden Gate Park, the Presidio and several smaller parks that had become shelters for the homeless and dazed. Puccetti and his bride returned to the city and took refuge with many others at the Presidio. There they cooked their chicken and settled into one of the tents that had been erected for the homeless.

The army oversaw the establishment of camps around town to house and feed the destitute. They inspected the dwellings, kitchens and latrines daily. The camp in the Presidio alone housed 16,000. Like a little city, the tents were laid out in numbered streets and residents' names and addresses were recorded. [2]

When Giuseppe Alioto escaped San Francisco, he boarded a ferry to Pittsburg, California, a city in the northeast Bay Area. He met the young Domenica Lazio on that ferry trip. Eight years later, they celebrated their wedding at the Fior. Giuseppe was to become the father of Joseph L. Alioto, San Francisco's mayor from 1968-76.

The city must have been terrifying for survivors who could not leave it. Most telegraph lines were silent and telephone connections had been cut. Water mains were torn up and there was no running water. Mayor Schmitz suspended the use of gas and electricity. He urged the public to stay in their homes at night -- those that had them! There was also a great deal of looting despite the Mayor's order to shoot looters on sight.

The Fior made an amazing recovery. Despite the chaos, within a week, the staff was serving the hungry homeless. The restaurant owners erected a structure down the street at 434 Broadway. The new wooden frame façade covered a shack with a rudimentary interior. Family tradition has it that the Fior was the first restaurant to resume operations after the disaster. Apparently other restaurants at the time also claimed this distinction. But the Fior was certainly among the first.

Besides overseeing resettlement at the Presidio, the U. S. Army was in charge of centralizing relief distribution and meting out supplies of water. Through his connection to an official at the Presidio, Del Monte had access to fresh water to make soup.

Ingenuity appeared everywhere. Those who weren't living rough in the parks or in the Presidio managed the best they could, huddling with family or other groups, contriving shelter and cooking on jerry-rigged devices, all without privacy or protection from the weather. [6]

From the makeshift shelter that became the Fior, Marianetti was quick to ladle out minestrone to the wretched who had so recently seen their lives crumble all around them.

In the months that followed the quake, eating and drinking establishments gradually resumed serving the public. As Baker described it:

> On Fillmore Street, on Van Ness Avenue, among former private residences and elsewhere in the unharmed districts of the city, such restaurants as Delmonico's, Tait's, Techau's and the Poodle Dog Café reappeared. Meanwhile in the Latin Quarter the old Bohemian haunts such as Matias's Mexican Fonda. Or the Buon Gusto, Fior d'Italia, and others of their ilk sprang to life in the little wooden shacks arising from the ruins of their former establishments. It was like the clusters of wild lilies and nasturtium that here and there have sprung from the ruins of former gardens in San Francisco, flecking the dismal ashes with gleams of color and fragrance. [7]

Giannini of the Bank of Italy had been at his home in San Mateo County the morning of the quake. As throngs of frightened citizens streamed out of San Francisco, he made his way into the city and found his bank in ruins. He entered the vault and retrieved the gold ingots that gave his bank its financial stability. He hoisted them onto a horse-drawn wagon and covered them with a tarp. Then the banker drove back to his home and buried the precious metal that would help rebuild the city under his home's hearth.

CARUSO ON THE RUN

What indeed happened to the great virtuoso, Enrico Caruso, that fateful night? Many supposed eyewitnesses asserted they saw the tenor clutching his bag and hurrying to the ferry, wailing and vowing never to return.

Photographer Arnold Genthe's recollected the morning after the shock:

> We decided that it would be a good idea to have some breakfast and went to the St. Francis Hotel which had not been damaged. When we arrived we saw that we were not the only ones who had had the brilliant idea of breakfasting there. The lobby and the dining room were crowded. Near the entrance we saw Enrico Caruso with a fur coat over his pajamas, smoking a cigarette and muttering, "Ell of a place! 'Ell of a place!' He had been through many earthquakes in his native Italy but this one was too much for him. It appeared that when he was awakened by the shock, he had tried his vocal cords without success. "Ell of a place! I never come back here.' And he never did. [3]

Caruso's own account is much different and considerably more dignified. He published his recollections accompanied by his own illustrations (he was an accomplished cartoonist) in London publications, *The Sketch* and the July 1906 edition of *The Theatre* magazine. Apparently, he wanted to waste no time setting the record straight. The article is recreated on the site of the Virtual Museum of the City of San Francisco.

Here are some excerpts:

> ....there have been many accounts of my so-called adventures published in the American papers and most of them have not been quite correct. Some of the papers said that I was terribly frightened, that I went half crazy with fear, that I dragged my valise out of the hotel into the square and sat upon it and wept. But all this is untrue. I was frightened, as many others were, but I did not lose my head. I was stopping at the (Palace) Hotel, where many of my fellow-artists were staying, and very comfortable it was....the night before the great catastrophe, I went to bed feeling very contented. I had sung in "Carmen" that night, and the opera had one (sic) with fine éclat. We were all pleased, and, as I said before, I went to bed that night feeling happy and contented.

> But what an awakening! You must know that I am not a very heavy sleeper – I always wake early, and when I feel restless I get up and go for a walk. So on the Wednesday morning early I wake up about 5 o'clock, feeling my bed rocking as though I am in a ship on the ocean, and for moment I think I am dreaming that I am crossing the water on my way to my beautiful country. And so I take no notice for the moment, and then, as the rocking continues, I get up and go to the window, raise the shade and look out. And what I see makes me tremble with fear. I see the buildings toppling over, big pieces of masonry falling, and from the street below I hear the cries and screams of men and women and children.

> I remain speechless, thinking I am in some dreadful nightmare, and for something like forty seconds I stand there, while the buildings fall and my room still rocks like a boat on the sea. And during that forty seconds I think of forty thousand different things. All that I have ever done in my life passes before me, and I remember trivial things and important things. I think of my first appearance in grand opera, and I feel nervous as to my reception, and again I think I am going through last night's "Carmen." [4]

Soon his valet rushed in and helped him pack and they ran into the street. The brave valet returned to bundle the rest of Caruso's belongings into chests and dragged them one by one down six flights of stairs. They made their way to Union Square, about five blocks from the Palace Hotel, and spent the day there. Caruso continues:

> So I lie down in the square for a little rest, while my valet goes and looks after the luggage, and soon I begin to see the flames and all the city seems to be on fire. All the day I wander about, and I tell my valet we must try and get away, but the soldiers will not let us pass. We can find no vehicle to carry our luggage, and this night we are forced to sleep on the hard ground in the open. My limbs ache yet from so rough a bed. [5]

Finally he hired a man with a car to take them to the Ferry Building. In Oakland, the singer boarded a train to New York where he embarked for Italy.

Giannini reopened his bank very soon after the quake by setting up a trestle table at Fisherman's Wharf and lending sums to the working people and merchants, so they could restart their businesses. He also financed vessels to ship in lumber and building supplies via the delta and the rivers that led to Northern California, thus helping San Francisco to achieve a swift resurrection from the ashes.

By the following year, 1907, Angelo had built another permanent building at 492 Broadway where he reestablished the restaurant. In 1909, he added a building next door on the corner of Broadway and Kearny. The restaurant was to stay there until the 1930s.

During this time, Angelo lived with his family in a building next door to the Fior on Kearny Street, which is a steep road that climbs up Telegraph Hill off Broadway. He kept a victrola playing in the Fior from the room nearest to Kearny Street. When he played something from his admired collection of opera recordings, he left the window open and neighbors sat on their steps enjoying the music.

This gem of a structure still stands, although it no longer houses the Fior. An elegant property, it featured an upstairs dining room with remarkable stained-glass windows and can be seen from the street. The owners imported artists from Italy to gild the moldings and paint murals of chubby cherubs and other Rubenesque figures on the ceiling.

"It cost $50,000 – a pile of money in those days. We were serving 35-cent dinners, so 50 grand was a lot of soup. It went over big, it was the talk of the town," Armido's son, Frank Marianetti, said of the decor.

It didn't take long for the restaurant to attract its fashionable clientele again. During the next 10 years, San Francisco would rise more brilliantly than before the earthquake. The Fior too achieved its own pinnacle of acclaim and elegance.

MINESTRA DI PASTA E FAGIOLI (PASTA AND BEAN SOUP)

This is a Venetian soup and thick enough for a meal. You may use canned beans and left-over pasta, if the pasta is firm and not overcooked. The olive oil and Parmesan are not optional. They make the soup!

1 tablespoon olive oil

4 ounces pancetta, chopped

2 stalks celery, finely diced

1 medium yellow onion, finely diced

3 anchovy fillets, chopped

2 cloves garlic, minced

2 teaspoons minced fresh sage

2 large tomatoes, seeded and diced,
   or 1 (15-ounce) can diced tomatoes, drained

6 cups brown stock (page 30) or canned low-sodium beef stock

2 (15-ounce) cans cannellini beans, drained

4 ounces elbow macaroni, cooked al dente (about 2 cups cooked)

Salt and freshly ground black pepper

Freshly grated Parmesan cheese, for garnish

Extra virgin olive oil, for garnish

In a large, heavy soup pot, heat the olive oil over medium-high heat. Add the pancetta and cook, stirring, 1 minute. Add the celery and onion and cook until the onion is translucent and the celery is tender, about 3 minutes. Add the anchovies, garlic, and sage and cook 2 minutes. Add the tomatoes and stock; bring to a boil. Lower the heat and simmer 20 minutes. Add the beans and cook 10 minutes. Add the pasta and cook until hot, about 5 minutes. Season to taste with salt and pepper.

To serve: Ladle the soup into warmed bowls, sprinkle with freshly grated Parmesan and drizzle with extra virgin olive oil. Serve immediately.

Serves four to six

CHAPTER 4: From the Depths to the Heights

The Fior was rebuilt at 492 Broadway, the corner of Kearny, in 1909. Later, the restaurant Vanessi's took its place. The building still exists.

During the second decade of the 20th century, when the Western World was embroiled in war, San Francisco was focused on the building itself. To celebrate its resurrection and to show it had achieved renewed acclaim, the city organized a grand party and invited the world. That party was the Panama-Pacific International Exposition of 1915. After three years of preparation, the mud flats of the Marina district were transformed into the grounds of palaces, lagoons, courts, arches, murals and statuary in the classical mold. Only one of these buildings still exists today, the Palace of Fine Arts. The Exposition's marketing brochure described the endeavor's scope:

> The Panama-Pacific International Exposition is an encyclopedia of modern achievement. You are afforded an opportunity to make a comparative study of the methods and manners of modern civilization; the conditions and means of living -- the hygiene, the religions -- in short, the objects and accomplishments of all the peoples of the world. Such an event will not occur again while you live.

Obviously, people believed the proclamations for the Exposition. It drew visitors from around the world during its 10-month existence. Many of the visitors ate at the Fior. On its walls, the Fior displays photographs of the banquets held at that time that honored royalty and foreign statesmen. One of those dignitaries was the esteemed Ernesto Nathan, a scholar and the first mayor of Rome after Italy's unification. Hanging on the Fior's walls is a photograph of the banquet held in

his honor, when Nathan appeared as commissioner and personal representative to His Majesty, King Vittorio Emanuele III, and hosted Italy's installation at the Exposition.

By this time, the restaurant was offering entertainment in addition to fine cuisine. The upper banquet room offered an orchestra and ballroom dancing. One of its musical programs has survived. The program featured soprano Helen Cole, pianist Jack Rogers, and Henry L. Del Monte, the son of Angelo's brother Francesco. He was a trap drummer and the master of ceremonies. Their descriptions in the program shed light on the restaurant's place in the city's life at that time.

Miss Helen Cole - Soprano

In the closing period of the Exposition, Helen Cole deserted Vaudeville to accept a lucrative offer from the Fior d'Italia management. She has remained at that famous resort of sybarites and connoisseurs since. Miss Cole was forging to the vanguard in vaudeville and those who should know say that a few more years would have seen her safely ensconced in a niche carved out by hard work among the bill-toppers; none who have seen her perform are skeptical of the Miss Cole's power to breathe the rarified atmosphere which only stars may absorb. Besides the ownership of an ineffable

This banquet during 1915 Panama-Pacific Exposition feted Ernesto Nathan, the first mayor of Rome after Italy's reunification.

Miss Helen Cole -- Soprano

Henry L. Del Monte
TRAP DRUMMER and ENTERTAINMENT MANAGER

Jack Rogers
AS A PIANIST

This was the first page of a musical program held during the Panama-Pacific Exposition.

to mind, still among so many successful clavier artists in local cafes, we hesitate to bestow the title upon any certain person. Still, Mr. Rogers attributes are varied, and if he is not the best at least he is among the very few whose names stand out as bulwarks against the encroachments of mediocrity.

His name is known to every cabaret-goer in the community. For Mr. Rogers, beside the twelve months and over he has been at the Fior d'Italia Restaurant, was at Stack's Café for three years in succession and in others of our best cafes prior thereto.

Self-congratulatory as most promotional literature usually is, these tracts are also rather literary. Surely the staff of the Fior d'Italia was not likely to have written such overblown Victorian prose, nor would they have written it for the residents of the neighborhood. Although there is no record of a publicist working at this time for the Fior, no doubt the owners hired such a person to convey a message that would reach well beyond the denizens of North Beach.

30th Anniversary

In 1916, the owners put on quite a show for the Fior's 30th anniversary. The special menu designed by architect and cartoonist, Luigi Mastropasqua (whose pen name, Lama, means blade), depicts Angelo, Armido Marianetti and chef Ireneo Cicchi leading the staff in a gastronomic parade. The trio press forward under the weight of platters of food, pots, ladles and ravioli cutters.

The legend in English reads: "The most up-to-date and largest Italian Restaurant in the United States." Below, the Italian text announces that meals are served every hour of the day. And further: "The meeting-place of epicures, the most vast and refined restaurant of our colony, the most select Italian cuisine of San Francisco, 30 years in business."

At this time, the Fior seated 750 people. The elaborate, gilt upstairs banquet hall alone accommodated 375 of that number. The restaurant boasted 15,012,280 dinners served in its three decades, averaging 1,400 daily. What a change in fortune for a young émigré who had failed to strike it rich in the gold fields almost 40 years earlier!

soprano, Miss Cole is blessed with beauty, both of physique and of disposition.

Henry L. Del Monte - trap drummer and entertainment manager

Henry L. Del Monte has held different positions at the Fior d'Italia for the past eleven years. About three years ago he suggested the installing of a dance floor; this suggestion was immediately acted upon by the management who appointed him as entertainment manager, which position he has held since.

Mr. Del Monte as a trap drummer, is a paragon of that species; and as the manager of the entertainment feature of this resort too much praise cannot be given to him, for to his judgment much of the Fior d'Italia's popularity and ever increasing business is due.

Jack Rogers - as a pianist

Casting about in our mind for the best pianist before the local public, several occurred to us as possessed of talent sufficient to claim the title. Jack Rogers was among the pianists whose names came

No prices were displayed on the special anniversary menu:

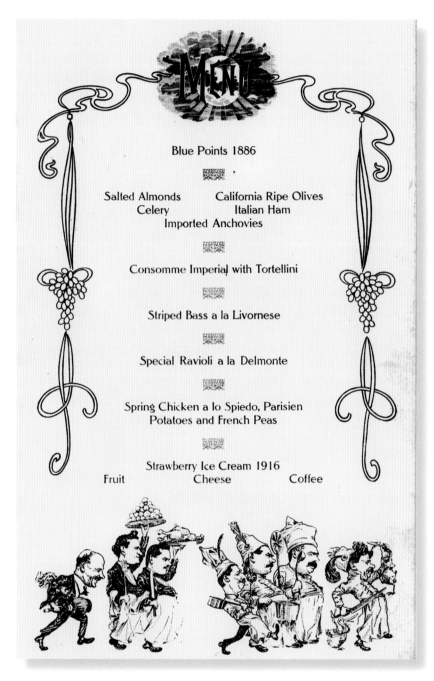

Menu

Blue Points 1886

Salted Almonds   California Ripe Olives
Celery   Italian Ham
Imported Anchovies

Consomme Imperial with Tortellini

Striped Bass a la Livornese

Special Ravioli a la Delmonte

Spring Chicken a lo Spiedo, Parisien
Potatoes and French Peas

Strawberry Ice Cream 1916
Fruit   Cheese   Coffee

For the thirty-year anniversary menu, the architect-cartoonist Lama again beautified the menu. The figure in the chef's hat might represent Armido Marianetti. And the drummer in the helmet? Possibly the Fior's leader Angelo Del Monte.

Virgilio Luciani

Sometimes fiction can illuminate fact. Italian poet and novelist, Virgilio Luciani, who was a Tuscan from Lucca, came to California as a boy in 1896 to join his father. He returned to Italy during World War I, and several years later wrote *Un italiano in America* (An Italian in America). An autobiographical novel, this book follows the daily life of a young immigrant with delightful detail.

In the novel, an adolescent, Omero Danti, takes a job as a busboy in the famed Fior d'Italia. This tract paints a picture so clear that one can almost smell the rosemary in the kitchen and the perfumes of its stylish patrons. Luciani describes Danti as follows:

His first job after school was a powerful exercise in learning the language. The restaurant was called "Fior d'Italia" founded by émigrés from Liguria and Tuscany and was the most luxurious spot on Broadway. A great door of crystal and brass, lucid as a mirror opened before a vast room divided by lines of white columns, filled with both rectangular and round tables.

Each table bore only with water glasses holding napkins pleated in the shape of a funnel and with glass vases full of fresh flowers. To one side, was an enormous mirror that appeared at the entrance to the kitchen. A great automatic organ played many of our operas on paper rolls: Boheme, Trovatore, Tosca, Traviata. Upstairs there was another room for banquets and weddings and small private rooms, each with a table and four place settings.

Omero had to obey and learn from his waiter and dress like him: The starched collar, a white shirtfront of special paper that shone like cloth, black bow tie, an evening waistcoat, a black jacket split at the hips and an ample white apron that bound him like a cassock. He learned quickly to take better care of his appearance, especially his teeth, nails and hair, his clothes and shoes.

He became immediately humble and servile in this grand place that had six owners: a manager, a barkeeper, two waiters, two cooks. All gave orders and he had to obey all and be impartial because they were all bosses. At times, the poor boy really did not know what to do. One wanted him to serve in one way and another in another. The good ones in the middle made him happy, the less good remained stubborn, irritating and irritated.

Those first days his hands trembled carrying three plates between the fingers, but then he got used to it. He carried the middle plates fine in the hand and the arm, walking quickly, leaning on the long banquet tables. God help him if he broke some kitchenware in his fervor to work. He would have to pay the cash register at the bar immediately. [1]

And here, Luciani lists a typical menu:

The meals fell into three categories: 25 cents, the regular dinner, and a la carte. For 25 cents one could satisfy one's hunger. Generally the Americans took the regular dinner which consisted of food not of the first quality but always ready: the soup and pasta that was cooked in the morning, remained in the double boiler until evening. But the numerous and select cosmopolitan clientele tasted the real Italian cooking:

Imported tortellini, chicken soup or beef
Lamb with olives, roasted pork and turnip greens
Chicken in gelatin or chicken cacciatore
Tortelli home-style that were cut out with glasses and sealed with the tines of a fork and filled with ricotta
Swiss chard
Chicken and nutmeg, served in giblet sauce
Beef roasted rare
Scaloppini in Marsala.
Various cheeses, zabaglione with liqueur
Assorted fruits with almonds, dates and bananas
And finally little squares of thick cream mixed with rum that were lit with a match. They quickly produced a beautiful flame that burned yellow, then blue and green. They made espresso coffee right at the table with a portable burner. The wines were from California, France, Italy, with champagne of the highest quality.[2]

The author takes us into the kitchen, exposing its mechanics and its dynamism:

The kitchen was large, rectangular, and very white and the pots of copper sparkled. The cooks dressed in white, all lined up next to the enormous red-hot stove. They repeated the orders of the waiters who practically shrieked. And when any main course was ready, a scullery boy gave a clap of the gong and the cook called the name of the waiter. When all the tables were occupied and the people standing waited for each to be finished, the work quickly turned to chaos!

Omero passed quickly with great trays of dirty dishes and carried clean tablecloths removing those stained with grease or wine. He used the napkin that he held in his arms as a handkerchief when his forehead perspired.

His quickness and his humble child's smile pleased the manager who after some months promoted him to the private rooms upstairs. These were quiet and restful haunts for wooing or for saying things deeply thought and meant during a meal. These attracted the coquettes with their men or lovers, girls from good or distinguished families, with their fiancés and their mamas, but often even alone. Rich parties who didn't like the music or the animated, noisy voices from the grand salon also chose private rooms.

This was the time of the First World War of 1914-18 and really that was the time of California's prosperity. From the Barbary Coast, the vice, the luxury, the dissolution together with strange passions and loves, entered the Fior d'Italia like a sharp and enervating perfume, like a slow and sweet melody that inflamed and excited the senses.

Beautiful women came to dine in these private rooms where Omero helped serve. They were heavily made up, clothed in silk, in velvet and satin. Décolletéed, they wore fake diamonds in their hair in the form of a diadem or plumes, and gold bracelets at the wrist, diamonds on the fingers with bright nails or red or pink with their tall, proud knights, so mocking and cynical. [3]

We have a novelist to thank for what is probably as true a portrait as one could paint of the life of the restaurant and its patrons.

Enter George and Frank

During the first and second decades of the 20th century, Armido Marianetti's sons, George and Frank, were brought in to the restaurant as youngsters to help out. From Doris Muscatine's *A Cook's Tour of San Francisco*, we learn about George:

It was his chore when he was very young to deliver the fresh, white aprons -- hot, and all rolled up -- to his father after school; his invariable reward was a dish of ice cream and a pastry. When he was in the first grade his teacher always dismissed him early so that he could fetch her an order of Fior's ravioli for her lunch. When he was twelve, George started to work after school. From the early 1900s through the First World War, when Fior devoted a second floor to revelry and entertainment, George was stationed at the bottom of the stairs to announce "Music and Dancing Upstairs."....

Every day his father drove the Chrysler to market to buy produce for the restaurant. He would dump the load on the family table in the rear of the restaurant, and the boys and Papa would start in shelling peas and stringing beans. Pretty soon Basilio Lippi, another partner (and a cousin) would join the group, and conversation vied in animation with the nimble fingers at work on the beans. Barsotti the butcher would bring in a couple of legs of veal, and Papa Marianetti would sing out a "*Come va?*" and a "*Vieni qua,*" and Barsotti, before he knew it, would be at work shelling peas. Salesmen who came in, Mr. Collins, the cop on the beat, Father Mario, and everyone else who entered, would be invited to sit down and talk, and nine or ten

This October 25, 1916 notice appears in *L'Italia.*

people would be shelling peas and stringing beans before the hour was up. [4]

World War I

We have few inklings of the effect on the Fior of the world's largest conflict till that time. The only scraps come from Muscatine and the Marianetti brothers. According to Muscatine:

The happiest time at the restaurant -- and the happiest time that George ever saw -- was November 11, 1918. The schools were closed because of the flu epidemic, and George was busily at work copying out the day's menu on the duplicating machine. About 11 A.M. the doors flew open. A bunch of workers from the biscuit factory nearby, flour flying in great clouds around them, burst in screaming, "The war is over!" They were followed without pause by crowds of hilarious and joyful citizens, who celebrated the end of hostilities until six o'clock the following morning. They jammed into the dining room, and crowded straight out to the curb, eating and drinking in long-awaited release. Signor Puccinelli, whose

PRANZI A TUTTE ... an advertisement. Since this advertisement appears in italian, it could have appeared in the Italian language daily, *L'Italia*. The translation appears below:

"Meals at all hours of the day
The haunt of epicures. The most vast and refined restaurant of our colony. The most choice italian cuisine of San Francisco. Thirty years of operation. Large dining rooms for clubs and weddings.
Faultless service at popular prices."

father had owned Il Trovatore in the early years of the century, arrived with a group of 50. The Marianettis opened the upstairs dining room and sent up a cook. Puccinelli, who knew the business, set it up and served. George, realizing after many hectic hours he had had nothing to eat since breakfast, grabbed a broiled steak, ran into one of the private booths designated for ladies, and gobbled it down. When the restaurant finally closed the next morning, after the most marvelous time in anyone's memory, it was completely out of everything: wine, bread, chicken, meat. Every crumb on the premises had been consumed. [5]

For his part, Frank described the euphoria he saw around him when he was nine years old: "I remember Armistice Day, everyone was so happy. Let's go have a drink, get drunk, make love!"

No wonder New Year's Eve marking the opening of 1919 was out of the ordinary. The Fior printed a special menu whose cover was enlivened by a lusty flamenco dancer. The price was not printed except for the notice that wine was $1.50 extra. The antipasto consisted of salame, olives and shrimp salad. Capon broth with pastine was followed by Lavasso a la Fior d'Italia, ravioli in mushroom sauce. The management served each patron a half-chicken broiled and sautéed peas, followed by dessert.

As Virgilio Luciani observed in his novel, World War I shattered the old ways, sweeping traditional relationships and rituals away. Women's suffrage and the temperance movement were affecting family roles and with it, fashions and mores.

During the war years, Victorian dress altered drastically, and it wasn't just because fabric needed to be conserved for the war effort. No longer were modest women swathed in yards of fabric, garlanded in braids and crowned by imposing chapeaux. The black and white photographs at the Fior display stern parents, papa seated, mamma standing, surrounded by children and babies. These images speak of a world of decorum where one knew one's station in life, where family honor and parents' dignity were valued.

Ponder how in a few short years, the corseted madonnas of the Old World who patronized the Fior with their bowler-hatted men were replaced by young people of a different planet. Women had lopped off their coiled chignons and braids. Brassieres now flattened bosoms formerly gathered and held lush above corsets. Necklines plunged as hemlines soared upward. The new flappers of North Beach were now seen in public places wearing lipstick and mascara and smoking cigarettes. Flaunting their sexuality. *Dio mio!*

But if the traditional Old World souls of North Beach were scandalized to see extra flesh, they would have been horrified to know that, virtually growing beneath their feet, was a force that would totally transform the community. Over a decade before the Eighteenth Amendment would be ratified in 1920, the movement for outlawing trade and transport in spirits was gaining momentum.

Would the Fior ever be so proud again? Could the owners have anticipated -- on the eve of Prohibition -- how its business and its clientele would change forever?

Il Fior d'Italia Restaurant
492 BROADWAY, SAN FRANCISCO

A HAPPY NEW YEAR

1919

New Year's Eve Dinner
$1.50 WINE EXTRA

ITALIAN SALAME
CALIFORNIA RIPE OLIVES
SHRIMP SALAD MAYONNAISE

CAPON BROTH WITH ITALIAN PASTINA

LAVASSO A LA FIOR D'ITALIA

RAVIOLI A LA GENOVESE
MUSHROOM SAUCE

HALF BROILED CHICKEN
GREEN PEAS SAUTE' IN BUTTER

VANILLA ICE CREAM   FRUIT IN SEASON
DEMI TASSE

A dinner program and menu for New Year's Eve 1919.

FONDO BRUNO (BROWN STOCK)

A rich, brown stock is essential to many Italian dishes, including zuppa pavese (Pavian soup, page 50) and zuppa di cavolo con formaggio (cabbage and bread soup, page 122).

You can prepare this for future use by pouring it into ice cube trays and freezing it.

3 pounds meaty beef bones, cut into 2- to 3-inch lengths
Olive oil
3 stalks celery, coarsely chopped
1 large yellow onion, coarsely chopped
2 large carrots, coarsely chopped
1 head garlic, cut in half crosswise
1 bay leaf
1/2 teaspoon dried thyme
1/2 teaspoon dried marjoram
2 tablespoons tomato paste
1 teaspoon whole black peppercorns
Salt

Preheat the oven to 400°F.

Arrange the bones in a large roasting pan and drizzle with olive oil. Roast until deep golden brown, about 1 hour. Leaving the oven at 400°F, transfer the bones to a large stockpot and add just enough cold water to cover. Bring to a boil over high heat. Lower the heat and simmer very gently about 3 hours, skimming and discarding any foam or grease as it rises to the surface.

While the bones are simmering, prepare the vegetables: In the same large roasting pan, combine the celery, onion, carrots, and garlic. Bake, stirring occasionally, until golden brown, 20 to 30 minutes.

After the bones have simmered for 3 hours, stir in the bay leaf, thyme, marjoram, tomato paste, black peppercorns, and the roasted vegetables and any pan drippings. Bring to a boil; lower the heat and simmer very gently about 1 hour. Vegetables must not go in until the last hour of cooking.

Strain the liquid through a fine-mesh strainer, pressing on the ingredients to extract as much liquid as possible; discard the solids. You should have about 1 quart of brown stock. Season and with salt to taste. Cool to room temperature. Cover and refrigerate for up to three days or freeze for up to three months.

Makes about 1 quart

CHAPTER 5: Red Coffee

What could be more frustrating for a business than to have its stock and trade outlawed? The Fior was not the only restaurant during the era of Prohibition to find itself caught between the government's mandates and customers' demands.

"One time during Prohibition, a guy had too much to drink. A couple of Sicilians said to my father, 'This guy's bothering you, we're gonna take care of him.' They had knives. So my father said, 'No, no, no please, don't do anything.' And they would've too. We have some real tough ones come in during Prohibition," recollected Frank Marianetti, Armido's son.

As so many restaurateurs and saloon owners did during that time, the Fior profited from the illegal trade in spirits. It was profit they would have preferred to come by legally and without danger. As Frank indicated, the contact with vice and hoodlums was unwelcome but almost inevitable.

While the Eighteenth Amendment's prohibition of the manufacture, transport and sale of spirits became effective in January 1920 (until its repeal in December 1933), the movement toward it had been intensifying for decades. Even so, few people in Northern California really believed the experiment called Prohibition would ever materialize. The wine industry and the culture of wine were so thoroughly engrained as to make prohibition seem most unlikely.

For years, the Women's Christian Temperance Union and their supporters had striven to rouse the nation's conscience to the evils of drink and its damage to family life. The momentum grew slowly but it eventually snowballed until it was politically irresistible.

Clifford J. Walker recounted in *One Eye Closed, the Other Red, the California Bootlegging Years.*

Money poured into prohibition campaigns from all over the country, dimes and dollars from church offerings, pennies and nickels from Sunday school children and huge sums from businessmen who believed strongly in prohibition and from those who found it advantageous to donate to the cause. [1]

Those who opposed prohibition, called the "wets," were weaker politically.

The wine industry, liquor companies and breweries did not organize as they could have. Individually, each struck sorties at the temperance enemy, wrote pamphlets, articles and gave money to campaigns. An example: the California Grape Growers Association collected $1,500 in December 1917 for their anti-prohibition fight in California. [2]

They planned to fight the ratification of the amendment and take the matter to the courts. However, they did not have the political power to carry the idea through successfully. At that time, states could vote themselves dry regardless of whether the amendment ultimately became the law of the land.

"By the time 1918 ended, 33 states had legislated themselves dry and voted for the amendment. Other states allowed cities and counties to decide. Many in California had done so," according to Walker. [3]

Actually, California never voted itself dry until the amendment became law. Nebraska, on January 19, 1919, became the 36th state to ratify the Eighteenth Amendment, making it part of the Constitution. It would become effective on January 16, 1920, when no one would again be able to make, sell, or transport liquor. But, in one of its many loopholes, the law did not forbid buying or owning booze. It was an irrational arrangement that would produce bizarre repercussions for the next 14 years.

After the amendment was ratified into law, Americans knew they had a year to stock up and they did. Del Monte and Marianetti amassed a tremendous stock of liquor at the restaurant. When the law took effect, they parceled out their stash among themselves and kept it at their homes. They meant to hold it for home use or to keep it until, they assumed, Prohibition would surely end one day.

Restaurants and saloonkeepers had to prepare for the run-up to the law taking effect.

By the summer of 1919, most saloon owners had applied to the city and county to turn their establishments into soft drink parlors. We know that John Tait, the owner of two famous night clubs, notified his patrons in 1919, the summer after ratification but before the law took effect, that Tait's at the Beach and Tait's Downtown would offer drink setups (ginger ale, lime rickey, soda) for patrons who brought their own liquor. Both establishments charged set-up and corkage fees and stored opened bottles for the client. [4]

The enforcement measure for the amendment, called the Volstead Act, handed the public plenty of opportunities to circumvent it. The act allowed families to make 200 gallons of wine (or apple cider) for their own use every year, a process that required about a ton of grapes. Families would go down to the Embarcadero to buy their supplies from the boxcars just arriving from the vineyards.

This was a boon for Italians and other Mediterranean peoples for whom wine was the traditional beverage. From childhood, Italians are taught to drink it at meals, first highly diluted in water and then gradually intensified as they mature. They found it unthinkable that the government would outlaw trade in spirits. They couldn't see the sense of it. The puritanical and largely Protestant spirit of the temperance movement was quite alien to them.

So Italians willingly and readily made their own wine when the country went dry. Then they went one step further and distilled the wine into grappa, a highly potent liquor made from the refuse of pressed grapes, the marc. This, of course, was not legal.

"'You could tell when people were making grappa because they pulled the shades down or they had black drapes," said Puccetti's daughter, Tecla Brevetti. "I remember watching my mother doing it. She gave me some grappa and it almost put me on my ear. We lived on Filbert Street and had a big enclosed back porch. There were lots of basins around. She pulled the shades down," she recollected.

The Fior, as did Tait's and countless other establishments, served set-ups for patrons when they came in and also hid their booze for them. It was legal for patrons to buy and drink alcohol. It was illegal for alcohol to be sold and transported. This preposterous state of affairs was the reason patrons brought it with them, hidden, to the restaurant.

Frank recalled a customer named Dobson and his wife who came in frequently. As a harbor pilot, Dobson guided foreign ships into San Francisco Bay. Every time he went out, he came back with expensive and forbidden whiskey, bottles of Old Grand Dad, Canadian Club and Old Taylor. Dobson was always a welcome customer thanks to his wooden leg.

"His hollow wooden leg had enough room for two quarts. He kept the restaurant supplied with good whisky. I never saw him pay a bill when he came with his wife for dinner….He'd pay for the bottles on the ships, and then we'd give him free dinners. He got drunk every night. There were many characters like that," Frank said.

The Fior continued to serve wine, as did other Italian restaurants, but in coffee cups to deflect detection. Fior owners referred to it as "red coffee." Armido's eldest son George who was just nine had begun helping out at the Fior. Patrons referred to him as "the wine kid" as he went about filling up coffee cups with deep red liquid.

As George told *San Francisco Chronicle* columnist, Stanton Delaplane, in 1967:

> My father built a plywood cover over the back room. I sat back there with a rubber hose for a siphon and a 50-gallon barrel of homemade wine. The waiters would come by and say in a loud voice: `Six cupsa coffee.' I would suck on the siphon, get the wine started. Fill six cups and slide them out under the plywood cover. Naturally…I had to suck up a mouthful of wine each time. I was always a happy kid. [5]

But the attempt at camouflage hardly mattered. One night, powerful hosts presided over a party of about 100 people. Mayor Sunny Rolph with District Attorney Matt Brady and Assessor Russ Wolden took over the upstairs dining room. Wine bottles littered the tabletops. For the opening toast, the Mayor raised a glass of wine and somebody snapped a photo, Frank recalled. The next day the picture was on the front page of a daily newspaper and caused a furor.

"From then on we were raided once a week," Frank said. "Very expensive, with lawyers and all."

Federal prohibition enforcers raided establishments with regularity in California, always in squads. They received thousands of tips in 1920. Their most concentrated flurry of raids occurred during the first two years of Prohibition.

> (They) closed stills and bootleg joints, arrested and convicted several thousand violators. Newspapers recorded victories as it (sic) had in the late war: small salients taken here, such and such roadhouse closed for selling liquor, biggest haul of moonshine in this or that county so far. Many trenches were overrun: bars closed, thousands of gallons of booze dumped down street gutters, buildings abated, bootleggers sent to county jails and evidence stored in basements of court houses. [6]

Barbara Nowicki, the daughter of Angelo Del Monte's son Guido, recounted how the Fior dealt with authorities when they raided the restaurant. Angelo's son Attilio would run into the kitchen and hide. Her father, Guido, was elected to go to the stationhouse as the designated defendant. A busboy, Guido sported a dark curly head of hair that attracted the affectionate fingers of many female patrons. However, for this assignment he had to use his head for other purposes.

"He went many times. He appeared before the judge and paid a fine and they started all over again. He never went into prison," Nowicki said.

The same could not be said of Puccetti, the waiter who had served Caruso the night before the earthquake and who was startled off his perch on a fire hydrant by the historic rumble. He had moved on by this time and opened his own restaurant. Though he later sold that establishment to his son-in-law, the former Fior partner continued to manage Ray's Place on Grant and Columbus.

One day the federal agents came in and somehow detected that he had been serving alcohol even though it had been well hidden. He was sentenced to a month in jail. A known chef, he wasn't behind bars very long before the constabulary incredibly asked him if he would cook for them. Puccetti explained that he could not do justice to any meal without herbs. They had none in stock in the county jail. But the resourceful restaurateur assured the officials he had all he needed in his garden at home on Filbert and Kearny Streets. His keepers let him go home every day to pick his rosemary and parsley and other greens for their table. Each day until his sentence expired he would return home from the hoosegow at mid-day, dine with his family and take a little siesta before returning, herbal bouquet in hand.

Stories like this one put in bold relief San Francisco's contempt for the Eighteenth Amendment, even at the official level. The city was flagrant in its disregard for the law.

Eventually, Armido tired of the constant harassing by the police. He closed the restaurant and when it reopened, across Kearny Street at the same intersection, the Fior no longer sold wine. Nonetheless, the public, excited by the publicity the restaurant drew from the Mayor's picture, continued to throng there, despite the fact that wine was no longer served.

"They'd go searching around the kitchen, but if people brought in their own (liquor), (the management) overlooked it," he said.

Frank began working at the Fior when he was ten years old. He recollected his first days fondly:

All the kids from the other partners worked there, too, and we got a silver dollar for each day that we worked. In 1920, my father said to me, come on down and wash these coffee mugs they used to serve wine in. (The mugs) didn't fool anybody though.

My job was to wash the glasses and wash the mugs. I worked my little ass off. After all, we had a two-story restaurant going. Family restaurant downstairs, the upstairs was for high rollers and big shots, dancing, what have you.

The first night I worked, I worked so hard. I went to the cashier, Del Monte's son. I asked for my silver dollar. Since it was only my first night, I only got 50 cents, not a silver dollar.

'Oh, Pop,' I moaned, 'I've waited all these years to get a silver dollar. '

'Not the first night,' he said. He was thinking back to when he started when he got paid only after one month.

The upstairs dining room was a nightclub after dark with a 10-piece band and two pianos. The Fior was "the hottest place in town," Frank reminisced. "We started a trend. Everybody wanted to come."

But the wrong people wanted to come as well. The Fior began drawing "real tough Damon Runyon, gangster-type guys. Mafia maybe. Murderers and gamblers. They were okay with us as owners because it was just their hangout," Frank said.

These patrons affected Frank, as he recounted:

One night a couple of detectives came in, looking around. There was a table with four or five of these tough guys sitting in the corner. One of the (tough guys) spots me, hands me a napkin with a gun in it. I take the gun with the napkin and stuck it in my locker. I wasn't really too scared, kind of excited actually. I was part of the gang. The cops went right to the guy and searched him. I got a dollar tip!

The young Frank also recalled one night when two rival gangs of thugs arrived. The place was packed and they were serving liquor upstairs, having closed the downstairs for security. Frank said:

One of the girls from one gang went into the lady's room and somebody else in the other gang called her a whore or something. It was a free-for-all. Like Hollywood. Everyone was fighting. The whole damn restaurant. Some people were flying out of the place. Punching, swinging. Bottles, everything. Bleeding. In about ten minutes it stopped. We called the cops but it was all over. Guys with split heads, bleeding. They're all tough bastards. I saw two or three of those gang fights. I don't like them. You don't know what you're going to get. Hit in the back? No point.

We had all kinds of gimmicks – secret doorways. The dishwasher lived behind the place. He had a pulley from his place down to ours. He'd send the wine down from his place to the restaurant....

During this frantic decade, Northern California supplied the rest of the country with a great deal of spirits. The state also imported liquor from Canada and Europe that entered as ocean cargo. At one time, as many as a dozen cargo vessels carrying liquor were moored off San Francisco. Smaller vessels, "rum runners," met them to take delivery of the potent shipments.

Frank's maternal grandfather, Giuseppe Corassa, was active in this trade as a "land shark." He picked up liquor off the beach and delivered it to those who stored and distributed it. This is the gentleman who was almost crushed by debris during the 1906 Earthquake and vowed he'd never work again. Apparently, he changed his mind.

Corassa and his family lived on 47th Avenue, near Ocean Beach, a convenient work address, where carriers would moor offshore to rendezvous with smugglers' boats. Frank said:

My grandmother told me they'd watch the ships come in. They were a block away from the ocean. And then she and her sisters and brothers would entertain the bootleggers.... whistle and sing for them. Then they'd get a silver dollar and they thought it was all the money in the world.

My grandfather just didn't understand Prohibition. That's why he broke the law. They knew you were doing it. Except when we got that big publicity in the front page, that was the end of the honeymoon for the Fior d'Italia. After that, every week or so we got raided.

We don't know what newspaper this was nor what the infraction he was charged with but it is easy to surmise. While the Fior was clearly in the wrong for breaking the law, Frank's attitudes show that many of the hospitality trade felt justified in their defiance. Not only did they feel the law was unjust but also that its enforcers were objectionable.

Frank rued:

Prohibition days were not glamorous like Elliott Ness....These people who worked for the Feds were scum. Nothing classy about them. You knew they were bums and mean. They came in and confiscated booze. They came in the kitchen where the big barrel of wine was stored. My father said, 'It's not ours. The customers brought their own.' And they said, 'Goddamn dagos.'

Quite a few (customers) came in from the dining room to see what was going on. 'We just wanted to see what you guys looked like,' said the Prohibition enforcers of the Fior.

One guy picked up a bottle of wine to hit the Fed. The customer says, 'Wait till I take my glasses off.' Then he hit the Fed on the head because they called him a rat. The Fed guy was out. I ran screaming out of the place. I was about twelve or thirteen.

The police in this era, and in San Francisco especially, were notoriously corrupt. In 1922, Federal Prohibition Director Samuel Rutter announced that he, along with Chief of Police Daniel O'Brien and Captain Charles Goff , "had uncovered a gigantic bootlegging conspiracy through which blind pig proprietors had paid money to police officers and prominent deputy sheriffs for protection." [7]

A "blind pig" was another term for speakeasy, an establishment which hid its serving and selling of liquor behind some other establishment, for instance, a storefront of some kind.

Speakeasies in North Beach frequently developed into restaurants after the amendment was repealed in 1933. One of those establishments is still operating, the Gold Spike on Columbus Avenue.

Because it was not hiding behind the façade of another business, the Fior d'Italia was not strictly speaking a speakeasy, even though it was breaking the law in selling spirits. And it was making money doing so. Even a lowly job, such as tending the hatcheck room, was not without its rewards. Bruno Lucchesi, son of Chef Giorgio, worked the hatcheck room and told of making as much as $200 in a night in tips.

G. William Puccinelli, a "land shark" and smuggler during this era, attested to the interdependence of the local police and the hospitality industry:

Everybody in the North Beach district who ran prostitution or bootlegged had to pay off the patrolman. Patrolmen in my district would meet each night on the corner of Grant Avenue and Pacific where they changed the guard and divided the money. Every night! between 12:30 and 1:00 o'clock....The shakedown ran from $2.00 to $10.00 a night, depending on the kind of place. [8]

We have no records of the Fior paying off the police. But the fact that they were raided so regularly leads one to believe that the owners had not been excessively cooperative in feeding the greed of petty officials.

The Fior was surrounded by prostitution during this era. To escape the Feds and the police, the restaurant built a passageway from the pantry to the hotel upstairs, an establishment that housed a brothel. Frank recalled:

> I discovered it when I saw this waiter Rocco go into the pantry to take food up to the girls. I wondered, 'Where the hell did Rocco go?' At Christmas time, Rocco would take all the busboys upstairs for the first time. You had to be thirteen years old. So the Christmas I was twelve and a half, my cousin told me about it. He was a couple of years older than me.
>
> So I told Rocco, I'm going this time. 'No way,' says Rocco. "Do you know what your father would do to me if he found out? He'd kill me!'
>
> My father did not go for that stuff at all, no way. Actually, I saw some of the girls. I wasn't too impressed.

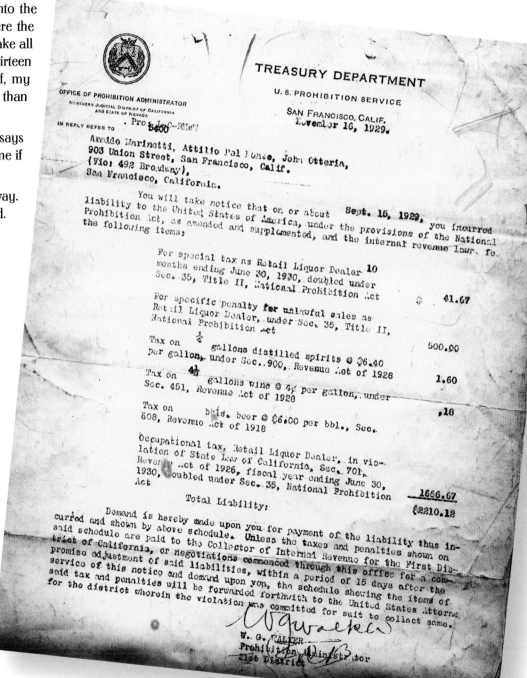

The U.S. Prohibition Service fines the Fior $2,210.18 for selling spirits in 1929.

CROCCHETTE DI PATATE (POTATO CROQUETTES)

These freeze well. When you cook them from their frozen state, cook at 325°F.

3 large eggs
1 cup freshly grated grana or Parmesan cheese
1/2 cup fine dried breadcrumbs
2 pounds russet potatoes, peeled, boiled, drained, and mashed, at room temperature
1 teaspoon salt
1/4 teaspoon ground white pepper
Pinch of freshly grated nutmeg
Peanut oil, for frying
Lemon wedges, for garnish

Line a large baking sheet with parchment paper; set aside. In a shallow bowl, using a fork, lightly beat 1 of the eggs. In a second shallow bowl, combine 1/4 cup of the grana cheese and the breadcrumbs; mix well. Set aside.

In a large bowl, combine the remaining 2 eggs, the remaining 3/4 cup grana cheese, the potatoes, salt, pepper, and nutmeg; mix well. Using your hands, shape about 1/4 cup of the mixture into a 1 by 3-inch croquette. Transfer to the prepared baking sheet and repeat with the remaining potato mixture.

Dip the croquettes in the beaten egg, then roll in the breadcrumb mixture, taking care to press the breadcrumbs on firmly.

Line a second large baking sheet with several layers of paper towels; set aside. In a large, heavy, deep-sided saucepan or Dutch oven, add oil to a depth of 1 inch and heat over medium-high heat until a thermometer registers 350°F. Fry the croquettes, a few at a time, until golden brown, 2 to 3 minutes. Using a slotted spoon, transfer the croquettes to the prepared baking sheet and let drain. Repeat with the remaining croquettes.

To serve: Garnish with lemon wedges and serve immediately.

Serves four

CHAPTER 6: Prohibition Be Damned. Celebrities Revel.

In one of life's great ironies, the puritanical Prohibitionist decade encouraged an outpouring of great ribaldry and passion, the Jazz Age. The Fior's 10-piece band entertained its audience of Charleston-dancing flappers. The famous stars of the day came to dine, dance and be seen. The fabled Rudolf Valentino, the Italian movie actor who intoxicated young women into swoons, was a patron.

The greatest female talent of the silent movies, Mary Pickford, and her film idol husband, Douglas Fairbanks, married in 1920. Pickford was both an actress and a producer and was one of the most popular stars in film history. Together with Fairbanks, D. W. Griffith and Charlie Chaplin, she founded United Artists Corporation. Fairbanks was also an actor and producer who was adored for his swashbuckling and athletic prowess in such films as "The Mark of Zorro, The Three Musketeers" and "Robin Hood".

On their honeymoon, the couple visited the restaurant disguised and incognito. Armando Lippi waited on them that Saturday night in a booth. The actors left him a $5 tip, well over a day's wages. The next morning Frank Marianetti came to clean up. At their table, he found that Pickford and Fairbanks had written a comment on the menu.

It said: "We had dinner here. Thanks for the wonderful evening."

Frank was impressed and stored the menu in his locker. Later that day he agreed to sell it to another waiter for a dollar, a sale he later regretted.

Years later when the place had changed completely and it was no longer a nightclub, Pickford came in with Buddy Rogers, the husband for whom she had left Fairbanks, and an entourage of friends. They took a booth just as she had with Fairbanks years before.

"I know she didn't come by accident," Frank reasoned later.

The upper crust, celebrities and foreign dignitaries made it a point to be seen at 492-494 Broadway. Broadway, the main thoroughfare of North Beach at that time, was a shopping paradise where boutiques and *negozi* (shops) remained open until well after midnight. The street began at the harbor where the boats and ferries that took passengers to Napa, Carquinez or San Jose were moored. Shoppers from as far away as Sacramento and Los Angeles (some ferries had sleeping accommodations) then disembarked on the Embarcadero. Out-of-towners would walk up Broadway to see what the city had to offer by way of food, entertainment, fashion and merchandise. All this traffic passed in front of the Fior regularly.

The Italian colony kept in touch through its daily newspapers, especially *La Voce del Popolo* and the *L'Italia*. The newspapers featured international, especially Italian, news on their front pages and devoted their inside pages to local news, gossip columns, serialized romantic fiction and news of births, deaths and marriages. A considerable amount of space was given to the activities of the many cultural societies of the Italian colony. [1]

In many ways the Italian colony was a world unto itself (often called "the Little City"), but the Italian colony still could not escape the pressures of the larger sphere. By the time the Great War was over in 1918 people wanted to return to the pre-war reality, but life had changed. Prices had soared. The specter of Bolshevism permeated the newspapers. Women now could vote. Fashions had altered dramatically. And Prohibition was now in effect.

Innovations in technology had changed everyone's worldview. The telephone had ceased to be a novelty and was now a standard fixture in many homes along with radio broadcasts from the new crystal sets. Horses and wagons were becoming less indispensable because of the automobile. Perhaps this was a blessing for the poor beasts that labored up Telegraph Hill bearing the loads of fresh produce and household goods. The emergence of automobiles and paved roads brought people closer to realms beyond their neighborhood. Some people had even flown in the air.

Theater -- A Participatory Sport

Now, with an ever growing number of sources for news from far and near, people enjoyed a bigger world. Still, the Old World and the new continued to overlap in many ways. The magical new experience that was cinema thrilled and brought with it the glamour of cinema stars. In North Beach, people still went to the live theater and the Fior was a meeting place for performers and artists. The incomparable Eleanora Duse played in San Francisco in 1924 and no doubt was feted at the Fior. Fellow actress, Mimi Aguglia, also toured the city and it is unlikely that she would have done so without a meal at the Fior.

San Francisco was a prominent stop in the touring itineraries of opera and theatrical troupes from New York and Italy. Opera in North Beach was not a highbrow entertainment of the elite. Even unschooled Italians knew the libretti of their favorite works. Opera groupies followed the careers of their idolized singers with avid interest. Enthusiastic patrons would stand and sing right along with the tenor or the diva.

Thus it was not unusual for a mechanic, such as Evaristo Alibertini, to sing in the opera. The basso had sung in Italy in the chorus in his hometown of La Spezia on the Italian Riviera and moved to San Francisco in 1904. When the San Carlo Opera Company from New York came on tour, during the mid-teens and early 1920s, it put out calls for extra chorus members. Alibertini stepped right up.

His daughter, Victorine Alibertini (who was a schoolmate of Eva Del Monte, the daughter of Fior founder Angelo), remembered how this troupe looked forward to meals at the Fior d'Italia:

This group of Italians had been on the train for five to six days, all they were hoping for was a good Italian meal. They got off at Oakland and a group of opera buffs would meet them at the train, and troupe members would say:

'Dov'è il Fior d'Italia? Vogliamo mangiare.' (Where is the Fior d'Italia? We want to eat.)

Meals were about 45-50 cents. (The Fior) was the meeting place. That was like home to them….they'd come to our home and they'd say, *'Oh, il Fior d'Italia, non c'è di meglio.'* (There's nothing better than the Fior d'Italia.)

Imagine having all the singers and chorus people there together….The *maestri* especially had so many stories to tell. It was wonderful to hear them, that group of people and all their enthusiasm. I remember a lot of noise, a lot of confusion and good times.

It was easy to encourage them to sing, singing without any music. It doesn't take much to get a bunch of singers going. When you have a group of Italian singers around the table, just one word from *La Bohème* is all. You say *"Che gelida manina"* and somebody will start singing it. It was spontaneous, not planned.

Alibertini recalled some of the great tenors who visited the Fior while she was growing up. Most of them had risen from the ranks in Italy to find careers at the Metropolitan Opera in New York:

Beniamino Gigli (1889-1957), Giovanni Martinelli (1885-1969) and Tito Schipa (1889-1965). Many of them were brought to the Fior by another notable artist, Gaetano Merola, the conductor who established the San Francisco Opera Company in 1923.

Merola came to San Francisco several times as the conductor of the touring San Carlo Opera Company, the same one Evaristo Alibertini had joined as a chorus member. According to John Ardoin, a music critic:

(Merola) believed that San Francisco should have its own opera company and, with the help from the city's Italian community, he put together enough money for three 'calling card' performances in 1922 in the Stanford Football Stadium. It lost $19,000, a good deal of money in those pre-world-War II days. But with a warmth and resilience that would become his trademark, he persuaded his backers to undertake another and longer season of opera, this time in the town's cavernous Civic Auditorium. [2]

There, in 1923, he formally launched the San Francisco Opera with a performance of Puccini's *La Bohème* starring soprano Queena Mario as Mimi and Giovanni Martinelli as Rodolfo. Merola was on the podium, as he would often be for the next 30 years until his death in 1953.

Another frequent patron was the esteemed editor of the daily paper *L'Italia*, Ettore Patrizi, who was one of North Beach's most distinguished characters for several decades. His editorial offices on Columbus near Broadway were quite close to the Fior. He could virtually pop out of his office and into the restaurant in seconds. His stature in the community attracted distinguished visitors from Europe and he brought them to the restaurant. He was in effect showing off his guests to the restaurant and showing off the restaurant to his guests.

Among the celebrities Patrizi introduced to the Fior was Pietro Mascagni, composer of the opera, *Cavalleria Rusticana*. Another was General Umberto Nobile, the great explorer.

Nobile had won fame piloting a dirigible over the North Pole in 1926. At that time, Italy's supreme leader, Benito Mussolino, would not risk supporting the trip in case it failed. Nobile found funding from Norway and named the flying ship, *Norge*. The feat was so successful that *il Duce* "ordered Nobile to tour the United States on the way home and tout his nation's glory before America's 'Italian colonies.'" wrote Philip Nobile, in the Italian-American magazine I-AM. [3]

This visit was most likely the occasion of his trip to San Francisco. No wonder Patrizi squired him around and showed him off at the Fior. Unfortunately, Nobile may have been dazzled by the fame of his accomplishment and the relative ease of achieving it. He planned another polar flight, but a longer one involving scientific explorations. This dirigible, *L'Italia*, flew under the flag of Italy with the dictator's enthusiastic backing. The vessel crashed and members of the crew died. There were even ill-founded rumors of cannibalism. Nobile and several crewmembers were rescued at the cost of other lives.

Ettore Patrizi, editor and publisher of the daily paper L'Italia, acted as host to famed Italian aviator General Umberto Nobile during his visit to San Francisco and to the Fior.

Mussolini, so eager to take credit for the first voyage that he had not supported, now discredited Nobile to the world to distance himself from the tragedy. The brave general, briefly a national hero, ended his flying career in disgrace.

Many celebrities who frequented the Fior were athletes, particularly, baseball players. At that time, the team in San Francisco was the minor league Seals. Frank remembered how the locally celebrated Seals players Burt Ellison, Pete Kilduff, Eddie Mulligan and William Cam would come in on Saturday nights to enjoy the entertainment on the Fior's second floor.

One night, the Seals players brought along one of the greatest hitters of all time, Ty Cobb, who was visiting the city. The restaurant owners were used to celebrities but this one mystified them. He stimulated enormous attention from the patrons but the management didn't know who he was. Frank recreated the staff's discussion:

"Who is this person?"

"I don't know."

"His name is Ty Cobb."

"Opera? I think I've heard of him. I think he's a German tenor but they don't care about him too much in his country."

When they found out he was a baseball player, Armido, the opera buff, was incredulous that someone who played the game he'd watched in the nearby playground attracted so much attention. He asked what Cobb got paid for playing professionally and he was told $50,000.

"This is impossible. This is insanity," he said shaking his head. "This is a crazy country. A wonderful country, don't get me wrong. The same country that's so wonderful you can't have any wine with your dinner in a restaurant and they give these guys who plays a kid's game $50,000."

In that same nearby playground, Giuseppe Paolo DiMaggio was practicing and improving his skills. Born in Martinez but reared in North Beach, Joe DiMaggio finally got a break when he joined the Seals of the Pacific Coast League in 1933, where he played through 1935. DiMaggio joined the New York Yankees the following year.

When Frank was selling Metropolitan Life insurance, he used to collect from DiMaggio's family, the home of Giuseppe, Joe's fisherman father. Frank remembered Joltin' Joe more for his dark side than for his home runs.

Every now and then I'd go to La Rocca's place on Columbus Avenue and shoot a little pool. Joe hung out there. I got to know him pretty well. It seemed to me that I did. As a matter of fact, I was in there playing one night and he wandered in with a prostitute. He was a young kid; he wasn't good yet. I think had just started to play with the Seals....Then he went to the big leagues where he got very popular. I was in the place bowling one night after work with a couple of guys and Joe DiMaggio walks in.

(I say,) 'Oh Joe.' I think I'm greeting an old friend. He must've had a lot of people putting the touch on him. Or maybe I looked like a bum. I don't know but he acted like he never saw me before. He didn't know me. I said, 'Hey, don't you remember?' I was embarrassed.

The famed athlete was also what restaurant people called a "fishhook" – he ducked when it was time to buy a round at the bar -- and he never tipped. However, after he joined the New York Yankees and left San Francisco, he continued to patronize the Fior from time to time and his autographed picture is proudly displayed near the bar.

Families Gathered Here

The Fior had always drawn North Beach families for important events such as First Communions, weddings and anniversaries. Many patrons celebrated their weddings there and came back 20, even 50, years later for an anniversary party.

In 1928, Angelo's daughter, Eva Del Monte, married pharmacist Fred Biagini. Eva had been studying Italian at the University of California at Berkeley and graduated with the intention of teaching, unusual for a young woman of that era. The situation was even more remarkable because none of her four brothers went on to university. But she changed her mind about a career when she met Fred and proceeded to devote herself to the family she had with him. As befitted a young woman of prominence in the Italian colony and the daughter of a famous restaurateur, Eva enjoyed the best the Fior had to offer. Her wedding reception was held in the upstairs ballroom.

Years later, when Eva passed by the former home of the Fior, she pointed out the upper story to her daughter, Janette, as the place her splendid wedding reception had been held so long ago.

The University of California, Berkeley, had an added significance for the restaurant. Its traditional rivalry with Stanford University in Palo Alto peaked every year when their football teams challenged each other at the "big game." Since neither university had a stadium built for some years, the game was played in San Francisco. For the Fior, the merry-making that followed the game was even more financially rewarding than New Year's Eve. Its dance floor, entertainment and food drew great crowds.

However, Angelo hated the "big game." The crowds were riotous and the youthful patrons relieved the restaurant of its creamers, salt-and-peppershakers and other tableware.

"All these wonderful, upstanding people would rob him. So the next day he would have to go down to Nathan Dorman's (a restaurant supply store) and buy all this stuff to replenish his stock," Eva's son Fred Biagini recalled.

Flying Parmesan

Many people know about the Italian sport of bocce ball, a game similar to bowling, which only men played in those days. But few have heard about the sport of cheese-rolling. Frank Marianetti relived his memories of the competitions on the lawns of the Marina's Funston Park, now Moscone Park. It was a sport also played by Armando Lippi, a Fior chef. According to Frank:

You take a Parmesan cheese – about 50 pounds – wrap a strap around it and take a run like you do in bowling and see how far you can throw it. You hold onto the strap and the cheese would roll out of the strap and go maybe 30, 40 or 50 feet.

I'm thinking of Lippi, my cousin. He was a hell of a guy, a good athlete and a great cook. He was a champion on this particular thing....They had a competition at one time to see who could roll the cheese the farthest. They started from Laguna and rolled toward Fillmore (a distance of three blocks). I was there watching. My cousin Lippi won the thing – he rolled it damn near all the way. He'd take a run, jump in the air and zing! The damn cheese would keep on rolling.

Frank surmised that the sport eventually waned when people realized Parmesan was too expensive to sacrifice on the lawns of Funston. But his cousin, Davide Lippi, the grandson of Armando Lippi to whom Frank was referring, put the site not at Funston but at Fort Mason, which separates the Marina from Aquatic Park:

"Many of them would meet there on Sundays to vie for the trophy that was also cheese," Davide recalled.

Rather than Parmesan, it was frequently peccorino or dry Monterey. And, according to him, sometimes a dummy cheese would be used since the real thing would tend to break. Armando won the city competition when his grandson, Davide, was about fourteen years old in the mid-1930s.

"We had a full house of cheese, all trophies he'd won," he said.

Shifting Sands

In 1922, the restaurant registered its trademark with the State of California as the Flower of Italy Restaurant, although it never used that name in commerce. Founder Angelo and his partners were prosperous men. Angelo continued to buy property around the restaurant at the corner of Broadway and Kearny. By 1929, he owned several buildings on the block.

Angelo retired in mid-1920s, selling his interest in the Fior to Armido Marianetti and his family. By 1926, the owners now included Angelo's sons, Attilio and Guido: Armido and wife Amelia; brother Giuseppe (Beppe) and wife Assunta; brother Alfredo and wife Albertina; Domenico Battistessa and wife Rose (Angelo's niece); and Giorgio Lucchesi and wife Emma.

Over the four decades since the Fior had opened for business, Del Monte and Marianetti had brought in their sons and brothers and their sons. Armido's sister, Teresina Marianetti, married Bondelo Lippi. Their sons Basilio, Armando and Ray Lippi grew up to work at the Fior where Armando became a respected chef. Basilio married his first cousin, Assunta Marianetti, the daughter of Zeffiro (Armido's brother), drawing the bonds between the Marianettis and the Lippis even closer.

Another family from Lucca also became part of the tapestry of those families that ran and operated the eatery. This was the Lucchesi family. Giorgio Lucchesi spent about 50 years as a cook at the Fior. His four sons, Bruno, Armando (not to be confused with Armando Lippi), Reno and Mario also worked at the Fior in various capacities. Giorgio's sister, Assunta, married Beppe Marianetti, a son of Armido.

The Del Montes, Marianettis, Lippis and the Lucchesis were the network whose impetus has kept the restaurant alive until today, although the ownership has changed more than once since the 1920s. Their success was exemplified by the changes in the Marianetti family. Armido, his wife and four children had owned and been living in one floor of a three-flat property at 1055 Montgomery Street near Vallejo Street in North Beach. His mother-in-law and her family lived in one flat while his maternal aunt, Clorinda, lived on the bottom floor with her husband and daughter.

The building was primitive but typical of the era: no electricity, no telephone and no heat except a wooden coal stove. It took an hour to get enough hot water for a bath, Frank remembered. He wondered how his mother and grandmother ever managed to run their households under such conditions.

"My father had this property because it was close to where he worked, the Fior d'Italia Restaurant, which has been a big part of my life since the day I was born. Running down after school to bring my father a clean shirt at work is still a strong memory for me," Frank recalled.

Many Fior staffers no longer lived in North Beach and had moved to the East Bay, especially the community of Elmhurst. At first, Angelo Del Monte bought property there for a summer home. His brothers and staff gradually bought property near his also. Assunta fed and entertained them in Elmhurst as the matriarch she was. Armido bought a quarter acre as did one of his brothers near the Del Monte's summer home and he constructed a three-bedroom cottage. Eventually Elmhurst grew more urban and many of the Fior staff, notably the Lucchesi family, settled there permanently.

Another Fior contingent moved to the Marina district of San Francisco. This area became a symbol of the rising expectations and new bourgeois status for the successful immigrants and the children of North Beach immigrants. In the late 1920s, when stock prices were roaring, Armido got a tip that paid off. It reaped enough to pay for a house in the increasingly attractive neighborhood that was being built on sand. The Marina was formerly flatlands and landfill that had become the grounds for the extravaganza of the Panama-Pacific International Exposition of 1915.

When that gala was over, developers razed the fantastic buildings, monuments and fountains and developed the land for housing. Fortunately, they spared the glorious Palace of Fine Arts. Armido bought one of the many single-family two-bedroom dwellings being built there. The family then left North Beach behind and moved to 2058 Beach Street.

With all his material success, Armido's open hand never faltered. Frank spoke highly of his father's compassion, for which he gained a storied reputation. When people came in who were obviously in need – and many had already figured out this was the way to Armido's heart – he would take them under his wing. Frank recalled that even though prices were already moderate, Armido would give the needy a break: "Take what you can spend and we'll feed you," he'd say. "We want you to come here, not elsewhere."

Frank recalled so vividly: "When I was a little kid, they built a special table that took care of twenty people, always filled with recent arrivals from Italy. Three or four hours at night, those 20 chairs were always taken. They turned out to be friends of my father. They came here and heard about my father being such a center for helping Italian immigrants. It really paid off well, a big part of our business."

One Christmas, after the owners had raised prices somewhat, Frank waited on a Mexican couple and their four children. They read the menu. It was obvious they were having a problem with the prices. They decided to stay, however, and the children were gleeful. Eventually, the family ordered two full dinners and two orders of ravioli.

Frank went to his father and advised him that the customers at that table shouldn't be ordering so much food. Armido looked in on them and remarked, "Look how happy and well behaved they are. What are you gonna do, tell them to leave?"

"Dad, if they can't pay, they shouldn't be here," Frank protested.

"Give them the dinner," Armido said, and Frank began serving them salad.

"This all comes with it today," the elder Marianetti told his customers. "You have a fine family here – nice looking little children."

They got the works: salad, soup, ravioli, turkey and a bottle of Chianti. Frank recalled they walked out as if "they were royalty."

Then Armido chided Frank, the first in his family to attend university (an English major at the University of California, Berkeley). Armido said: "Is that what they taught you (at school), to be cruel to people? Would you have sent them out, made them feel sick, to have their Christmas spoiled?"

While Armido's largesse persisted throughout his life, the Fior and its owners did not escape the growing cataclysm. The end of the twenties marked the end of good fortune for the entire country.

CREMA FRITTA ALL'ITALIANA ALL'EVA BIAGINI (EVA BIAGINI'S ITALIAN FRIED CREAM)

Custard
4 large egg yolks
1/2 cup all-purpose flour
1/4 cup granulated sugar
1/8 teaspoon salt
1 teaspoon vanilla extract
2 cups half-and-half

All-purpose flour, for dusting
1 large egg, lightly beaten
1 cup fine dried breadcrumbs
Peanut oil, for frying
Powdered sugar, for garnish
Jam, for garnish

Lightly butter a 6 by 8-inch baking dish.

To prepare the custard: In a medium bowl, combine the egg yolks, flour, sugar, salt, vanilla, and 1/2 cup of the half-and-half; whisk until smooth.

In a medium saucepan, bring the remaining 1 1/2 cups half-and-half to a boil over medium-high heat. Remove from the heat and slowly whisk into the egg mixture. Return the mixture to the saucepan and cook over medium heat, whisking continuously, until the custard is very thick and smooth, about 10 minutes. Pour no deeper than 3/4 inch into the prepared baking dish and smooth the top. Place a piece of plastic wrap directly on the surface of the custard and refrigerate until firm and chilled, about 4 hours or overnight.

Lightly flour a work surface and place the beaten egg and breadcrumbs in separate shallow bowls. Carefully tip out the custard onto the floured work surface and, using a sharp knife, cut into twelve 2-inch squares. Lightly dust the squares with flour. Dip each square into the egg, then into the breadcrumbs, pressing the crumbs on gently but securely.

Heat 2 inches of oil in a large, heavy saucepan over medium-high heat until a thermometer registers 360°F. Cook the custard squares in batches without crowding, turning occasionally, until crisp and golden, 3 to 4 minutes. Drain on paper towels.

To serve: Dust with powdered sugar and garnish with a dollop of your favorite jam. Serve immediately.

Serves four to six

CHAPTER 7: The Great Depression

By the end of the 1920s, all America was flying high and so was the Fior. The twenties had been a period of conspicuous prosperity. Amateur investors were wildly putting their cash into stocks, buying on margin and bidding up stock prices to heady heights.

The Giannini Break

When share prices on the New York Stock Exchange plummeted by $6 billion on Black Tuesday, October 24, 1929, the event marked America's definitive break with unreality. However, for many West Coast investors the stock market had already crashed in 1928. Their savings had already evaporated and their lives were in tatters -- a consequence of the success of one of the Fior's most prominent patrons, the banker A. P. Giannini.

Giannini, who had started the Bank of Italy almost three decades before, had grown his North Beach bank into a respected Californian institution. He didn't stop there. He pushed long and hard to realize his vision of a national bank, acquiring institutions around the country and including them into his scheme of a single coast-to-coast bank.

A. P., as he liked to be called, had pioneered branch banking in the United States – directly in the face of the resistance of the East Coast banking establishment. An institution that could lend and take deposits in more than one location had not existed before in the country.

Giannini's humanity and his business vision had excited many since the birth of the Bank of Italy. The West Coast Italian-American community, in particular those in agriculture and small businesses, were both his loyal customers and investors. He transformed the Bank of Italy into the Bank of America (BofA) through various acquisitions and, for a few years, the two entities co-existed while he also launched a holding company, the Bancitaly Corporation. At one period, the shares of the three entities were trading simultaneously. Bank customers and investors, impressed with this growth, pushed more and more money into the entities whose unifying figurehead remained A. P. Giannini. Angelo Del Monte, his brothers and several of his partners were active investors.

During the late 1920s, Giannini warned his investors and his employees not to gorge themselves on BofA, Bank of Italy or Bancitaly Corporation shares but, to his horror, investors continued to indulge in a feeding frenzy. By 1927, those stocks had doubled and tripled their values from the year before. While the market in San Francisco allowed no buying on margin, financial institutions emerged that would lend money to speculators who greatly inflated share values to sell stock.

In May of 1928, the Federal Reserve raised the discount rate to four from three and a half percent. Nonetheless, the share prices of the Banks of Italy and America and Bancitaly kept climbing. Then, at the end of May the Federal Reserve pumped rates up again to four and a half percent just as news began circulating of Giannini's illness.

A. P. Giannini

He had been vacationing in Rome where he was stricken with pleurisy and neuritis. This news sent the West Coast market into a tailspin.

"Monday, June 11 (1928) – 'Blue Monday' – was a wild day on the San Francisco Stock Exchange. Bancitaly opened at 175, off 20. That was enough to make the bankers with stock under escrow agreements look in the direction of their vaults…. there was no holding (the stock's price) any longer against the flood of selling. It dropped to 170 and the dumping began," according to the James's *Biography of a Bank.* [1]

A day after this huge break in prices, A. P. Giannini wired a colleague, "everything tiptop. Don't worry." [2]

But the visionary was wrong. This was just a taste of what was to come.

Angelo Del Monte had sold his ownership of the Fior by this time to Armido Marianetti and also rented the restaurant's premises to him. But Angelo still owned the restaurant property on 492 Broadway, the contiguous buildings, the parking lot and the two flats he and his family lived in around the corner on Kearney Street.

Over the years, Angelo and his brothers had made the same mistake as so many others and invested in Bank of Italy stock as its price spiraled upward. When its price tumbled, the Del Montes found themselves squeezed for funds.

Here the trail gets murky. Whether, after the break in its share value, the bank foreclosed on Del Montes' mortgages or Angelo had to sell his property to pay the money he had borrowed to buy the stock, we do not know. The Bank of America claims its policy during the Depression was not to foreclose on property owners. But the result was the same. Angelo and his brothers were ruined. They were left with only the parking lot that still sits next to 492 Broadway and is still owned by his heirs. He lost the two buildings the Fior occupied, the nearby buildings and his two-flat home around the corner on Kearney Street.

However, it happened that the Del Monte family lost their fortune, the family felt abused by the bank. Angelo's son, William Del Monte, asserted that his father "had been one of A. P. Giannini's original 28 accounts" when he established the Bank of Italy and "must have known Giannini well as one of the first depositors."

William claimed the bank supported its largest and most troubled debtors after the 1929 crash, sacrificing the small business owners who gave the Bank of Italy its first breath of life. However, by this time, the Del Montes had no longer any ties to the restaurant since Angelo had sold out to Armido a few years before.

"During the depression years, Marianetti announced that the Fior d'Italia would never close. 'If you think this is a depression,' he would say, 'you should see Italy!' " [3]

Seeing it through as the sole owner, Armido and his crew vacated the premises abruptly in 1930. Overnight they moved the restaurant to a building across the street at 504 Broadway at Kearny Street.

George Marianetti asked his father Armido how long he thought they would have to remain closed in order to move and resume their business?

"Closed?" was Papa's indignant reply. "Tomorrow we will serve in 504 Broadway." They fed their dinner guests as usual, including three friends whom George had brought for a farewell meal in the old place. As soon as the last customer left Papa began giving commands to the whole family, all of the personnel, and George's friends included. They moved everything: food, liquor, iceboxes, boardwalks, tables and chairs quickly refurbished with silver spray. By three A.M. they had finished. The next day at 11 A.M., the Fior served lunch at 504 Broadway. [4]

The new location was smaller. No more second-floor entertainment. Those days were gone.

The Fior d'Italia is all on one floor. It is simple, dignified and has an air of refinement and reserve. It has one private dining room, private booths which have their own entrance and with an open dining room and bar. Some 200 customers can be accommodated at one time. Lunch and dinner are served daily from 10 in the morning till 10 in the evening. Regular lunches and dinners or service a la carte is the schedule for all days, except Sunday, when all orders are á la carte. [5]

This building remained standing and was home to Finocchio's upstairs and the space the Fior occupied on the ground level became Enrico's in the following decades. The 492 property eventually became home to another much-loved restaurant, Vanessi's. Though Vanessi's has disappeared today, the building and its sumptuous stained glass windows still shining from the second floor – built by Del Monte -- have been preserved.

Giorgio Lucchesi, an immigrant from Lucca, had been a cook at the Fior since the turn of the century. He had become a wealthy man through his investments and quit the Fior, selling his share in the restaurant in the late 1920s. When he lost his shirt from the downturn in stock prices, Giorgio went once more to the restaurant to ask for his job back. Armido Marianetti rehired him the same day.

Despite the 1928 crash of the Giannini empire, the rest of the city expected good times to continue. From the beginning of 1929 until the October crash, bank deposits increased 13 percent in San Francisco and summer employment reached a peak. The Depression's impact

504 Broadway exterior

on the rest of the country was enormous but it did not make itself felt in the Bay Area until 1930, when it started hitting home in San Francisco. [6]

Within the first two years of the 1929 crash, manufacturing in the city slipped 34 percent. As per capita income in the nation declined 28 percent from 1929 to 1933, income levels fell 29 percent in California. [7]

Employment evaporated. An annual wage in 1927 had averaged $1,460 but it reached only $1,080 in 1933. Retail sales fell accordingly

and the cost of living teetered. Bank deposits also fell precipitously, leaving the institutions less to lend, a factor that may have figured in the Del Montes' financial misfortunes.

During the Depression, the hungry would appear occasionally outside the side door to the restaurant on the Kearny Street side adjacent to the kitchen, asking for food handouts. The Fior's cooks always gave them something.

Fortunately, San Francisco had a champion during these dark days. Coincidentally, he was a good patron of the Fior. Mayor Angelo J. Rossi was originally the owner of the floral business, Carboni and Monti. Rossi had a head for business and finance. He started a league of merchants called the Down Town Association and became its president from 1920-21. He had been a finance chairman of the Board of Supervisors under his predecessor, Mayor James "Sunny Jim" Rolph. By all accounts Rossi was a popular mayor and well liked.

Mayor Rossi was just what the city needed during the most trying years of the Depression. Rossi strove to maintain the city's fiscal balance and to improve the range of services offered to its citizens.

Rossi did leave some time for levity, however. When New York Mayor Fiorello H. LaGuardia came to San Francisco, Rossi gave him a dinner party at the Fior.

At one point, the relief rolls were bulging heavily from the jobless middle class who had used up their savings, sadly at the same time as

504 Broadway interior

the city's relief budget ran dry. Rossi saw to it that the city borrowed from the Community Chest rather than run up a deficit. He funded relief efforts with bonds and by asking city employees to take pay cuts.

While the city was suffering, the Port of San Francisco remained vital, exporting almost 80 percent of the state's agricultural output. Its 82 docks could handle 250 ships each working day. In 1933, 7,000 ships docked and departed. The streets teemed with truckers, stevedores, and merchant sailors. Fior sat but a few blocks from the Embarcadero, the center of this heavy activity that streamed past its doors.

As work became scarce, the longshoremen began to organize. They had neither voice nor leverage with the shippers and property owners who controlled the work hours and wages. With the leadership of firebrands such as Harry Bridges, the longshoremen demanded decent hours, better pay and decent working conditions.

San Francisco's maritime workers planned a general strike that would be honored up and down the western seaboard. All West Coast dockworkers belonging to the International Labor Association struck on May 9, 1934. Because the seamen and the teamsters soon joined them, the strikers halted ocean traffic from San Diego to Seattle. For weeks the workers, management and the police challenged and confronted each other.

When the teamsters voted to strike and to abandon the waterfront and its businesses, their pickets turned away most trucks heading into the city although food and dairy deliveries continued. The industrialists and shipping companies affected were furious and they calculated their lost receipts at $1 million a day. [8]

July 5, 1934, came to be known as Bloody Thursday. On this day, a crowd of many hundreds gathered on and near the Embarcadero where they confronted 800 policemen armed with riot sticks, firearms and nausea gas. The police confronted a crowd that could retaliate only by throwing the stones that lay in the street. Two of the unionists were killed. The somber and huge funeral march up Market Street on July 9 commemorated the fallen.

Mayor Rossi, along with the Governor and those who represented management on the Embarcadero, believed the strike was the work of Communists. Rossi, in an emotional and strident address on the radio, vowed to end the strife which he believed was meant to overthrow the city's and the country's governments. He appealed to President Franklin D. Roosevelt to intercede. The president did not.

After considerable negotiations, on July 19 the teamsters returned to work . On July 31, after an 83-day strike the longshoremen up and down the coast followed suit and voted for arbitration. They won major concessions from their employers in a struggle that electrified the nation.

A LA CARTE

Oyster Cocktail --------------- 30

ANTIPASTI
Italian __ or Salami -------- 15
Tonno .. Olive Oil ---------- 30
Green Onions or Pickles ----- 1u
Celery en Branch ------------ 15
Pepperoncini di Verona ------ 10
Italian Anchovies ----------- 30
Antipasto "Il Sole" --------- 40
Assorted Antipasto ---------- 50

SALADS
Lettuce or Romana ----------- 15
  With Eggs or Tomatoes ---- 25
  With Anchovies or Tonno -- 40
Combination 30; with Shrimps,
  Crab, Anchovies or Tonno -- 40
Asparagus with Mayonnaise --- 35
Shrimp Salad ---------------- 30
Sliced Tomato, Green Peppers- 25
Chicken Salad --------------- 50

SHELL FISH
Shrimp Cocktail ------------- 25

COLD MEATS
Assorted Cold Meats --------- 50
Cold Sliced Chicken --------- 75

SOUP
Consomme -------------------- 10
Vermicelli ------------------ 15
Pastina 15; with Eggs ------- 25
Minestrone ------------------ 15
Maritata -------------------- 30
Pavese ---------------------- 40

ITALIAN SEMOLINO PASTE
Spaghetti a la Napoletana --- 40
Ravioli a la Genovese ------- 40
Mostaccioli a la Napoletana - 40
Tagliarini a la Napoletana -- 40
Farfalle a la Parmigiana ---- 40
Risotto a la Milanaise (to order) 50
Any Paste with Mushrooms 50c

CHICKEN
Half Broiled Spring Chicken - 65
Half Chicken, Fried or Saute
  a Sec --------------------- 65
Chicken Saute a la Cacciatora 1.25
Chicken Saute with Artichokes,
  Green Peppers, Peas or
  Potatoes, Zucchini ------- 1.50
Chicken Saute, Mushrooms --- 1.50
Chicken Saute a la Casserola 1.75
Chicken a la Fior d'Italia -- 1.75

VEGETABLES
Cauliflower Saute ----------- 25
Spinach Saute --------------- 25
Fried Artichokes ------------ 40
String Beans ---------------- 25

POTATOES
Italian Fried --------------- 15
Saratoga -------------------- 15
Long Branch ----------------- 20
Shoestring ------------------ 20
Cottage Fried --------------- 25
Hashed Brown ---------------- 25
Au Gratin ------------------- 30

STEAKS AND CHOPS
Club Steak ------------------ 50
Sirloin Steak --------------- 75
T-Bone Steak ---------------- 1.00
Porterhouse Steak ----------- 90
Tenderloin Steak 1.10 Half-- 65
Veal Chop ------------------- 40
Lamb Chops ------------------ 50
Veal Cutlet a la Milanaise -- 40
Broiled Ham or Bacon -------- 40
Veal Saute with Potatoes ---- 50

ITALIAN SPECIALTIES
Scallopini with Peas or Potatoes 50
Scallopini with Mushrooms --- 50
Fritto Misto ---------------- 50
Rovelline a la Luchese ------ 50
Sweetbreads Saute ----------- 50
Frittata a la Genovese ------ 40
Veal Saute a la Cacciatora -- 40

SANDWICHES
Swiss Cheese ---------------- 30
Salami ---------------------- 30
Ham ------------------------- 30
Chicken --------------------- 40
Turkey ---------------------- 40

EGGS and OMELETTES
Fried or Boiled Eggs (2) ---- 30
Scrambled Eggs on Toast ----- 30
Plain Omelette -------------- 30
Spanish Omelette ------------ 40
Ham or Bacon and Eggs ------- 40

CHEESE
Fresh Monterey -------------- 15
Imported Swiss -------------- 15
Imported Gorgonzola --------- 15
Imported Parmigiano --------- 15

DESSERT
Orange, Pear or Apple ------- 10
Vanilla Ice Cream ----------- 20
Baked Apple 10; a la Mode --- 20
Preserved Peaches 20; a l'Mode 25
Apple Fritters -------------- 30
Banana Fritters ------------- 30
Mixed Fresh Fruit in Season - 25
Zabaione -------------------- 30
Coffee (per cup) ------------ 10
Milk ------------------------ 10
Pot of Chocolate ------------ 20

REGULAR DINNER 75c

Oyster or Shrimp Cocktail
Or Shrimp or Lettuce Salad   Salami

Chicken Soup, Minestrone or Consomme

Paste, Italian Style

Roast Chicken   Lamb Chops and Potatoes
Scallops of Veal and Potatoes

Ice Cream
Glass of Beer   Cup of Coffee   or Glass of Claret

DE LUXE DINNER -- $1.00
Oyster Cocktail or Salad

Assorted Antipasto a la Fior d'Italia

Minestrone Soup or Chicken Broth with Pastina

Special Tagliarini or Ravioli with Mushroom Sauce

Chicken Saute a la Fior d'Italia
Scallops of Veal with Mushrooms and Potatoes
or Club Steak

Fresh Fruit   Ice Cream
Coffee, Beer or Pint of Claret

SPECIAL ENTREES

Veal Fricandeau, Ravioli ------ 40	Roast Veal with Vegetables ---- 40
Fresh Cod Fish -------------- 40	Brains with Brown Butter ---- 40
Veal Fricandeau, Spinach ---- 40	Veal Cutlet Breaded with Fried
Boiled Beef, Vegetables ------ 40	Potatoes ---------------- 40
Sea Bass -------------------- 40	Roast Chicken and Vegetables - 50
Roast Beef, Vegetables ------- 40	

FISH
Sandabs and Potatoes -------- 40   Rex Sole and Potatoes -------- 40

BEER LIST
(Half Bottle)

Pabst Blue Ribbon 25   Regal Amber 15   Globe 15
Golden Glow 15   Lucky Lager 15

BEVERAGES

Grenadine 25   Syphon 15
Canada Dry 40   White Rock 40   Belfast 30

February 10, 1935 menu

the nation.

ZUPPA PAVESE (PAVIAN SOUP)

This is a typical soup of Pavia, a city south of Milan. Easily multiplied, this is a hearty dish eaten with Italian bread.

1 cup brown stock (page 33) or chicken stock
1 large egg
2 slices Italian bread, toasted and buttered
Freshly grated Parmesan cheese

In a small saucepan, bring the stock to a boil over high heat. Decrease the heat to maintain a low simmer, crack the egg into a small bowl, and carefully slide the egg into the stock. Poach at barely a simmer until the whites are firm, but the yolk is still soft, about 4 minutes. Gently transfer to a warmed large soup bowl.

To serve: Crumble the buttered toast into large croutons over the soup and sprinkle with the Parmesan; serve immediately.

Serves one

CHAPTER 8: *I Clienti* (The Customers)

Armido always became excited when Joseph Di Giorgio entered the restaurant. The president of Di Giorgio Fruit Corporation and a prominent individual in North Beach society, this patron was also an official of Associated Farmers, a group that suppressed the farm workers toiling in California's fields during the Depression. Surely this distinction was not what caused Armido such joy; rather, it was the importance the man exuded.

When Di Giorgio walked in, always accompanied by a group of colleagues or family, Armido would cry out, *"Ecco Di Giorgio"* (Here comes Di Giorgio), alerting the kitchen that the powerful food magnate had arrived in the restaurant and was approaching.

Armido would then "dash down the aisle to greet him," recalled Davide Lippi, who was a young busboy at the time and the nephew of Fior's chef, Basile Lippi. The patron would wield the menu like a potentate and do all the ordering for his table.

Clients are of course the life blood of any business. At the Fior, they formed a kind of set, a familial coterie that made life make sense to the owners and the staff.

The Regular

Anyone who's dined in the Fior's smallest dining room, the Godfather Room, will have seen a copy, much enlarged, of an entry from the long-lived cartoon, *Ripley's Believe It or Not.* The portrayal features the likeness of Luigi Scaglione, who ate at the Fior every day for 54 years.

While the *Ripley's* representation claims that Scaglione was a customer twice a day, Lippi, who waited on him at 504 Broadway, said he came in only once daily.

"He sat at the same table and same chair every day. Nobody else would dare sit in that seat. He sat at a round table that seated maybe eight people. He was there by himself every evening, but eventually the table would fill and they would seat single people at the same table. He was a very quiet man but forceful. The waiters were very respectful of him, impressed by his manner," Lippi said.

Maybe the waiters didn't know what Armido knew about this loyal customer. Doris Muscatine told what went on behind the scenes:

(Scaglione) worked as a tailor at the fine gentlemen's haberdashery, Bullock and Jones, and put most of his funds into stocks. When the 1929 crash came, he lost almost everything. He asked the owner, then Papa Marianetti, if he could charge his meals and pay at the end of the month. Papa obligingly kept a record, entering vague marks on a pad to satisfy his customer, but charging only a very modest sum when payment day came around. The last

Ripley's Believe It or Not portrayed
the Fior's most regular customer, Luigi Scaglione.

three years, he wouldn't allow Scaglione to pay at all, reassuring him with an offhanded "Pagherà" ("You'll pay some day.") [1]

Scaglione obviously had very strong ideas about food and was unwavering in his patronage of the Fior. He said he ate at his niece's once a year but dreaded it. Scaglione wasn't alone. Local attorney Renzo Turco was also a Fior devotee, dining there every Thursday for 50 years. Turco was one of the founders of the men's club, *Il Cenacolo*, which in later years became strongly identified with the restaurant.

Was it the highly praised food that drew the patronage? Or was it the camaraderie and ambiance of the Fior itself?

For the lunch trade at 504 Broadway, management set a long table set right by the front window facing the street. It accommodated perhaps 20 people. Merchants, attorneys and other businessmen would drift in and take a seat, frequently the same spot every day. They all knew each other and would freely discuss timely topics.

"Some had the habit of going into the kitchen to look around and sample a little. The owners didn't like it but let them do it," Lippi remembered. They might look over the rim of a pot or a pan and say to the cook, *"O, fammi provar un pò di quello"* (Let me try a bit of that) to help them decide what to order.

Famous visitors to the city were also frequent guests at the Fior. One was Guglielmo Marconi, the inventor of the wireless radio, who came to San Francisco in 1934, an arrival that stirred the neighborhood. Following established custom, any distinguished visitor from Italy (though Marconi was as much an Englishman as an Italian) had to visit the clergy at the church first. He was photographed at St. Peter's and Paul's, the religious heart of North Beach facing Washington Square. Eventually, the then consul general of Italy brought him to dine at the Fior.

And long-time Fior patron, photographer Alessandro Baccari, took his portrait. Apparently, the Italian consulate had decided Baccari should photograph Marconi but they had not alerted the photographer. Before the appointment took place one day, a group of men burst into Baccari's studio and began to dismantle his cameras and other equipment. Baccari erupted and protested, "what the hell do you think you're doing?"

The intruders revealed they knew he was going to take the inventor's picture. It turned out they were security personnel checking his equipment for possible weapons.

"He has no appointment and I make the decision whether I want to photograph or not," Baccari shot back.

Later, the consul called Baccari and asked to make an appointment for Marconi "at 9 in the morning."

"But I don't get up before 10 and I don't function right until around 11:30," the photographer asserted. Marconi was amused by the photographer's assertiveness when the conversation was relayed to him.

The inventor was concerned about his photograph, which was to be a portrait. Marconi had a glass eye, the result, Baccari surmised, of some of his experimental work. However, Baccari was able to photograph him softly, through a mirror and using only a single source of light.

Marconi wouldn't leave before he saw the results. He followed the photographer right into his darkroom. The security guards began to trail in as well. But Baccari shooed them outside the studio door. He developed the film with Marconi looking over his shoulder, by all accounts, pleased with the images as they darkened.

Much of Marconi's pioneering work was done in the Bay Area, particularly in the Tomales Bay region, and from his Bolinas transmitting station. The city awarded Marconi honorary citizenship in 1933, four years before he died.

Let's Have Fun in San Francisco, a 1939 tour guide, commented on the Fior's clientele:

> During the Opera season you are apt to find the entire cast there, for it is a tradition for singers to go to Fior d'Italia when they are in town…in the old days it was Caruso, Salassa, Mascagni, who wrote Cavalleria Rusticana. These led the procession. Today you may see Pinza, Gigli, Martinelli, Maestro Merola and perhaps Tibbett. [2]

Frank Marianetti remembered Gaetano Merola's frequent appearances at the Fior. The founder and first general director of the San Francisco Opera would acknowledge Frank when he entered but the maestro refused to order from him. Instead, he would demand, "Where's your father?" – meaning Armido.

"He would go through the same ritual every time he came in. He was a ham. He would give me his coat to hang up. He would tell my father what he wanted for his group: Spaghetti. He'd give him the recipe: 'Tomatoes, skinned, seeded, passed through a machine. And not too ripe. And please, no garlic. Plain tomato sauce.' Anyway, he'd strut and make sure everybody knew he was in the place," Frank said. Merola was in large part responsible for the careers of such luminaries as Licia Albanese and Ezio Pinza, so it was perhaps fitting that he strut.

Davide Lippi remembered him as of average height, medium build with a good-sized moustache. "He was a kind of potentate sitting at a table," he said.

Frank recalled the maestro was pictured on the cover of TIME magazine with an interview inside the publication. Merola told the reporter there were only two restaurants in the United States he would go to. One was the Fior d'Italia, the other was in Los Angeles.

Frank recalled Merola's account of a trip he made to that very Los Angeles restaurant once. When he appeared there one night, the owner said it was quite busy and gave Merola $10 to eat elsewhere. The maestro was impressed with the owner's largesse. He said it was the first time anyone had given him money to eat elsewhere.

But Frank interpreted the transaction differently: "The reason he got the 10 bucks is because he was a pain in the ass. Very demanding. All the olive oils and everything."

A View from a Youngster

Young restaurant guests sometimes have a different experience of restaurants than their parents. Giovanna and her brother, Giorgio Andreini, remember during this era that the Fior had two entrances, one only for ladies. When her family entered the restaurant with her mother, they would use only the ladies' entrance. Married women and their families were led into a section where the booths were curtained with flowered material, creating a protective, intimate atmosphere.

"Mom and the children would be put in there and Daddy would go to the bar with his friends. Most of the men would do the same thing. Men who had their 'other women' would meet them in the bar. A mom would never leave the booth," Giovanna said.

Giovanna's father, Professor Giovanni Andreini, was an executive at Occidental Life Insurance. A close fried of A. P. Giannini, Andreini, played a key role in the Bank of America's acquisition of Occidental Life Insurance Company, the offices of which were in the bank's headquarters building. Because of his close relationship with A.P., Andreini arranged to get Giovanna a summer job in the bank's central files when she was sixteen. When Andreini dined with A. P. and the other bank executives, the daughter joined them for lunch at the Fior.

"He was from Italy and very protective of me so he would not let me go out to lunch by myself," she remembered.

One of the luncheon diners from the bank was Giannini's right-hand man, Virgil Dardi. Giovanna recalled Dardi as flamboyant and expansive. When she entered the restaurant, he would call out to her from his seat, "Oh Giovannina!" While this was a warm and familiar atmosphere for a young lady, the bank executives were too solicitous about her welfare to suit Giovanna.

"They were trying to find me a husband. They'd discuss it over the table right in front of me. It made me so mad, I didn't want to go anymore," she said.

A few years later, she would find her own husband, indirectly thanks to the Fior. She was in the cast of a passion play being produced at the College of Notre Dame in Belmont either in 1949 or 1950. The college was a women's school, so male roles had to be filled from outside. They recruited Paul Marianetti, George's son, and a Dick Stockman from other schools to play two men.

"We sat in the back of the stage in the dark, waiting for our turns to be onstage. Paul introduced me to Dick. We were married a few months later and stayed married for 50 years," Giovanna said.

It Comes back to the Food

While Muscatine was praising the Fior during this era, so were other writers of the decade. In *Eating around San Francisco*, by Ruth Thompson and Chef Louis Hanges limned a sharp portrait of the restaurant in the 1930s:

A fact which draws those who know good Italian food to this place is that such typical dishes as capretto are served. Capretto is a young goat or kid and is a favorite meat of the Italians. It is a dish especially enjoyed in the spring and at Easter tide. At the Fior d'Italia it is prepared in all its delicacy with proper herb flavorings and is served daily to those who desire it. The tender young goat is butchered preferably at the age of two months, but certainly never after three. When braised and cooked with herbs and wine it is a considered a food fit for the gods.....

The cooking is done by Chef A. Luccessi (sic) who has been there for 30 years. He uses imported oils, cheeses and such. It is the boast of the management that no canned goods are ever used. ....

59

Each day, besides the varied menu of Italian foods, has its specialty. It may be something like this:

Monday: Polenta with (Belgian hare)

Tuesday: Calves' feet or tripe

Wednesday: Bocconicini cravatine

(veal with paste in bow-tie shapes)

Thursday: Osso bucco (marrow bone) with rice

Friday: Ciopino (sic)

Saturday: Pot roast and home-made ravioli

This is the place where the favorite pan grissini (bread sticks) are served. When walking through the pantry to the kitchen, the row upon row of glass containers with the pan grissini on the shelves made me feel as if I were walking through a forest of bread sticks. Minestrone, the popular Italian pastes and sauces, were all to be seen in the kitchen, which is large, light, airy and beautifully sanitary. The huge refrigerators, stored with fresh, chilling foods for dinner, were appetizing in appearance. Fish, tender young chickens, racks of lamb, luscious looking steaks – the variety at hand ready to cater to almost any order is a treat to see. [3]

A menu from Sunday, February 10, 1935, the year Thompson wrote the review in her book, described the Regular Dinner available for 75 cents. This dinner included a choice of seafood cocktail, salad or salami. One chose chicken soup, minestrone or consommé. A pasta dish followed and then came the entrée: roast chicken, lamb chops or scallops of veal. Ice cream gave pleasure to the finale.

The De Luxe $1.00 dinner offered more choices but in addition included an extensive à la carte list of antipasti, salads, pasta, meats, vegetables and side dishes, omelets, sandwiches, cheeses and desserts.

Some of the entries, such as brains with brown butter, or the soups *maritata* or *pastina* with eggs, or chicken sauté à la casserola are authentic Italian dishes but rarely seen anymore on menus in this country.

Three Cheers for the Cook

Armido and his brothers, Zeffiro (Cook-oh), Alfredo and Giuseppe, could all cook well but Armido took the prize, recalled his grandson Paul Marianetti who later became known as Paul Mantee.

"My grandfather could bone a squab without removing the knife. He used to go 'boompa dee-dee boom boom' and take out the bone," said Paul.

In 1956 Paul's father, George, told the *Pacific Coast Review*, a trade magazine, that Armido "was the best cook I ever knew."

By this time, Armido's cousins, Armando and Basilio Lippi, worked at the Fior as well. Basilio cooked while Armando was a waiter. Davide Lippi, Armando Lippi's son, had begun helping out as a child by washing glasses. An apprenticeship at the Fior had its set course: Wash glasses, then graduate to busboy and then perhaps to some other illustrious post such as waiter, bartender or cashier.

Armido had started his sons, George and Frank, washing glasses also about 15 years earlier. The soap was a harsh soap made of abrasive particles, important for washing glassware perhaps, but cruel to little boys' hands. When George had his baptism by sand soap, he returned home that night bleeding from his palms. Armido's wife Amelia scolded her husband but it didn't dissuade George.

"It was a kind of blood initiation he had to have. He talked about it with pride," said his son, Paul.

Armido was loved and respected even though he wasn't overly demonstrative. His sons, his daughters, Stella and Rina, and his wife idolized him. Paul remembered his grandfather as a man who "operated with a quiet grace." He loved being the patriarch but he didn't talk much and wasn't effusive with children.

"He never hugged me or anything. His way of relating to me was to give me a dollar for ice cream. In those days, that was 10 scoops, a lot of ice cream," Paul said. "But I had respect for him. I got the message: He's the provider of all these bounties, all of this."

Frank and George

By the Depression, George and Frank were grown men. They had never intended to join the restaurant in their youths. Yet two people never became more closely identified in modern times with the restaurant than these brothers, so different in temperament and style. George was convivial, extroverted and charming while Frank was quiet, internal, gracious and wise. After they had each spent their adolescences helping out at the Fior as busboys, cashiers and doing other functions, they struck out on their own.

Frank went to the University of California at Berkeley, a very uncommon choice for a young man from North Beach to do at the time, where he majored in English. He was one of only two in his graduating class. But he never attained the type of white-collar job he was qualified for because of the Depression. He worked variously for a hospital delivering X-rays, setting tile and selling insurance.

Frank eventually came to hate selling insurance and couldn't wait to get back to the restaurant. He didn't mind the long hours for he felt he was always learning at the Fior. He used to arrive at 9 A.M. to do preparatory work. "My father ordered maybe three dozen (live) chickens. Now they come in clean and eviscerated. That's not the way we got them. We had to cut off their heads, pull their guts out and separate the liver from the rest of the insides. They were fresher. You did it yourself. You washed them out. You knew what you were doing," he said.

His parents wanted him to go to Europe. Instead, in his early twenties he married Ruth Corsiglia. His brother had married Olive Foss and had a son, Paul, in 1931. George had gone to work for the Bank of California. He hoped to rise into the executive ranks.

George apparently was disgruntled at the Bank of California. Paul explained that his father felt "that since his name was Marianetti that he was not going to get very far at the bank. Never mind A. P. Giannini. He felt that Italians were discriminated against in the business world. His buddies were all getting promoted and he was not."

Then George did an unfortunate thing. Frank recollected an incident as revealing about himself as it was about George:

(George) had no taste for the restaurant business, long hours or working the holidays. (At the bank) he worked in the booking department and foreign exchange. He pulled a couple of fast ones at the bank and that really cooked his goose.

One of the senior officers at the bank -- very hard-boiled guy and by the book -- my brother was able to forge this guy's signature. (George) took about six guys up to a bar, ran a tab having drinks, and signed this fella's name. How stupid! When the guy got his bill, he knew he wasn't even there.

Word got back, somebody popped off. But my brother someday thought he'd be in an officer in the bank, but that killed it. (He) saw how much my father was making, very considerable, so he asked my father if he could come in as a partner. In my father's eye, my brother could do no wrong.

I think I was kind of a disappointment. (They) sent me to school but I didn't end up as a doctor or dentist. I wanted to be a waiter. I liked it. Isn't that strange? No desire to be a dentist.

George returned to the Fior later in the decade when Armido told him the place was doing exceptionally well and asked him to come back to work as a waiter. He did, perhaps reluctantly and looking for a refuge from the bank. Yet George was well suited to the restaurant business. Suave and welcoming, he had the glad hand always out and he was good at keeping the books. He had already been doing the Fior's bookkeeping once a month for years.

Ron Edwards, who ran the Fior's valet parking service for many years, recalled that George dressed the same way at the restaurant as he had at the bank, "with the swallowtails, white carnation and the Toscano," a large, dark Italian cigar.

Frank and George gradually took over the running of the restaurant from Armido and they stayed at the helm until the late 1970s. But there was always bad blood between them, a fact that they disguised before patrons but it was apparent to all the staff, many of whom were relatives.

Paul recalled that "most of my childhood, they weren't speaking to each other. I loved my Uncle Frank, he was very soft and very sensitive, a fabulous guy."

Paul believed that Frank, as the youngest of Armido's four children, received a lot of attention which George, the first-born, may have resented. By the mid 1930s, both men were fathers. While Frank remained married to Ruth the rest of his life, George and his first wife Olive divorced in 1936 when their son Paul was five. George took Paul to live with him at Amelia and Armido's house, just around the corner from where he had been living with Olive in the Marina.

Restaurant Life

Paul had warm memories of the restaurant during that period:

I was in awe of the restaurant. When I was very little, we would go in for dinner and the waiter, Oreste, always caught me with this trick. I would be sitting at the table and he would come in back of me with a napkin folded. He was a tiny little guy. He looked like an Italian Jack Gilford. He would come up in back with the napkin unraveled so the points stood out. Then he would just touch the back of your neck (with the edge of the napkin), very lightly, it felt like a fly. Then he would touch it again. I don't know how many times he would do it before anybody turned around. He did it every time and he got me every time.

Oreste wasn't the only prankster at the Fior. So was the cook, Basilio Lippi. He would take advantage of the waiter, Nandino, who adored tuna salad. When he determined that Nandino was just about to tuck into one, Basilio would take a cork and chop it finely and add it to the dish of greens.

Ever mischievous, Basilio also preyed upon one patron, a Mr. Solari. There was a lottery run by a Chinese outfit on Kearny Street. It was Davide Lippi's duty to go down to Kearny Street to bring the lottery tickets to the Fior. After the lottery was drawn, the Chinese proprietor would come to the restaurant with a big sheet of numbers with holes in it. The holes indicated which numbers had been drawn.

One time, Basilio grabbed that sheet as soon as it came in and punched extra holes for the numbers that Solari had played. Solari was ecstatic and cried out: *Oddio, ma guarda li, ho vinto, ho vinto!* (Oh my God, look, I've won, I've won!)

Paul learned from the Fior men. Domenico Batistessa had been part-owner during the twenties and thirties. While he no longer retained his equity by the forties, he kept his reputation among the staff and management. Paul Mantee remembers him as an inconspicuous figure that dressed like a waiter but operated as a busboy.

I got the impression (in the mid-forties) that he was the elder statesman of the Fior and possessed of a kind of restaurant wisdom. My dad said offhandedly that…if Batistessa suggested I do something, it would be wise for me to do it….Batistessa taught me how to slice French bread – zing, zing, zing–leaving only a quarter of an inch at the bottom connected to the loaf. I don't remember him saying anything except that he engendered reverence.

North Beach Means *Mangiare*

By all means, the Fior was not alone among the popular dining places of San Francisco. North Beach was honeycombed with excellent and beloved eateries. Jerry Flamm's memoir about the Depression in San Francisco, *Good Life in Hard Times*, recalls the abundance of wonderful restaurant and nightlife during the period, much of which still exists, such as the Gold Spike, Bimbo's 365 Club, the New Pisa and Julius' Castle.

The Gold Spike, still on Columbus Avenue, began as a candy store that accommodated some gambling activity in the back during Prohibition. Food and whiskey were served to keep the games going and after the Eighteenth Amendment was repealed, the establishment dropped the cover of selling confections and became a restaurant and bar.

Recounted Flamm: "During the thirties, after repeal, one of the specials of the house was seven Coffee Royals lined up on the bar for a dollar. This was a popular draw for the laborers who would drop by in groups for a drink after work." [4]

Flamm quotes a patron as saying: "Dinner was 50 cents with lots of French bread, which cost six cents a loaf then. Pasta like spaghetti was 10 cents a pound. Dried beans for the minestrone soup were five cents a pound. Guys who worked at the cement plant and lived around here used to come a lot." [5]

Pierino Gavello was a partner in, or owned outright, several establishments. He sold his interests in the dinner clubs, Lido and Apollo, when he opened his own Lucca's near Fisherman's Wharf. Lucca's had a winning strategy -- enormous portions of very good cooking at only 50 cents. People lined up around the corner to eat there. Lucca's was renowned for its pastries, especially the petit fours that its own bakery and pastry shop produced.

While Armando and Basilio Lippi were partners in the Fior, they also owned a small share in Lucca's and worked at each.

In the late 1930s, Gavello opened the Riviera on Washington Square in North Beach across from St. Peter's and Paul's Church. It would figure in the Fior's destiny in the coming years. [6]

In 1936, Joe Finocchio and his wife, Eva, opened a nightspot at 506 Broadway, upstairs from the Fior that became a worldwide tourist attraction. Finocchio's featured female impersonators as the sole entertainment. This was considered quite outré at the time and its attraction endured until changing real estate prices forced its closure in 1999. There was a good relationship between the owners of the Fior and the Finocchios. Sometimes Davide was sent upstairs to bring dinner to Joe Finocchio whom he remembered as a good tipper.

"I'd go up before the show started but I'd see performers coming in and out. Before the customers would start coming in, they'd have all these glasses lined up with shots already in them so they could speed up the making of the drinks," Davide said.

One could imagine young Davide looking intently about, eyes wide as spaghetti platters, as he went upstairs to see what he could see.

He was never called to wait on the female impersonators, however, because only the owner, Joe, ever placed an order.

The Bigger Picture

Despite the economic misery of the decade, large projects were launched that glorified the city and gave San Francisco and North Beach their defining characteristics. Construction on the Golden Gate and the San Francisco-Oakland Bay Bridges commenced in 1933. The Bay Bridge was completed in 1936 and the Golden Gate the year later. Both were accomplished under the mayoralty of Mayor Rossi (1931-39), partly with the support of A. P. Giannini, who agreed to buy bonds for the Golden Gate.

It was also in 1933 that the monument overlooking North Beach, Coit Tower, was erected. It was designed to mimic the nozzle of a fire hose. Appearing to watch guard over the community below, it was funded by the estate of eccentric and moneyed Lili Coit, who, as a child, spent much time chasing fire engines and cheering firemen as they put out fires on Telegraph Hill. A monument, which she erected, honors the city's firefighters and stands in Washington Square across from the current site of the Fior.

SALMONE AFFOGATO (POACHED SALMON)

Do not overcook.

2 small shallots, finely chopped
2 small leeks, white part only, cleaned and finely chopped
2 small carrots, peeled and finely chopped
2 stalks celery, finely chopped
1 bay leaf
4 (7-ounce) fillets of boneless, skinless salmon
Salt and freshly ground black pepper
2 cups dry white wine
1/2 cup unsalted butter, at room temperature, cut into 8 to 10 pieces

Scatter the shallots, leeks, carrots, celery, and bay leaf in the bottom of a large saucepan. Place the salmon on top of the vegetables; season with salt and pepper. Add the wine, cover with a tightly fitting lid, and bring to a boil over medium-high heat. Decrease the heat to medium-low and cook until the salmon is just opaque in the center, 7 to 9 minutes. Do not overcook. Transfer the salmon to a plate and keep warm.

Strain the pan juices through a fine-mesh strainer into a small saucepan; discard the solids. Cook the sauce over medium-high heat until reduced by half. Whisk in the butter piece by piece, whisking until the each piece of butter has emulsified before adding the next.

To serve: Arrange the salmon on 4 warmed serving plates, spoon the sauce over the top, and serve immediately.

Serves four

CHAPTER 9: Lock the Doors. Lock the Windows. 1940-50

Frank Marianetti remembered the onset of World War II as the time "when life got terrible." A frightening tunnel of uncertainty bored through North Beach for reasons quite unlike the problems suffered by the rest of the country.

When Japan bombed Pearl Harbor on December 7, 1941, terror-stricken San Francisco plainly felt vulnerable. The next day, Ocean Beach was thronged with people staring at the Pacific as if they could find some answer in the great expanse. At 11 A.M., less than an hour after the attack, the military began laying mines in the bay. The police stopped all soldiers and sailors on the streets and sent them back to their stations of duty. Mayor Angelo J. Rossi proclaimed an emergency and pledged the city government's cooperation with the Civil Defense Council.

On December 9, enemy warplanes flew over San Francisco. Western Defense Commander Lt. General John L. DeWitt spoke stridently to the Mayor: "You people do not seem to realize we are at war. So get this: last night there were planes over this community. They were enemy planes. I mean Japanese planes!" [1]

Blackouts were imposed along with the rationing of food, gasoline, rubber and metals. But people lived and did business throughout this hysteria. Frank recalled the mood in the restaurant:

Holy God, lock the doors…. lock the windows. We had big plywood things we used for the restaurant windows when the blackout started. Walk down Columbus Avenue, and people were getting in fights all the time, crazy people, screwy….

When the Japanese bombed Pearl Harbor, they talked about the possibility of bombing San Francisco too, so we had eight pieces of plywood, different sizes, to cover the windows. We had them all lined. [There was talk of] the strong possibility about an attack. One night, everything was going fine at the restaurant, then the scary sirens started. Little Oreste puts plywood on the wrong window, hammered it in. The whole goddam thing was a mess, nothing fit right. (We) had to turn out all the lights in the restaurant, but nothing happened. It was a test! And we had all this plywood nailed to our walls. We were fine. (We had) two candles in the dining room and kept serving dinner. We took the plywood off when it all was over, and then lined them up right. (Everyone was) very excitable.

Japanese submarines were detected off the coast of California several times in the ensuing days. On December 24, a Japanese submarine was poised to shell the city, but apparently on orders from its Japanese superiors, it turned around and returned to its base in the Marshall Islands. The next week, agents of the Federal Bureau of Investigations were given the authority to search the homes of enemy aliens if they suspected contraband to be on the premises.

The danger posed by the enemy was perceived within the very fabric of life in San Francisco and the West Coast. U.S. Treasury agents told the army in San Francisco that "an estimated 20,000 Japanese in the San Francisco metropolitan region were ready for organized action." [2]

The respected newspaper columnist, Walter Lipmann, wrote that the West Coast, "is in imminent danger of a combined attack from within and without…It may at any moment be a battlefield. Nobody's constitutional rights include the right to reside and do business on a battlefield." [3]

Many in the military felt compelled to avert a perceived danger by means that today are considered to have been unconstitutional as well as cruel and unjust. In February and March of 1942, President Franklin D. Roosevelt signed Executive Orders 9066 and 9102, respectively. The first order authorized the designation of "military areas" from which persons could be excluded. This authorization meant that people who lived or worked in a military area could not return there. The second order created a War Relocation Authority to carry out the removal and relocation of excluded residents. Under this provision, excluded residents were taken from their homes and interned in camps.

Soon after the orders were signed, General DeWitt issued Civilian Exclusion Orders pertaining to all enemy aliens over fourteen years of age and all persons of Japanese ancestry. His first order imposed a curfew on all persons of Japanese ancestry, all alien Germans, and alien Italians who resided within the designated military area.

Throughout the Bay Area, thousands of such families had to evacuate areas close to sensitive facilities, including military bases (of which there were several in the Bay Area), and the industrial and waterfront areas as well. Even Joltin' Joe DiMaggio's fisherman father was restricted from fishing beyond local waters. The city of Pittsburg, northeast of San Francisco was decimated when 2,000 of its 7,000 residents were forced to leave.

Of the millions of Americans of Italian origin, about 600,000 had remained, for various reasons, resident aliens. These people suddenly had to register as enemy aliens even though many had lived in America for most of their lives and had long ago considered themselves Americans. Many had given birth to U.S. citizens who were now in the U.S. Armed Forces.

In February of 1942, Italian and German aliens were subject to a curfew from 8 P.M. to 6 A.M. They could not travel more than five miles without special permission and could not enter designated "strategic areas." [4]

Within a year, over 1,250 Italian aliens had been arrested, many simply for violating the curfew. Countrywide, about 228 non-citizens were sent away for up to two years to camps in Montana, Oklahoma, Tennessee and Texas, according to Rose Scherini, an historian of this era of Italian-American history. And 254 naturalized citizens were excluded – that is, sent to live in inland states.

Whether any excluded or interned were Fascists or spies is unclear. Those interned were not informed of the charges against them. They were not allowed legal counsel. Because one resident of North Beach, Carmelo Ilacqua, was an employee of the Italian consulate, he was wrested from his family and interned.

"In San Francisco, about 20 Italian Americans, both men and women, were excluded. They were community leaders, Italian-language school instructors, staff of the pro-fascist Italian-language newspaper, *L'Italia*, and members of the Italian War Veterans," recounted Lawrence DiStasi, who is editor of *Una Storia Segreta: The Secret History of Italian American Evacuation and Internment during World War II.*

The movement to rid the Coast of enemy aliens rattled the Fior community as well as North Beach. Several of the Fior's most notable and most loyal patrons were interned and/or relocated. The American-born Mayor Rossi, as well as the naturalized Ettore Patrizi, editor of the daily *L'Italia*, and Renzo Turco, the international lawyer and founder of *Il Cenacolo* (a club which figured later in the Fior's history), were the most notable among the Fior circle to be targeted and uprooted.

All the residents of Italian ancestry in North Beach felt the disgrace of being seen as traitorous. Rossi's Market in North Beach (not related to the former mayor) carried the sign: "No Italian spoken for the duration of the war." The garbage collectors of San Francisco, mostly Genoese, painted on their trucks: "Italy is in our veins, but America is in our hearts."

Excerpts from an article, by James O. Clifford, filed by the Associated Press on December 18, 1999, paint the sad picture that made this particular official acknowledgement important. Early in the '40s, the State of California held secret hearings to investigate ``un-American activities''. These hearings eventually led to the relocation of citizens. California-born Rossi was among those called to the stand and humiliated.

> The records show (Mayor) Rossi was asked pointedly if he had any sympathy for fascism.
>
> "Absolutely not," he replied.
>
> "Have you always been against it?" his inquisitor persisted.
>
> "I have only one form of government, and that's the American form of government," answered Rossi, who was born in the United States.
>
> The mayor reacted angrily when he was asked if he had ever given the outstretched arm salute favored by the black-shirted followers of Italy's Fascist dictator, Benito Mussolini.
>
> Rossi shot back that the hearing represented "government by poisoned platitudes and scandalous generalities." He said the lawmakers were "creating religious and racial bigotry in a city world-famed for its tolerance."
>
> Still, Rossi got off easy compared to Ettore Patrizi, editor of an Italian newspaper,
>
> *L' Italia*, in San Francisco. He was asked if he felt American soldiers of Italian descent would fight against Italy. "No matter how they loved their mother country, they will do their duty," Patrizi said in testimony that filled 27 transcript pages.
>
> But the 77-year-old Patrizi, a naturalized American citizen since 1899, was forced to move and to stay out of military areas that covered about two-thirds of California. Accusations against both men came from Carmelo Zito, publisher of the city's rival Italian language newspaper, *Il Corriere del Popolo.*
>
> Zito claimed Rossi gave the fascist salute, and testified that Patrizi sponsored a radio show in the late 1930s that gave "the message of Mussolini to the Italian-Americans of California." [6]

Officers of the Federal Bureau of Investigation entered Italians' homes, searched their belongings, confiscated shortwave radios, cameras and any objects that could conceivably be employed as signaling devices. The usually lively streets of North Beach must have been much quieter. We have no record but one can imagine that several waiters at the Fior must have had tough decisions to make about whether to serve the dinner shift and risk violating the curfew.

After several months of lobbying by Italian-American politicians, the restrictions were rescinded. The U.S. Attorney General chose Columbus Day, October 12, 1942, to lift the restrictions on Italian aliens.

It could be said that these privations were not severe since they lasted less than a year, but it was a period of shame, family separation, loss of livelihood and property whose effects were felt for generations thereafter.

Not until November of 2000, did the U.S. Government finally acknowledge the injustices by passing the Wartime Violation of Italian American Civil Liberties Act. But the language included no apology.

Dining out during World War II

The U.S. Office of Price Administration introduced food rationing to avoid price inflation and ensure that food would be equitably distributed while it was being diverted to the war effort. Sugar and meat were especially restricted. Still, while food was rationed for consumers and corporations, the hospitality industry seemed to get off scot-free. John Mariani, in his book, *America Eats out*, painted one picture of how the general public and restaurants conformed to rationing limitations:

Americans were limited to one pound of sugar per person per week, four ounces of butter and four ounces of cheese, and there were cutbacks on coffee and flour as well. Sugar bowls disappeared from restaurant tables, while molasses, honey and saccharin were substituted in desserts and pastries. Restaurants were allowed to use only one pound of coffee for every hundred meals and one pound of sugar for every thirty-three customers in 1943. Chefs were reminded to conserve fats, oils and shortenings, not only because they were energy foods but also because they were ingredients in munitions. [7]

However, Amy Bentley, assistant professor of food and nutritional studies at New York University, said restaurants had much more

leeway than the official line would indicate. Bentley's book, *Eating for Victory: Food Rationing and the Politics of Domesticity,* studied the connections between eating and American life during World War II. In an interview, she said restaurants were to abide only by the principle that they mustn't buy more than they did before the war.

"But there was a lot of fudging and restaurants got away with it," she said. There was a big black market.

"You may know a local butcher that you could buy from, a farmer with an arrangement to slaughter cattle. You could get around it," she said.

While consumers had to buy ration coupons to buy food at grocery stores, they did not need to use them to eat at restaurants. This difference meant that those with the means to eat regularly at restaurants hardly suffered from the rationing system. There was a great deal of resentment about this loophole among those less well off and groups such as labor unions. According to Bentley:

Bread and wheat were never rationed during the war. It was more canned goods, butter and dairy products but not eggs. But after the war when there was global famine, the U.S. started a voluntary rationing campaign on wheat so wheat could be diverted to newly freed countries. The U.S. called on restaurants voluntarily to remove breadbaskets and cut down on wheat. There was one wheat-less day a week. The *New York Times* said restaurants were not complying with this. It was too hard to enforce.

According to the Museum of the City of San Francisco, the Office of Price Administration set new ceiling prices for fresh produce, dropping the price of lettuce, for instance, by 2 cents. In February, 1945, just weeks before Germany surrendered to the Allies, a midnight curfew was imposed on San Francisco restaurants "to save fuel, keep wartime production high and factory absenteeism low." [8]

All Was Not Totally Grim

There were vibrant, hopeful moments during wartime too, of course. Alessandro Baccari, Jr., an artist and photographer and son of the Baccari who had photographed inventor Marconi two decades before, tells the story of the famed black athlete, singer, actor and activist, Paul Robeson. A leftist who was accused of being a member of the Communist Party, Robeson was as often maligned as he was adored.

In 1943, he opened on Broadway in *Othello*, a role with which he became strongly identified throughout his career. In an era when racial segregation was an unquestioned reality of life in America, Robeson took the show on the road and so came to San Francisco. Unfortunately, he was denied entry into a well-known Italian restaurant in North Beach during his stay here . However, he dined at the Fior d'Italia without incident and was served with dignity, as a guest of Alessandro Baccari, Sr.

One delightful incident developed during the war, when Lynette E. de St. Croix, a corporal in the Marine Corps, was stationed in Menlo Park, California. She reminisced:

My roommate, Martha Jacob and I, we went through boot camp together. We wandered into the Fior with two friends of mine from Minneapolis…. We kept going there. We liked it and they treated us well. After the war, I went back home to Minneapolis and got married. My husband, John Trux, got a job in San Francisco. We bought a house in Menlo Park but we didn't have enough money for a babysitter. We would take our baby Sara (to the Fior) in her car bed. In those days it was a little cloth cradle thing with two metal stands on each end. We brought her up (to San Francisco) and were going to have her sitting out in the restaurant. Frank or George suggested, 'Why don't we slip her in the linen closet where it's quiet and dark?' She'd continue sleeping. We'd put her bed on the floor of the closet. So they would seat us outside the linen closet. They always gave us an extra something, a free drink or extra dessert.

Eventually, the family moved to Portland, Oregon, and later back to Los Altos, south of San Francisco. On Lynette's fifieth birthday, the family celebrated at the Fior. By this time the little Trux infant Sara was a grown woman with two brothers. Lynette and John entered with their adult children to learn that by this time George Marianetti had died. They saw Frank Marianetti again and explained who they were.

Frank looked at Sara and remarked, "Oh, this is the linen closet baby."

Sara said, "I knew exactly what he meant because I had heard this (story) my entire life. The food was always good. The waiters always had a white napkin over their arm, as a kid you think that is wonderful. We always went there because we felt special and they knew us."

In 1945, at the end of the war, people were in an expansive mood. The Fior decided to celebrate its heritage rather than hide it or apologize for it. Its owners commissioned the painting of a mural that remains in the restaurant in its present location. Paul Rockwood, the painter, was instructed to depict the many landscapes of Northern Italy. The cover of a Fior menu described it rightly as "a fantasy" of Italy including "the topmost peaks of the Appenines," the Arno winding through Florence, ruined turrets, baronial estates and the town of Assisi.

Fior mural commissioned in 1945

GAMBERONI INVOLTATI IN PANCETTA
(PRAWNS WRAPPED IN PANCETTA)

No salt is used because pancetta is already very salty.

3 tablespoons olive oil
2 shallots, minced
2 cloves garlic, minced
1 tablespoon freshly squeezed lemon juice
1 teaspoon grated lemon zest
Freshly ground black pepper
16 extra large prawns, shelled and deveined
16 thin slices pancetta
4 (8-inch) bamboo skewers, soaked (metal skewers can work)
Chopped fresh flat-leaf parsley, for garnish

Preheat the broiler. Generously oil a large baking sheet.

In a medium sauté pan, heat the olive oil over medium-high heat. Add the shallots and garlic and cook until lightly browned, about 3 minutes. Stir in the lemon juice and zest. Season to taste with pepper. Keep warm over very low heat.

Wrap each prawn in a slice of pancetta, then skewer 4 wrapped prawns onto each bamboo skewer. Arrange the skewers on the prepared baking sheet and broil, about 4 inches from the heat source, until the pancetta is golden, 2 to 3 minutes. Turn the skewers and broil until the pancetta is golden and the prawns are opaque throughout, about 3 minutes.

To serve: Arrange the skewers on a serving platter and pour the sauce evenly over the prawns. Garnish with the parsley and serve immediately.

Serves four as an appetizer

CHAPTER 10: Cold War on a Plate

On February 12, 1945, San Francisco was selected as the site of a conference to forge a charter for the United Nations. That famous meeting lasted from April 25 to June 26, drawing large numbers of diplomats, stimulating huge reams of print and hours of broadcast news.

Frank remembered how the Fior was drawn into this event. However, since he could not name the document or the exact group involved, we cannot verify his account. All he remembered was that the Soviet bloc was preparing to sign a treaty.

"The emphasis every day on television was that these countries will not sign the treaty. It so happened that about five of them used to come to our place for lunch every day. I think they liked the boiled beef we had at the time. It must be like the Russian something or other," Frank said.

As the U.N. conference drew to a close, the Soviet big shots came to lunch on a Saturday.

"My fertile mind was working," Frank said. He asked the interpreter if the dignitaries would give him an autographed menu. They graciously accommodated him. Armed with the menu, Frank wrote to the famed columnist Herb Caen of the *San Francisco Chronicle* that while 'the delegates couldn't get the Russian contingent to sign the agreement...I got them to sign a menu.' It was the lead item in his column. That's when I became aware of the power of Herb Caen."

It certainly drummed up business. "People came in asking, 'who was the asshole that got the goddamn Russians to sign?' I was the bad guy," Frank said. These earthy words reflected the contempt in which the Soviet Union was held at the time.

When Angelo Del Monte had sold the restaurant business the previous decade, he didn't sell the building. Instead, 492 Broadway was not sold until 1945. At the time of its sale in 1945, there were several owners, including the estate of Assunta Del Monte, Angelo's wife, who had died in 1943. They sold the building to the owners of Vanessi's restaurant, which remained in that spot for decades.

The Changing Salad Bowl

In 1946, a young student of architecture from Weed, California, was persuaded to buy a failing grocery store on Grant Avenue in North Beach. He then gave up architecture forever. Bruno Andrighetto was having trouble making the grocery succeed so he did a wise thing. He turned to wholesale. At that time, most restaurant owners went themselves early each morning to buy produce at the farmer's market. A shrewd salesman, Bruno believed he could convince them to pay him for the convenience of supplying their needs. He snagged New Joe's restaurant as his first customer when its owner asked him to pick up a box of mushrooms for him.

"I bought a box of mushrooms for $7 and sold them for $8. It was the easiest dollar I ever made in my life," he recalled.

He tapped on the Marianettis' kitchen door as well. "George wanted me to get him *radicetta* (a variety of lettuce). He couldn't get it," Bruno said. But Bruno could. From then on, George asked him for two dozen bundles of *radicetta* a day. Finally, George asked the wholesaler if he ever supplied any other kind of produce. From then on and for years to come, Bruno supplied the Fior with Swiss chard, carrots and peas -- the ones the Fior habitués sat around the kitchen shelling while kibitzing. His business eventually became Lee Ray Tarantino, one of the largest produce wholesalers in the state of California.

Bruno recalled that the Fior's menu changed over the years and was reflected in its changing demands for produce. "In the old days, they'd use *radicetta* for salad...Then they went into red lettuce. Then into romaine and then into the baby salads, just like everybody else because times change. In the old days, you ate boiled beef. Where now are you going to find boiled beef?" he said.

Antipasto Memories

Chef Giorgio Lucchesi's grandson, Bill Lucchesi, started eating at the Fior when he was a child. He remembered the décor clearly: aged pea-green booths enclosed by curtains. "It was rather austere, not very ornate," he said.

But especially he remembered the tastes and rhapsodized about a dish rarely seen in America anymore, *cima alla genovese* (pronounced CHEE-ma) or stuffed veal pocket, cooked in the Genoese style. Veal pocket is made by creating a hollow below the calf's ribs. It was frequently filled with chopped spinach, pine nuts and other vegetables. At the Fior, it was served cold, as part of the antipasto.

Bill remembered, "They had absolutely incredible antipasto

plates, incredible because they were so huge. They had prosciutto and calamari cooked a certain way I'd never had since, cold but sautéed. And the raviolis they had there were unbelievable, tasted like my grandmother's. The filling must have been a *genovese* derivative."

Davide Lippi recollected that during the war years the Fior offered three menus: a 50-cent dinner, a 75-cent dinner and a dollar dinner. The dollar dinner provided a fifth of a bottle of wine, antipasto and the regular courses, including prosciutto.

While Lucchesi was of Genoese background and remembered fondly the Genoese dish *cima*, Paul Mantee, George Marianetti's son, remembered most warmly the Tuscan dishes that reflected his family's background. He said the "cooking was the way they did it in Maggiano, real Provençal."

He remembered the pasta known as *lasagnette* (lazan-YEH-teh). The Fior used these inch-wide ribbons of pasta in many of its dishes, particularly in a specialty of the restaurant at that time, chicken with *lasagnette*. Paul recalled:

My grandfather (Armido) said he didn't put it on the menu because he said Americans don't like this kind of food. I said they love this kind of food. My father (George) convinced him otherwise. So they put it on the menu and it was a huge seller. During the war, sailors and soldiers were coming from the East coast ordering lasagne and what they wanted was what they got at home, the (wider) Sicilian kind…. I don't think it's as good. So when they were served lasagnette, they'd say this isn't lasagne. It wasn't, it was better. So my father learned how to make the other lasagna. They'd do it as if you were to make chicken sauté, brown chicken in olive oil on both sides, smash and brown some garlic, chop tomatoes. You make a sauce with a chicken base and then you put it on the pasta…with some Italian mushrooms, porcini.

Three soups were cooking at all times at the Fior. At 6:00 A.M., a staffer came to chop the vegetables for the minestrone. Beef consommé and chicken and barley soup were also always on the stove.

"They had a clam chowder on Friday which was a killer. It was not white or red, it was orange, an Italian clam chowder," Paul said.

Like Bill Lucchesi, Paul felt the Fior's was the "best antipasto in town," enormous platters piled with the *cima* and cracked crab. "The food was delicate and simple. From the provinces. Risotto Milanese, and done to a turn. Many things were made to order, chicken sauté sec on the à la carte menu," he said.

He particularly relished that part of restaurant life the clientele never sees, the life in the kitchen and among the staff. The skill among the cooks and the kitchen crew was admirable and athletic. If, for instance, a cook was working on two orders of chicken sauté sec, he'd put two portions in the frying pan and fling salt at it from a distance. With a flip of the wrist, he'd toss the chicken and all the pieces would go up and come back down again finding their original places in the pan. The kitchen held a 32-gallon corrugated metal garbage can full of salt. When the restaurant was busy, five cooks would be running back and forth, and they'd dip into the salt and throw a pinch here, a handful there.

As Paul said: "They didn't taste, they'd throw it in -- bang! They had a bell when something was done, 'Bing bing bing!' It was charming but they lost that when they moved," he said referring to the Fior's change of address in 1954.

He praised Ray Lippi's skill with a knife: "(Ray) used to sharpen a knife so that it would sing on the knife sharpener. He used to make zabaglione the way most people scoop ice cream…. eggs and a little wine over the double boiler. And they would stand just like that."

Paul Mantee got a ringside seat for all this action because like so many of the family members he started working young at the restaurant.

I was a busboy when I was seventeen. My father thought it was a good idea. I thought I could make some money and eat. I ate more than I was worth. I used to come at five o'clock and have dinner. We'd finish at 10:30 and I'd have dinner and I'd eat all night long. If there was something in a platter, a little risotto Milanese from a big platter would come back, I would go in the kitchen, boom-boom-boom, (mimicking how efficiently he finished what was left). Of course, I was seventeen, skinny as a rail. I never got yelled at for dropping a dish. Never, never, never. Finocchio's was upstairs, and I heard the drums. I wondered what went on there.

The Fior had a family table in the corner that sat eight comfortably. All the regulars, such as Louie Scaglione, would sit there alone. A Mr. Orobbio probably ate there four times a week. ("He was a pleasant gentleman who had a side-to-side motion to his walk, as if he were aboard ship during a storm," Paul remembers.) The atmosphere at this table was just like eating Italian cooking at home.

Paul still recalls the eternal shelling of peas.

When the vegetable broker came, those in the kitchen would be shelling peas. When the guy from the bakery would come, my father would be shelling peas. The guy from the bakery would sit down, have a coffee royale and start shelling peas. The meat guy, Figone, he would come in, sit down shelling peas. There were eight guys shelling peas for the Fior d'Italia and they were shooting the bull and it was great. That's out of style. Nobody does that today….

John Figone was a nice man. When my father took over, the restaurant was in debt some, and Figone told my father, 'Don't pay till you can.' When my father and Frank took over, they may have got in debt when they moved . But they had the bread guy say, 'Don't pay till you can.' Because they knew these people for years, there was a real family atmosphere and the food like was family.

Since then, people's needs have changed. People have become more interested in quick food, a Coke and a smoke. No more the three-hour lunches with daily specials such as the *baccalà* (salted cod) and *ceci* (chick peas) on Friday.

The smells just for lunch were fabulous…. They'd open at 11 o'clock and the bar would be three-deep in 20 minutes. By two o'clock, it would all be finished. There was a rush for lunch but the bar was making all the money.

Shifting Loyalties

By 1936, George and Olive had been divorced for four years, in part due to the stresses of restaurant life and the attention it drew from George, away from his family. Paul went to live with his grandparents.

Four years later, George married Emily Kobsef and the new couple reclaimed Paul from Armido's and Amelia's house. They set up housekeeping in the Sunset District. Emily was difficult. Paul avoided his new stepmother and George apparently suffered from her as well. Paul observed that his father apparently liked to work nights more than ever at this time.

Emily didn't like Frank's wife, Ruth, and the two wives did not speak to each other, driving the wedge between Frank and George even wider. The restaurant staff could see these dynamics quite clearly.

Meanwhile, Paul and his Uncle Frank grew close. They would take drives and have long talks together. Paul trusted and loved his uncle. He found in Frank the sensitivity and understanding he couldn't experience with his father and stepmother.

It would seem Frank and George couldn't get much farther apart but a tragedy intervened to bring them constantly in contact. Armido and Amelia had a little cabin in Monte Rio on the Russian River. Armido would often go up there with his family for a day in the country but he never took a real vacation. One day in 1945, Armido and Amelia went to Monte Rio for a real holiday, his first ever. Swimming in the Russian River, Armido suffered a heart attack and died. Amelia was inconsolable.

"She almost jumped in the coffin," Paul said of his grandmother.

George appealed to Frank to become his partner even though there was discord between them, saying "Papa would love it." Paul believed that Frank agreed because he was married with a child and needed to make more money than he did as a waiter. Now Frank and George were at the helm without the buffer of Armido. They made a partner of Armando Lippi, the younger brother of Basilio, who had been Armido's partner earlier.

While so much of the interaction at the Fior had developed over decades and could be called familial, the families behind the Fior were changing, splitting up and reconfiguring. This shifting of alliances set the stage for the next era in the restaurant's life.

The August 14, 1948 wedding party joining the families of Del Carlos and the Moores at the Fior d'Italia.

ANATRA ALLA FIOR D'ITALIA
(DUCK FIOR D'ITALIA)

This is good served with either wild rice or a sauté of vinegar and pancetta. Or consider saving the duck fat in the pan to sauté with potatoes.

If you don't have duck stock, use beef or veal. Chicken is too light. If you cook the duck past medium rare, it will be tough and chewy.

1/2 cup balsamic vinegar
2 tablespoons granulated sugar
2 cups duck stock (page 59) or brown stock (page 33)
Salt and freshly ground black pepper
4 (6- to 8-ounce) duck breasts

Preheat the oven to 400)F.

In a small saucepan, combine the vinegar and sugar. Bring to a boil over medium-high heat and cook until reduced by half, 6 to 8 minutes. Add the stock and bring back to a boil over medium-high heat; cook until reduced by half, about 12 minutes. Season to taste with salt and pepper. Keep warm over low heat.

Preheat the oven to 400°F. Using a very sharp knife, score the duck skin, taking care not to cut into the meat. Season generously with salt and pepper.

Heat an ovenproof sauté pan over medium-high heat until very hot. Add the duck breasts, skin side down, and cook until most of the fat has rendered and the skin is golden brown, 3 to 6 minutes. Turn the duck over and cook 2 minutes. Transfer the pan to the oven and continue cooking until medium-rare or until an instant-read thermometer registers 135°F, about 5 minutes. Remove from the oven and let rest for 10 minutes before slicing.

To serve: Ladle a spoonful of sauce onto each of 4 warmed serving plates. Slice the duck breasts and fan over the sauce and serve immediately.

Serves four

DUCK STOCK

2 (4 1/2-pound) ducks
1 medium yellow onion, diced
1 stalk celery, diced
1 medium carrot, diced

Preheat the oven to 400°F. Rinse the ducks with cold water and pat dry with paper towels. Using a sharp boning knife, remove the duck breasts and set aside for the Duck Fior d'Italia recipe (page 66). Remove the duck legs, wrap tightly in plastic wrap, and refrigerate or freeze for another use.

In a large roasting pan, combine the remaining carcasses, onion, celery, and carrot. Bake, stirring occasionally, until the duck and vegetables are nicely browned, about 45 minutes.

Using a slotted spoon, transfer the duck to a large stockpot. (Set aside the roasted vegetables and pan juices; they will be added later.) Add enough cold water to just cover. Bring to a boil over medium-high heat. Lower the heat and simmer very gently for 3 hours, skimming and discarding any foam or grease as it rises to the surface.

After the carcasses have simmered for 3 hours, stir in the roasted vegetables and pan juices. Bring to a boil; lower the heat and simmer very gently about 1 hour.

Strain through a fine-mesh strainer, pressing on the ingredients to extract as much liquid as possible; discard the solids. You should have about 2 cups of stock. Cool to room temperature. Cover and refrigerate for up to three days or freeze for up to three months.

Makes about 2 cups

CHAPTER 11: A Place to Be Seen

Frank and George had every reason to think they could make a success of the Fior. After all, they grew up in the restaurant. The clientele they had enjoyed in their first years of ownership seemed to validate this conviction. During the 1950s and 1960s, the Fior was political flypaper. Local, national and foreign politicos patronized the establishment with regularity. When Richard M. Nixon visited San Francisco during his vice presidency (1953-61), a member of the Di Giorgio family (of the Di Giorgio Fruit Company) recommended the Fior d'Italia to the vice president, who was staying at the Fairmont Hotel. The Fairmont's owners at the time escorted the vice president to the restaurant along with about half a dozen FBI personnel and security people, some of whom Frank knew. Word of Nixon's arrival got around and a healthy-sized crowd greeted him at the restaurant when he arrived and gave him a standing ovation.

In the Fior, Nixon demanded of the waiter, "I want some good pasta."

Someone in his group suggested, "Spaghetti and meatballs."

"No. No. I was in Italy. I didn't have any spaghetti and meatballs," Nixon insisted, adding that what he wanted probably wasn't even on the menu.

However, the cook was able to prepare a dish quickly and invented a sauce made of ground filet mignon and imported dried mushrooms just for the vice president and his party. Nixon "cleaned it," in Frank's words, and he made a special point of raving about it to his group.

"This is the best sauce I've had outside of Italy. The last time I had anything (Italian) it was not quite as good," he said.

"It was very tasty, very good, contrary to the popular notion that you have to cook a sauce for an hour and a half or two hours," Frank remembered.

Frank and many of the guests requested and received autographed menus from the vice president. A week or so after Nixon's departure, Frank asked one of the police officers, who had been escorting Nixon through the city, what he thought of the vice president. The officer allowed that Nixon was a "nice guy" but one thing bothered him. When security personnel accompany someone of his stature for several days, the great one usually tips each of the officers at the end of the trip, he said.

"When Eisenhower was here, we each got an envelope with a hundred bucks in it. Very nice," said the officer.

"How about with Nixon?" Frank asked.

"We got a little autographed photograph," the policeman said.

Soon Frank wrote and asked the vice president for his permission to name the dish he had been served, Spaghetti Nixon, and put it on the menu. But Nixon responded that he didn't want his name attached to the dish lest many other chefs decided to do the same.

A Place to Be Seen

Fior employees had their own interactions with the great. Ron Edwards, a law student who, while in the midst of a divorce and having to support three children, found a job parking cars at the Fior. He was to stay with the Fior for 11 years and then started his own parking and car service company.

Edwards said at the time, "the Fior was a place to be seen."

Once he spotted Nixon walking down the street on Columbus Avenue.

I just happened to be coming around the corner by the Bohemian Club Cigar Store, and a reporter grabs a hold of us, (me and a) street sweeper...I wish I could remember his name because I love him. He's sweeping the street, and one of the guys grabs a hold of him, like this, and said, 'Come on. You have a chance to have your picture taken with the Vice President.' And he took one look and said, 'I'm not going to.' And he walked right around the corner. All the political types used to come in there at that point."

Edwards remembered the several politicians who patronized the restaurant, such as Judge John Molinari, once a candidate for mayor, and Dianne Feinstein who, during the 1970s, was President of the Board of Supervisors.

"She's somebody who'd wink and smile at you," Edwards reflected.

Later, as a U.S. Senator, Feinstein reminisced about the meals she had had at the Fior during her days as a San Francisco supervisor. "The Mayor (George Moscone) used their rooms many times to have luncheons. I remember they had the biggest, best, crispiest calamari. Everybody was warm and welcoming, always. Frank Marianetti greeted me at the door," she said.

San Francisco Mayor Joseph Alioto (1968-76) and his Deputy Mayor, John A. De Luca, entertained at the Fior on many occasions for civic, personal and professional reasons. During Alioto's mayoralty, there were approximately 35 strikes involving workers, such as the teamsters, machinists, bus drivers and teachers, to name a few.

"Sessions were held (at the Fior) with labor to formulate positions for the city….We would meet there with our police department, the captains and deputy chiefs of police to formulate positions," De Luca said. Alioto and De Luca also went to several restaurants on Fisherman's Wharf for these city-labor summits. But because of the mayor's background in North Beach, the Fior was one of the restaurants they frequented.

De Luca eventually left city government to become president of the Wine Institute. Headquartered in San Francisco, the Institute represents over 90 percent of wine growers and other wine trades in California.

"In last 25 years as head of the wine industry, I entertained (at the Fior) with the (U.S.) Treasury Department and with outside guests from other countries in the meeting rooms," De Luca says. The Institute meets with Treasury on a regular basis because that department oversees the Bureau of Alcohol, Tobacco and Firearms that regulates trade in liquor.

The curious thing was that although the Fior attracted the heavy hitters like politicos and entertainers, at the same time it maintained its family atmosphere and Italian tradition.

"The Italian community was treated like kings and queens. The ladies came here, I don't care if they were eighty years old, they still were looking thirty-five at that point. And the guys tried to look at least forty," the parking attendant quipped.

Frank and George ran the restaurant along with their partners, Armando and Basilio Lippi and Leo Quattrin. Armando and Leo were both gifted chefs and hardly needed to invent a dish with a president's name to draw interest to their fare. The *Pacific Coast Review* in May 1956 sketched a typical menu of the time:

Among the delicacies that bring customers to Fior d'Italia are its minestrone soup, frittata with meat and vegetables, antipasto Fior, baked cima a la Genovese, gnocchi with branciuoli, Italian pot roast, boned jumbo squab casserole stuffed with wild rice, crab legs bordelaise, chicken with fettuccine Fior, ravioli with mushroom sauce, cannelloni a la roscana (sic) and innumerable other appetizing creations including many tasty items from the charcoal broiler. Surprisingly, a favorite entrée at the Italian restaurant is – corned beef and cabbage, and this is a regular feature on Thursday luncheons. [1]

By 1959, the same restaurant trade magazine took a new look at the Fior and noted that its dinner entrees also included veal scaloppine Marsala with fresh mushrooms and Beef *Cenerentola* (che-neh-REN-tola, Cinderella in Italian). This dish consisted of the heart of the filet and artichoke bottoms filled with truffles. The chefs also liked to serve flambé desserts, such as fried cream, cherries jubilee and crepes suzettes, in addition to the standard Italian ices, spumone and tortoni. By 1959, prices ranged from $2.50 à la carte to a complete roast dinner of roast tenderloin of Beef Gaidano for two for $15.00.

George Marianetti lets the customers spoil him.

The world of entertainment was still happy to take notice of the Fior and to be noticed there. During the 1940s and 1950s Hollywood's brightest stars wanted to be seen at the Fior when they were in San Francisco. Filmdom's "love goddess" Rita Hayworth (1918-87), known to all at the time for her staggering beauty and her sultry performances in "Gilda" and "The Lady from Shanghai", dined at the restaurant.

Another Hollywood celebrity and Fior customer during this era was Eva Gabor, whose career was overshadowed by that of her sister Zsa Zsa, until Eva got the starring role in "Green Acres" on television. Raymond Burr (1917-93) who played sleuth Perry Mason on TV was also a revered patron. The long-lived, prolific actors, Gregory Peck (1916-2003), noted for his roles in "Moby Dick" and "To Kill a Mockingbird", and Robert Preston (1918-87), star of "The Music Man" on stage and screen and "Victor Victoria" on screen, were regularly welcomed by the Marianettis and staff.

"To me, movie stars were like God at that time in my life," Frank said. He also liked to remember the jazz singer, bandleader and comedian Phil Harris. Harris's very long career included working on Jack Benny's radio show and in the movies with Bing Crosby. Harris had been introduced to the Fior by a mutual friend of his and Frank's, Johnny DiPaolo.

The Fior's 75th anniversary in 1961, from left:
Chef Leo Quattrin, George Marianetti, Police Chief Thomas J. Cahill, Mayor George Christopher, Maitre d' Armando Lippi, and Frank Marianetti.

A World War II pilot in the military, DiPaolo would do "crazy stuff", according to Frank. He once telephoned Frank and said, "Hey, Frank, I want some polenta and chicken. But I'm up in a plane right now. Can you hear me?"

Frank was tickled to receive an order from someone piloting a plane and told his friends of his high-flying patron. He later learned that DiPaolo had not been aviating at all but shaving. He had fooled Frank by putting his electric shaver next to the telephone to simulate the sound of engines. For Frank, that made even a better story.

A Literary Tribute

The Fior d'Italia has also been fortunate to capture the imagination and passion of writers, as we saw in Chapter Four with Virgilio Luciani who, in the decade after World War I, described the experiences of the young waiter, Omero, in his novel, *Un italiano in America*.

Another unabashed celebration of the culture of Italian cuisine and the Fior is found in the 1956 account, *Americans by Choice*, by Angelo M. Pellegrini. [2]

Born in Italy, Pellegrini came to the United States with his parents when he was ten. While an Associate Professor of English Literature at the University of Washington in Seattle, he achieved fame through his books on food, *The Unprejudiced Palate* (1948) and *Americans by Choice* (1956). In *Americans by Choice*, Pellegrini described *Food Lover's Garden* (1989) and in his autobiographical works, *Immigrant's Return* (1951), his visit to the Fior d'Italia, where he had arranged to dine with the greatly respected Louis M. Martini, the founder of Martini wines.

Pellegrini's account rhapsodizes about the quality of the fare at the Fior. But more than that, he illustrates the high expectations of its patrons and their intense identification with the restaurant. Here is a short excerpt:

When I arrived at the Fior d'Italia a few minutes before twelve, Martini was already there, strolling leisurely in front of the entrance, enjoying the cool autumn sun, detached and observant, greeting the early luncheon arrivals, the solid San Franciscans of Italian extraction – lawyers, bankers, doctors, merchants. Dressed in a dark double-breasted suit, white shirt and conservative tie, bareheaded, the erect well-proportioned body a pedestal for his magnificent head, he radiated well-being and breezy confidence. As soon as I approached he came briskly toward me with outstretched hand.

'Buon giorno, Signor Pellegrini. Did you enjoy yourself? Have you dispatched your business? I hope you are hungry – *qui si mangia bene* (for here we eat well).' He opened the door for me and we entered the restaurant. The Fior d'Italia is neither large nor pretentious. In a city noted for its excellent cuisine, there may be better restaurants – although it is reasonable to ask whether mortals deserve better fare than is served there from day to day. [2]

Besides highlighting the esteem in which the restaurant was held, Pellegrini observes how deeply the community identified with it.

Martini had chosen that restaurant spontaneously, as if no choice whatever were involved. Men of his generation, Italian immigrants who came directly west and who have been in and around San Francisco for half a century, feel a proprietary interest in it. They grew up and became a part of America together. It is their restaurant. It has never betrayed them nor they it. In that modest dining room they have celebrated important events, planned community affairs, entertained celebrities from the Old Country, cemented friendships, courted their women, brooded over the reverses of the market, quarreled and hated and loved and had memorable times in the boisterous, uninhibited manner of Italians when they tuck in their bibs and gather at the table.[3]

The visiting Pellegrini notes that the Fior's public held an exacting standard of fresh, wholesome, uncontrived food.

They feel perfectly at home in the restaurant they have molded to their own tempers and upon which they have virtually imposed their standard of culinary excellence. It is a very sane standard. Let there be caldrons of soup, bushels of green and leaf vegetables, always cooked just so with the appropriate condiment. The olive oil must be pure, virgin, nutty in flavor. The meat, fish and fowl always fresh. Bring the salad to the table in half-barrel bowls, with an uncomplicated dressing of olive oil, wine vinegar, salt and pepper. (Reserve the fancy dressings with cheeses and eggs, and so on, for foreigners and country yokels.) Good bread, good wine, genuine cheeses, ripe fruit, regional dishes, such as polenta or gnocchi at regular intervals, male waiters – and cleanliness. Hearty, discriminating eaters, more prone to castigate for a failure than to praise for an achievement, they have insisted upon all this – and they have got it. Woe unto the management should it ever show signs of slipping! I once saw an articulate Tuscan rise to his feet during the lunch hour and with compelling eloquence scourge the management for having served him a withered pear with his Bel Paese. [4]

It's interesting that the restaurant's denizens abjured "the fancy dressings" of "foreigners" and yokels. Was he making a reference to French cooking and its American devotees? There has been a disdain for French cooking among Italians and the sway it holds over the American palate. The Fior customer demands freshness. He regards food products and condiments with a zest and aestheticism for their natural goodness.

Nor do they take the menu very seriously. They pick it up, of course; and as they appear to scan it they mutter to themselves, '*Vediamo un pò cosa c'è di buono oggi* (Let us see what's good today.) Having gone through this ritual, they lay it aside and call the waiter. '*Cameriere, sentà*. (Waiter, listen): 'Tell the cook I want a piece of boiled chicken – not a piece of skeletal carcass, understand, but a piece of chicken. Or else a piece of boiled beef, *magro magro* (very lean). With that he may send me a beautiful portion of spinach, well drained and not cooked to death, and with a dressing of good olive oil, salt, pepper, and the juice of half a lemon. But first bring me a beautiful bowl of broth with some pasta in it.' It is not unlikely that the diner may then turn to his companion, or to anyone who is sitting nearby and shows any inclination to listen, and offer a dietetic postscript in explanation of his choice. 'Rich sauces, roast and frys (sic) and always *pastasciutta*, day after day – they are not healthful. One must exercise a little prudence at the table, otherwise...' And the hands move in contrapuntal harmony, all tending to suggest the horror of graves, worms, and epitaphs. Meanwhile, the broth has arrived, steaming and savory. The *cameriere* uncovers the bowl of grated *parmigiano*. The patron scatters a spoonful on his soup. And as he catches the fragrance of the broth, flavored with parsley and celery and carrot and tomato and onion, he salivates feverishly in anticipation; worms and epitaphs are forgotten. He sees life as beatitude. 'Ha-a-a-a! Now we live! And you, *Signor Cameriere* – you are a gentleman!' [5]

COSTOLETTA DI VITELLO CON FUNGHI ALLA CREMA
(VEAL CUTLET WITH MUSHROOMS AND CREAM)

Preparation should begin with soaking the dried porcini mushrooms for one hour.

Ask the butcher to french the chops for you.

4 tablespoons olive oil

2 shallots, minced

1 1/2 ounces dried porcini mushrooms, soaked for 1 hour in water, drained, and coarsely chopped

1/2 cup white wine

1 tablespoon freshly squeezed lemon juice

2 cups heavy cream

Salt and freshly ground black pepper

4 (12-ounce) veal chops, bone in, frenched

All-purpose flour, for dusting

In a medium sauté pan, heat 2 tablespoons of the olive oil over medium-high heat. Add the shallots and cook until translucent, about 2 minutes. Add the porcini and cook 2 minutes. Add the wine and lemon juice; cook 2 minutes. Add the cream and cook until reduced by half. Season to taste with salt and pepper; keep warm over very low heat.

Preheat the oven to 400°F.

In a large ovenproof sauté pan, heat the remaining 2 tablespoons olive oil over medium-high heat. Season the veal generously with salt and pepper. Dust lightly with flour and shake gently to remove any excess. Arrange in a single layer in the hot pan and cook until golden, about 4 minutes per side. Transfer to the oven and bake until medium, and an instant-read thermometer registers 155°F, 10 to 15 minutes.

To serve: Place one veal chop on each of 4 warmed serving plates. Pour the sauce over the top of the chops and serve immediately.

Serves four

CHAPTER 12: The New Fior

In December of 1954, the Fior abandoned Broadway, the street that had been its home for 66 years. Broadway had become honky-tonk with the opening of topless restaurants and nightspots that dimmed the special elegance that had characterized that thoroughfare for so many decades. The Fior took up residence a few blocks away at Union Street on the corner of Stockton Street where it remains today. Here it faces Washington Square and the Italian church of Sts. Peter and Paul. The Fior leased the ground floor of a building owned by Elmer Gavello in 1954. This same space had been the site of the Riviera Restaurant and before that, the Gianduja. Gavello owned and operated both. Gavello had also owned Lucca's, the highly popular North Beach eatery opened by his father, Pierino, in the 1930s.

Entrance to the new Fior designed by Mario L. Gaidano.

The group's partners, the Marianettis, the Lippis and Leo Quattrin, now completely rethought the restaurant's ambiance, driven by a desire for modernization. They had it redone in an award-winning design. As reported by the *San Francisco Call Bulletin*:

Fior d'Italia celebrates their 68th year moving to their new, $100,000 restaurant on Union nr. Columbus on Wednesday of this week. Architect Mario L. Gaidano is very likely to win another national design award as he has really outdone himself on the new Fior. The motif is Italian modern. Italian red, black and white have been beautifully combined with wood, brick, stone and Italian wrought iron to achieve breath-taking beauty. [1]

In fact, Gaidano did win an award. His design for the Fior won *Institutions Magazine's* first prize in 1955 for interiors in a national competition. The May, 1956, edition of the restaurant trade magazine, *Pacific Coast Review*, described it:

The main dining room is enormous and generally circular in shape. It gives an impression of spaciousness and at the same time suggests sociability. Booths are built for comfort, and the whole atmosphere is one of friendly hospitality and festivity. The cocktail lounge also has an air of roominess and has an inviting appearance.

Special interest centers in the restaurant's large banquet quarters, the Plaza Room, which overlooks St. Peter's and Paul's park and the historic church beyond. This generations-old church is the scene of many weddings which are followed by receptions in the Plaza Room. [2]

The award-winning interior.

J. L. Pimsleur, a reporter for the *San Francisco Chronicle* also reviewed the new restaurant interior:

'The materials used for the walls,' explains Mario, such as brick, burlap and wood were suggested to suggest solidity and naturalness. The quatrefoil design on the cast iron grill work, the chandeliers and the sculpture – though contemporary – are reminiscent of the classical spirit.'

But the most intriguing facet of the interior is Gaidano's 'folded ceiling' – low in two corners, high in another, designed to "create areas within areas, high and low levels lending intimacy to a large room which could not be achieved by an ordinary, flat ceiling.[3]

Another elegant feature was an eye-catching fountain, with petal-like fronds that brought patrons' attention to the center of the dining room.

A world-renowned architect, Gaidano, in 1961 was the first in the world to employ an outside electric elevator and he did it in San Francisco's Fairmont Hotel, where it still operates. He topped that accomplishment by installing an underwater outside electric elevator at the first Marine World when it was built in Redwood City in 1968.

However, he was especially well known for restaurant design and he prided himself on the fact that his restaurants – unlike so many newly established eateries – never failed.

Mario Gaidano shows his award to George on the left and Frank on the right.

The Fior was "memorable for all the family" said the architect's son, Scott Gaidano, because the Marianettis named a steak dish after him, Beef a la Gaidano. The chefs were eager to use the names of celebrities on the menu even though they had been forbidden to use Nixon's name.

Out the Backdoor

In that era, Frank was tending bar, a job he detested. He hated seeing people at their worst, and having to be, in his words, "a psychiatrist," listening to the customers' troubles or indulging their need for attention. "The thing that really got me is that I just couldn't stay behind the bar. If it got too busy, I'd just walk away. I got to shaking. I didn't drink at all before I tended bar. My father stuck me back there. I didn't want to be a bartender. I didn't like it. I don't know how to make a drink," he said.

Frank also couldn't stomach watching bartenders steal from the house. "We'd have bartenders get very fat on us. I kept getting back to my brother. He didn't give a damn. I didn't know at the time he didn't give a damn. He liked the bartenders 'cause they discussed fighters. One of the bartenders was an ex-fighter," Frank said.

He also bewailed the elaborate schemes staffers devised to fill their pockets. Even years later, when the Fior introduced computerized ordering and sourcing, he felt no owners could be completely free of miscreants on the payroll. "Get rid of as many as you can. But you're never going to get rid of them completely," he'd say with disgust about a time when there was no cash register control.

However, there was one thief Frank seemed to admire, a bartender named Freddie Angel. Frank called him "a real nice guy" who "looked like an all-American kind of kid." Every month or so, Freddie's wife would call and say he had a migraine headache and he couldn't come to work that day.

One day, Freddie's wife called to excuse him. It turned out it wasn't a headache that had incapacitated him but a gunshot wound to the leg.

"He was robbing a bank in Sacramento. He got caught. He wasn't alone either. Better that he steal from somebody else than steal from us. He came back as an old friend when he came out of jail. He never took a dime from us," Frank insisted. But the Fior never hired him again either. Still, every time thereafter when Freddie came in, the bartenders served him on the house.

Edwards liked to spin a tale that he said came from George about a situation that came to light right after the Fior moved to Union Street.

At that time, a busboy, with great embarrassment, told George of a practice that had been going on at the former address on Broadway. The busboy hadn't the courage to tell him at the time because he didn't want to be seen as informing on his colleague, who had not followed the Fior to the Union Street location. Now that he was no longer around, the busboy screwed up his courage and revealed that particular waiter would steal four napkins every day in the early shift and four more every evening shift. Here is the story in Edwards's inimitable phraseology:

And (the busboy) says, at the end of the month, the waiter sent them all back home to Italy…thousands of boxes of those God-damned things. But they were worth money over there, you see… You know what those napkins cost? Well, they cost thirty-eight cents apiece just to launder. And if you lose one or burn a hole in one, that's going to cost you three dollars. And so what happens is year after year, you start building up an account with your laundry. It was owned by 'the family,' by the way. You know what I mean by that?…They owned all the laundries. So, at one particular point in time .…when George just wanted to change the laundry because he could save money, he finally got the bill. And he owned them something like twenty-six, twenty-seven thousand dollars. We're talking over a period of twenty years. They keep all these little notes, that's how they kept everybody in mind….for the items that were lost, they were all noted though.

Edwards observed that the theft of food was also an unfortunate fact of life in the restaurant. He described an associate of George's,

Fior D'Italia

SINCE 1886

Our mural of Italian landscape, dotted with hills and plains, with slender trees ascending into the air and here and there a ruined turret, is a fantasy painted by the artist Paul Rockwood in the year 1945. From the topmost peaks of the Apennines, gradual sloping lines descend to find peace and quiet in the valleys below, flecked with towers and relics of baronial houses. Through the sallows and gray poplar trees winds the Arno, spanned by ancient arches and guarded here and there by castellated towers. Overlooking this entire panorama stands the Church of St. Francis of Assisi.

04 BROADWAY - SAN FRANCISCO, CALIFORNIA

Fior D'Italia

Dinner

(Choice of Entree Determines Price of Dinner)

ASSORTED ANTIPASTO

SALAD

COMBINATION SALAD SUPREME

Or CRAB OR SHRIMP COCKTAIL

SOUPS

| MINESTRONE | CONSOMME | VEGETABLE |

CHICKEN BARLEY (Sunday)

PASTE

RAVIOLI BOLOGNESE

ENTREES

ROAST CHICKEN, VEGETABLE & POTATO 2.50
POT ROAST, POTATOES & VEGETABLE 2.35
SWEETBREADS SAUTE SEC WITH FRESH MUSHROOMS 2.85
LAMB CHOPS, VEGETABLE AND POTATOES 2.75
CHICKEN SAUTE FIOR D'ITALIA 3.00
VEAL SCALOPPINE MARSALA — FRESH MUSHROOMS 2.85
BREADED VEAL CUTLET 2.85
NEW YORK CUT STEAK 3.85   FILET MIGNON 3.85
MINUTE STEAK 3.00   GROUND SIRLOIN 2.75
(STEAK WITH FRESH MUSHROOMS 50¢ EXTRA)
ROAST PRIME RIBS OF BEEF 3.85
(SATURDAY & SUNDAY)
SQUAB CASSEROLE — WILD RICE 4.00
CALF LIVER WITH BACON 3.00
WHOLE CHICKEN CASSEROLE, POTATOES & VEGETABLE 4.00
EXTRA CUT LAMB CHOPS, VEGETABLE & POTATOES 3.75

DESSERTS

| ICE CREAM | CHEESE | FRIED CREAM | FRESH FRUIT |
COFFEE

SALADS

CRAB LOUIS 1.00   CRAB OR SHRIMP COCKTAIL .75   SHRIMP LOUIS 1.00
SLICED TOMATOES .60   MIXED GREENS .50   (With Anchovies .65)
AVOCADO .65   COMBINATION VEGETABLE .65
MIXED GREENS & IMPORTED TUNA 1.00
ASSORTED ANTIPASTO AL FIOR D'ITALIA 1.00
HEARTS OF ARTICHOKES IN OLIVE OIL 1.35

SOUPS

MINESTRONE .30   PASTINA IN BRODO .30   MARITATA .50   CONSOMME .20
RICE SOUP WITH HALF CHICKEN 2.00

•

ITALIAN SPECIALTIES

SPAGHETTI BOLOGNESE 1.00
RAVIOLI A LA GENOVESE 1.25
MOSTACCIOLI A LA MARINARA 1.25
SPAGHETTI SALSA NAPOLI 1.25
SPAGHETTINI WITH MUSHROOM SAUCE 1.50
RISOTTO MILANESE 1.25, with Mushrooms 1.50
CHICKEN LIVERS SAUTE WITH MUSHROOMS 2.00
POT ROAST & RAVIOLI 1.50   FRITTATA 1.25
HALF CHICKEN FRIED, WITH SHOESTRING POTATOES 1.50
WHOLE CHICKEN CASSEROLE WITH VEGETABLES
& MUSHROOMS 3.00
HAMBURGER STEAK WITH SPAGHETTI 1.35
SWEETBREADS SAUTE 1.85
ROVELLINE A LA LUCCHESE 1.85
SQUAB CASSEROLE WITH WILD RICE 2.75
SPAGHETTI WITH MEATBALLS 1.25
CALF LIVER SAUTE WITH MUSHROOMS & WHITE WINE 1.85
VEGETABLES — IN SEASON

STEAKS AND CHOPS

NEW YORK CUT 3.25   FILET MIGNON 3.25   RIB STEAK 3.25
GROUND SIRLOIN 1.75   MINUTE STEAK 1.75
LAMB CHOPS (2) 1.75   Extra Cut Lamb Chops (2) 2.75
(Steak with Fresh Mushrooms 50¢ Extra)

DESSERTS

FRESH OR DRY MONTEREY CHEESE .30   CAMEMBERT .30   PROVOLONE .30
WISCONSIN SWISS CHEESE .30   BLUE ROQUEFORT TYPE .30
ICE CREAM OR SHERBET .25   FRIED CREAM IN FLAME .60
ZABAIONE .60   RUM OMELETTE 1.50
COFFEE .10   TEA .15   MILK .15

1955 Menu.

who had access to the big freezer where they stored frog legs, frog legs that became suddenly ambulatory. Not to mention the pantry man who would arrive an hour and a half early for work so that he could park his car right outside the kitchen exit on Stockton. When he walked out, he "had those God-damned sticks of salami stuck down the legs of his pants," Edwards said.

No establishment wants to admit that underhandedness ever goes on. The Marianettis were educated men. It is easily argued they should have known better and exerted more control. But family owned businesses in those days did not adhere to the rigorous standards of transparency demanded today. Many were content to run their enterprises as the family's piggy banks. Without computers, sleight of hand was a common state of affairs.

Armando Lippi serves green peas to Tenessee Ernie Ford just the way the singer likes them.

CRESPELLE CON GRANCHIO (CRABMEAT CREPES)

You can make the crepes ahead. They heat up best if the crab filling and the sauce are used relatively soon. Never use virgin olive oil for cooking. There are a of vegetable solids in virgin olive oil and it will burn. Use virgin olive oil for cold dishes or for topping off cooked dishes.

Crepes
1 cup whole milk
2 large eggs
2 tablespoons clarified butter (see next page), plus extra for cooking
3/4 cup all-purpose flour
Pinch of salt

Mousseline sauce
(hollandaise sauce with whipped cream)
3 large egg yolks
3/4 cup clarified butter (see next page),
2 to 3 tablespoons freshly squeezed lemon juice
Salt and freshly ground black pepper
1/2 cup heavy cream

1/4 cup freshly grated Parmesan cheese

Filling
2 tablespoons olive oil
1 shallot, minced
1 red bell pepper, seeded and diced
1 green bell pepper, seeded and diced
1/2 teaspoon Madras curry powder
1 1/2 cups mayonnaise
1 1/2 pounds lump crabmeat, picked over to remove any bits of shell or cartilage
Salt and freshly ground black pepper

To make the crepes: Place the milk, eggs, and butter in a blender. Add the flour and salt and blend until smooth. The batter should be the consistency of heavy cream; if it's too thick, add a little additional milk. Let rest at least 30 minutes or refrigerate overnight.
Heat an 8-inch cast-iron or heavy nonstick sauté pan over medium-high heat. Lightly brush the pan with clarified butter and carefully pour 2 to 3 tablespoons of the batter into the center of the pan. Immediately pick up the pan and, using a rocking action of the wrist, swirl the batter to cover the surface of the pan. Return to the heat and cook until just lightly golden, about 1 1/2 minutes. Gently turn the crepe over and cook until just lightly golden, about 1 1/2 minutes. Transfer to a large plate and cover with a kitchen towel. Repeat with the remaining batter, stacking the crepes directly on top of one another. You should have 12 to 16 crepes. Crepes can be made ahead to this point and refrigerated, tightly wrapped, up to five days or frozen up to three months.

continued

To make the filling: In a large sauté pan, heat the olive oil over medium-high heat. Add the shallot and bell peppers and cook until tender, about 3 minutes. Add the curry powder and cook 2 minutes. Remove from the heat and let cool.

In a large bowl, combine the sautéed vegetables and mayonnaise; mix well. Gently fold in the crabmeat. Season to taste with salt and pepper.

To make the mousseline sauce: Start with a hollandaise base: Fill the bottom of a double boiler with 2 inches of water and bring to a boil over high heat. Lower the heat and maintain a simmer. Place the egg yolks in the top of the double boiler and set over the simmering water. Whisking continuously, slowly dribble in the butter, little by little, until the consistency of mayonnaise, about 5 minutes. Whisk in the lemon juice and season to taste with salt and pepper. Transfer to a medium bowl and let cool 10 minutes.

In a medium bowl, using a whisk or electric mixer, whip the cream until soft peaks form. Using a large rubber spatula, gently fold the whipped cream into the hollandaise base.

To assemble the crepes: Preheat the broiler. Generously butter a 9 by 13-inch shallow baking dish. Select the 12 prettiest crepes.

Place a crepe on a flat work surface. Dollop about 1/3 cup of the crab filling down the center of the crepe. Roll the crepe to encase the filling and arrange in a single layer, seam side down, in the prepared baking dish. Repeat with the remaining crepes.

Carefully spoon the sauce over the top of the rolled crepes, taking care to completely cover the surface. Sprinkle with the Parmesan and broil, about 4 inches from the heat source, until golden brown, 4 to 5 minutes. Serve immediately.

Serves four

TO CLARIFY BUTTER

In a heavy saucepan, melt 1 pound of unsalted butter over medium-high heat just until it boils. Remove from the heat and let sit two minutes. Skim the foam off the top and discard. Carefully pour the butter into a small bowl, taking care to leave the milk solids in the bottom of the pan. Cover and refrigerate until ready to use. Clarified butter can be refrigerated up to one month or frozen up to six months.

CHAPTER 13: The Next Generation

A Beat North Beach

In the 1950s, North Beach was transformed. As Italian-American families grew prosperous, they began leaving Little Italy, moving to other parts of the city and the Bay Area. Newcomers filled the vacancies and the relatively low rents attracted artists and bohemians.

North Beach was the epicenter of what came to be known as the San Francisco Renaissance. Writers, poets and philosophers, who drew their inspiration as much from political activism and drugs as from Buddhism and mysticism, were the forces behind this blossoming of North Beach intellectual life. For instance, poet Lawrence Ferlinghetti opened a bookstore and started publishing under the name City Lights, just a few blocks from the Fior. Grant Avenue drew young people who had no stake in the Italian community but who identified with the Beat Generation or, as columnist Herb Caen eventually christened the group, "beatniks."

Meanwhile, many Italian-American residents had gained a degree of professionalism through the G.I. Bill's tuition assistance. With this increased economic ease, they were moving to the suburbs, just as the McCarran-Walter Act 1952 severely limited new immigrants from Italy.

Low-cost establishments, such as the family-style Half Moon Café, attracted radical sculptor Beniamino Bufano, who would beautify San Francisco in the coming years with his creations. A violinist from the Central Valley, Enrico Banducci, was lured to North Beach, where he established his own attraction for artists and intellectuals with the nightclub known as the hungry i. Coffee shops and bookstores became magnets for this new wave of creativity. Still, Italian family-style restaurants remained very viable and managed to survive in the midst of this sea change. New Joe's, Vanessi's, Three Little Swiss and the elegant Blue Fox all thrived amid a parallel world throbbing around them.

Il Cenacolo

While the surrounding culture was veering off in many new directions, some people still retained their love of tradition. During this era, a long-lived men's club chose the Fior as its regular meeting place. To this day, *Il Cenacolo* meets at the restaurant every week. *Il Cenacolo* (eel chen-AH-colo) means supper room in Italian and, by extension, it means a group of like-minded people who dine together and share similar intellectual interests. The word also refers to the famous painting of "The Last Supper" depicting Christ's last meal with his apostles, painted by Leonardo da Vinci.

This men's club has met regularly since a group of Italian professionals, recent arrivals from Italy, founded it in 1928. They were an elite group and included Alberto Mellini Ponce de Leon, the vice consul of Italy; Renzo Turco, a Piemontese attorney who was one of those Italians investigated during World War II; Ettore Patrizi, editor and publisher of *L'Italia*; Luigi Filiasi, from Naples and commander in the Italian Navy; Armando Pedrini, vice president of the Bank of Italy, which later became the Bank of America, and other prominent academicians, businessmen, artists and men of letters.

The society is not restricted to Italians. But its meetings, while in English, explore and highlight aspects of Italian culture. They usually feature a speaker or a program on that theme. Its members are particularly interested in Italian opera and *Il Cenacolo* has over the years honored several classical singers.

The society met at the Fairmont Hotel for the first half of its life. A founding member, Alberto Campione, was an assistant manager at the hotel. This connection might have accounted for the fraternity finding a venue there.

When it moved to the Fior in the 1960s, the group drew not only its members to the restaurant but the dignitaries, professionals and entertainers who spoke at its luncheons. Among the speakers were Mayor Alioto and his deputy DeLuca, who was also a member.

"I used to practice my Italian there. There was a sense of neighborhood and bonhomie," DeLuca said. On a number of occasions as deputy mayor, DeLuca addressed *Il Cenacolo* on matters of city policy, jobs, transportation, and housing.

Since it has been meeting at the Fior every Thursday for over three decades, the group has drawn some people who have become great friends of the Fior, including photographer Tom Vano and Bill Armanino of Armanino Foods of Distinction, who would eventually become a Fior owner.

Family Matters

By the 1950s, George's son, Paul, had become an adult who had no intention of entering the family business. Paul did remain throughout his life a perspicacious observer of its management and reputation. Later in his life, he wrote a semi-autobiographical book about growing up surrounded by the restaurant business, cooking and food.

He was not impressed by the new location on Washington Square. Paul rued the loss of the old look characterized by its cane chairs and the breadsticks presented in water glasses on the tables. "They went fancy-schmanzy. I think the era changed and it was sad....If they'd kept it like it was...but I didn't work there. It happened while I was in the Navy. I came back to it. I looked at it and said, "Yes it's very nice, the people are very beautiful but that's not the place that I remember. And it's not the place that Louie Scaglione ate every meal of his life for 50 years. That was family," he said.

Paul started a career in journalism, reporting on sports for the *San Mateo Times* before he entered the navy in 1950 at the age of nineteen. He was also attending San Mateo Junior College at the time and received an Associate of Arts degree in journalism. Studying journalism held less appeal than actually plying the trade so he switched to San Jose State College for the last two years to major in marketing, seduced by the media and movies of the era that glorified advertising professionals. But the course work bored him.

"So I joined the navy. Best thing I ever did in my life. It took me away for four years," said Paul, who was eager to leave his uncomfortable family situation. The ironic note was that the stepmother he feared, Emily, died just weeks after he left home for the U.S. Navy in 1951.

I was stationed for the last two years in Hawaii. I met some incredible Bohemian people, pre-beatnik people. A large influence on me was (Marlon) Brando and (Montgomery) Clift. These guys were so real, they were not afraid to be soft, not afraid to weep. I thought to myself I could be a part of that. I'd done a few plays in high school and had a great time doing them (although) I didn't know what I was doing, except for learning lines.

When I came back from the navy I went to (the University of California at Berkeley) for the last two years. I had a wonderful teacher, Walter Boughton. He cast me as Armand Duval in *Camille*, also in the *Lower Depths*, which I loved. He said. "You have some talent here." And I thought I really wanted to do that because it was a way of expressing myself and I was never allowed to. Ever. I was very quiet about everything. So I came to Hollywood and got a job scooping ice cream at Baskin and Robbins.

I got into a very good workshop. I was lucky....And I was a big good-looking kid. And I got a part and then I got another part and pretty soon I was an actor. And I loved it. I love the camera. Right here up close, over your shoulder. I needed some applause in my life and you do get it as an actor.

Governor Edmund G. (Pat) Brown congratulates Frank on the Fior's 80th anniversary.

George was proud and frequently would boast to his associates about his son's accomplishments despite the fact that Paul changed his name. Paul found the surname Marianetti was too difficult for the Hollywood of the mid-50s to appreciate. "People were calling me Martinelli, Manghinucci. Nobody looked at it or listened to it," he said.

He changed it to Mantee, the surname of Humphrey Bogart's character, the cold-blooded killer, Duke Mantee, in the 1936 film, "Petrified Forest".

"It felt great. I never liked my last name anyway. When I was in school, all the girls were Irish with short names...I wanted a name like Brick Bradford," he said.

Meanwhile, Frank had inducted his sons, Bob and Rick, into the business of the Fior when each reached twelve. Some restaurant staff speculated that he wanted his adored elder son, Bob, to take over the business from him in the future. But it didn't happen that way. In his late teens, intelligent and sensitive Bob suffered a psychic breakdown. He was diagnosed with schizophrenia. The family sheltered him for many years and he was eventually institutionalized without ever reaching his potential.

Frank puzzled until the end of his days how this anomaly could have stricken his family. He recalled that his fathers and uncles were hardy and resilient. They had succeeded despite the odds, unschooled though they were. How a youngster from "his background," as Frank put it, could have psychological problems never made any sense to him.

In 1962, when he too reached twelve, Rick was thrilled to be put in charge of the cash register. That first year at the till, the young cashier went gaga when actress Kim Novak walked in one day. She had appeared four years earlier in Alfred Hitchcock's thriller film, "Vertigo". Rick, whose hormones he said were "raging big-time," was awestruck by her cool, unattainable beauty. The fact that "Vertigo" was also set in San Francisco must have lent a special poignancy to her appearance at the Fior.

He was also delighted to serve Roy Orbison, the "Caruso of Rock," whose music Rick admired deeply. The man put his everlasting imprint on popular music and led the way for the Beatles. Orbison struck him as a polite and gentle man, when Rick had the opportunity to serve him.

During his teens, Rick sometimes irritated his uncle George. He wasn't always reliable. There were times when he didn't show up on time for his shift after partying the night before. Yet George was able to train his nephew to follow him in one tradition: Rick was smoking Toscano cigars by the time he was fourteen.

Later, in the 1960s, George's son, now Paul Mantee, was enjoying what he thought would be his big break. In 1965, he was cast in the movie "Robinson Crusoe on Mars". Paul dominated the film with a performance that still inspires fans' loyalty after all these years. The film was acclaimed for its cinematography and special effects and it remains a cult classic of the science fiction genre. However, Paramount marketed the film unenthusiastically and it never boosted Paul to the heights of fame he had been led to expect.

In the film, Paul plays an astronaut who crashes on Mars, losing his co-pilot and ship. He faces a desolate existence on the red planet until he encounters another creature and adventures ensue. He recalled:

It was a dreadful title. But I was on screen for about an hour with this monkey then another guy came on. It was considered a cult classic and I still go to sci-fi conventions to sign my picture. It was shot in 1966, a long time ago, and it flopped. By the time it was released and cut together, Paramount had changed hands and (the new) Paramount didn't know what to do with this. So they gave it a terrible release and it died. And I was disappointed because people said, 'Hey kid, this is going to do it for you.' And I bought that.

Frank and George and Armando Lippi at the Fior's 80th anniversary.

The Marianetti clan was terribly proud of Paul's dramatic accomplishments. Rick remembered, "It was a major event every time he was on TV. When Crusoe came out, the whole family went to the local drive-in to watch it."

Getting the Word out

Harkening back to J. L. Pimsleur's August 9, 1959, story in the *San Francisco Chronicle*, we see the Fior is associated with the introduction of several recipes to the local table:

> Through the years the Fior made a number of significant contributions to the Nation's culinary vocabulary, introducing several dishes which today are standard items on menus throughout the country. Many were known in the Italian home but none had ever before been served publicly in a restaurant. Veal Scaloppine, for instance, started here in 1886. So did Risotto with Clams. In 1931 Lasagne with Chicken and Mushrooms was introduced, soon became one of the most popular dishes on the menu. And a scant four years ago, the king of them all, Saltimbocca (aptly, "jump in the mouth") was introduced after Herb Caen had raved about it from Italy and a retired East Bay restaurant man brought back the recipe. [2]

Paul said George had told him many years ago the Fior was responsible for introducing these dishes to the American palate.

"I would kill for the risotto and clams recipe in his own words. Or Frank's. Or Leo's (Quattrin). I believe Saltimbocca was introduced while I was overseas during the Korean War. There are many scaloppine variations. Scaloppine Marsala was on the 'dollar dinner' when I was a busboy in 1947," Paul said.

Rick however was more cautious in confirming that the Fior introduced these dishes in this country:

> One thing my years in the culinary business taught me: there are more exaggerated, fabricated, and fanciful stories about the origin of menu items than there are legs on all the calamari that's ever been served at the Fior. I really can't say for sure which dishes were first served there, although I remember Frank telling me it was his idea to serve the Saltimbocca like a Cordon Bleu, i.e., the veal and prosciutto rolled with the cheese in the middle, served with a mushroom sauce and wild rice on the side. Traditionally, it's served flat with plain rice, potato, or pasta. Besides the Chicken Fior (sauteed with mushrooms, artichoke hearts, and white wine), that Saltimbocca was

one of the best dishes the Fior did in my experience….All the flavors and textures on the plate worked together in a magical synergy that I still remember to this day.

While these news stories were great plugs, during the 1960s Frank and George fell derelict in maintaining the Fior's elegance and reputation. Even Edwards, the parking attendant, said he watched the restaurant as "it went downhill…right in front of my eyes."

Lulled by complacency, the brothers failed to promote the business adequately. Rick was dismayed by the lack of persistent effort devoted to keeping quality high and marketing and publicity efforts at the forefront of the business.

"I noticed from the time I was twelve, it was very busy and over the years, it was less busy. As I was able to go around to different restaurants and sample different food, I could see the quality went down. They were cutting corners…and they weren't taking any steps to do anything about it," Rick said.

Curiously, the owners added one exotic feature, the kimono-clad hatcheck girl Kioko Moser, a native of Nagasaki City. Having just lost her husband at the age of thirty-three, Kioko was grateful to have a second job at the Fior, where she found Frank and George were always gracious to her.

Hatcheck girl Kioko Moser.

90

Kioko was bashful as the only female on staff. "They told me to have something to eat in the kitchen before I start work, to join them eating. But at the time I was the only girl and was too shy. I say, 'Thank you, thank you. Sometimes they give me spumoni," she recounts now.

George's humor left her uncomprehending but she did certainly understand that he drank to excess.

"One Thanksgiving, I gave Frank one bottle *sake* and to George I say, 'This is rice wine for the holiday.' A few days later, Frank gave me some dessert with cream inside. The New Year I give them *sake* again. I told them it had to be warmed but I think they drank it cold on ice," she surmised. "I think so because George was a drinker."

Kioko in a kimono was certainly a charming addition to the restaurant but hardly constituted what was necessary to keep the restaurant in the public eye. Rick managed to capture the attention of Herb Caen, the *San Francisco Chronicle* columnist, but there was no consistent policy for marketing.

"The management was nothing like restaurants built these days where everything is done with lawyers, accountants and it's scientific. (Fior management) was done in the old style. They hired a guy if he walked in off the street. The training was on-the-job. Frank and George …didn't really know what they had. I just realized it in my twenties. They didn't know the history of the thing and what you could do with it…how you could exploit it," Rick recalls.

Meanwhile Rick, who was heir apparent, did not step into his father's or his uncle's shoes. He spent time at the University of California at Berkeley debating about an academic career. Even while working at the Fior, he showed no interest in the restaurant. So Frank and George were left without willing successors. George's son, Paul, was in show business. Frank's son, Bob, was incapable, and it would be years before Rick developed an interest in cuisine and food service.

"Everyone was getting older and they got tired. Maybe if I'd expressed more of an interest in it when I was younger, things would've been different," Rick said.

Now losing money, the brothers eventually came to the conclusion it was time to sell. Apparently it was George who to advanced the idea and as the big brother and head of the clan, he persuaded everyone else to go along, although reluctantly.

On January 17, 1977, Herb Caen reported that Gino Biardelli, owner of Cafferata Ravioli had bought the Fior for "a bargain $90,000." But in the end, this deal did not go through. The Fior became instead the prize of a group of investors.

ANIMELLE CON FUNGHI E CREMA
(SWEETBREADS WITH MUSHROOMS AND CREAM)

2 pounds sweetbreads
2 tablespoons clarified butter (see page 69)
All-purpose flour, for dusting
1/2 pound button mushrooms, sliced
1 cup chicken stock
1 cup heavy cream
2 tablespoons unsalted butter
Salt and freshly ground black pepper

To prepare the sweetbreads: Soak the sweetbreads in cold water for at least 6 hours or overnight, changing the water twice; keep them refrigerated during soaking.

Fill a large bowl with ice water; set aside. Bring a large pot of water to a boil over high heat. Add the sweetbreads and cook until firm and just cooked on the outside, about 5 minutes. Using a slotted spoon, carefully remove the sweetbreads and immerse in the ice water until cold. Using your fingers, remove any membrane covering the sweetbreads and discard. Cut the sweetbreads into bite-size pieces.

In a large sauté pan, heat the clarified butter over medium-high heat. Lightly dust the sweetbreads with flour and shake gently to remove any excess. Arrange the sweetbreads in a single layer in the pan and cook, turning occasionally, until golden, about 4 minutes. Using a slotted spoon, transfer the sweetbreads to a plate and set aside. In the same pan, add the mushrooms and cook until the liquid they release has evaporated, about 5 minutes. Add the stock and cream and cook until the sauce coats the back of a spoon, about 5 minutes. Add the unsalted butter and whisk until incorporated. Return the sweetbreads to the pan and cook until just heated through. Season to taste with salt and pepper.

To serve: Divide the sweetbreads and mushroom sauce among four warmed serving plates and serve immediately.

Serves four

CHAPTER 14: Leaving the Family Fold, 1977-90

When the Marianetti brothers finally let go of the restaurant, the Fior passed into the hands of five men: William Armanino, brothers Larry and Sergio Nibbi, Charles Ramorino and later, Achille Pantaleoni. They were all respected men in the Italian-American community.

William Armanino

Armanino's great grandfather farmed herbs. "We were always in the crop business," he recalls In 1957, his father founded G. Armanino & Sons, Inc., the holding company of Armanino Farms of California. The business specialized in growing, processing, and distributing fresh, frozen, and freeze-dried herbs, spices and vegetables. The business today is called Armanino Foods of Distinction in Hayward, California, and now also produces food products, such as pesto sauce.

An athlete as a young man, Armanino always retained his interest in baseball and baseball players. He is an imposing man who enjoys entertaining and is an active fund-raiser for his many political interests. The Fior proved to be an appropriate place for him to entertain groups from his various circles.

"We really didn't need to make money at the Fior. We wanted to be successful but we had our own businesses. It was almost an extension of my social being and my being involved with the community," he explained.

His company's needs for trucking services eventually led him to Charles Ramorino, the owner of Bob and Rich Schroeder Trucking Company. Armanino became one of Ramorino's important clients and eventually a friend. Charlie and Bill lunched together frequently in North Beach.

On October 8, 1977, author and historian Kevin Starr quoted Armanino in the *San Francisco Examiner*.

'There is a renewal of pride and optimism in the Italian community,' William Armanino told me recently over lunch at the Fior d'Italia. 'Pride in the Italian heritage, pride in the Italian contribution to San Francisco.' [1]

Starr continued with his own comments:

Bill Armanino was a go-getter. Born in 1927 to a family active in the produce business, Armanino learned English under the Sisters of St. Joseph of Orange at St. Joan of Arc Elementary School in Bayview. His early morning hours were spent helping his father at the Produce Mart. At Commerce High School he led a dance band, Armanino's Music Makers. Over the years, Farms (sic), started by Guglielmo Armanino, Bill's father has grown into a multimillion-dollar enterprise, producing chives and a variety of herb and spice products.

Bill Armanino sought, worked for, and attained financial success, but he wanted more – he wanted to get involved….[2]

And he did. At the time he owned the Fior, he was active in many charities, a member of several associations and a regent of the University of Santa Clara.

The Nibbi Family

Marino Nibbi, a native of Lucca, brought his wife and infant son Sergio to San Francisco in 1940 where he landed a job as a carpenter. Ten years later, he started his own contracting business that eventually became known as Nibbi Bros.

The man who served San Francisco as chief of police and from 1992-1996 as mayor, Frank Jordan, remembers Marino, as cutting a dashing figure and entertaining patrons after his sons became Fior proprietors.

"He was one of those old style Italians, impeccably dressed with a little white pencil moustache and a strong accent," Jordan says. "People would come in and ask, 'Where's La Felce (a restaurant across the street)?' and Marino would take them into La Felce and make sure they were taken care of and met the people they were looking for."

Nibbi Bros. became one of the largest privately owned construction companies in the Bay Area and the most active in San Francisco proper. His sons, Sergio and Larry, eventually joined the business.

Today, as the heads of the family business, the Nibbi sons are active in civic and philanthropic endeavors. That is how they eventually came to meet Bill Armanino.

Charles Ramorino

Ramorino's parents came from Piemonte in Northern Italy and settled first in the gold country of California. Later, they moved to San Francisco's Mission District, where Charles was born.

Ramorino was a bright student who won a scholarship to St. Ignatius High School and saw World War II interrupt his hopes for higher education. After his discharge from the U.S. Navy in 1946, necessity led him to pumping gas. After a couple of years, he and his brother launched their own service station business, specializing in serving trucks. The business proved to be inadequate to support two families and his brother finally withdrew, leaving Charlie as the sole owner. Charlie married Joann, a Utah native of North Italian extraction, and they had two sons, Robert and Richard.

Through the 1950's Charles made a transition to the trucking business and bought the Schroeder Trucking Company. He renamed that business after his two sons, the Bob Rich Schroeder Company. Charlie assumed larger prominence in his industry, eventually serving from 1997-99 as President of the American Trucking Association

The Fior's *Roshomon*

While the backgrounds of these gentlemen are fairly clear, how and when they decided to come together to buy the Fior is less certain. Like the classic Japanese film, *Rashomon* in which each individual's recollection of an event of long ago differed based on the role each played in the drama, Armanino, Ramorino, and the two Nibbi brothers have indeed recounted their separate versions of how they learned the Fior was for sale and how and why they decided to buy it. Curiously enough, all the versions may be true.

The Nibbis' story was based on their employee, carpenter Achille Pantaleoni. Pantaleoni was a brother-in-law of Fior chef, Leo Quattrin. Quattrin told Pantaleoni, who passed on the information to his employers, that the restaurant was going to be shut down if no buyer was found for it. This news had shock value in the Italian-American community. The Fior was an icon in their culture. It was an institution that immigrants and their children had shaped with their earliest memories in North Beach.

'Flower' Has Bloomed For 85 Years

Fior Is A Family Affair

By Timothy J. Guiney

Fior d' Italia — the "Flower of Italy."

To do justice to this famed San Francisco restaurant would really require a book. Too much has happened, and there's too much to write about to properly cover its 85 years as one of the city's outstanding gourmet institutions.

For it is 85 years old. Or should we say 85 years young, and while the old traditions of the finest in quality and service, as well as warmth and cordiality still prevail, there is nothing "musty" about the Fior.

Behind its romance with yesterday, the Fior has always been conscious of the changing mores of "today" and "tomorrow." In these respects, the management not only keeps abreast, it keeps ahead.

To illustrate: It has patrons who have literally been going there for decades. At the same time, newer generations are much in evidence, too, with all sharing the same admiration for good food, good drinks, and genuine hospitality.

Family Affair

The Fior is a family affair, one that has passed from father to sons as you would a precious jewel.

The brothers, George and Frank Marianetti, are the sons of Armido Marianetti, and the nephews of Alfredo, Zeffiro and Giuseppe, who joined their brother after he first became an owner of the restaurant. The other partners — and a congenial partnership it is — are Armand Lippi and Chef Leo Quattrin.

We mentioned that some customers have been going to the Fior for decades. This is literally true. Renzo Turco, for instance, a local attorney, has dined there every Thursday for the past 50 years! How many other restaurants could make that statement about a customer?

If you want to use the expression, "born to the purple," this certainly applies to the Marianetti family. George Marianetti, the personable host, actually started working at the restaurant when it was located on Broadway at the age of nine, and was known as the "wine kid," the little fellow who hid behind the walls and filled coffee cups with a product far more enticing than coffee, under the noses of the unsuspecting revenooers.

Unglamorous

Later he had the unglamorous role of dishwasher—"there must have been 10,000 glasses, all waiting for me, the night that I started," says George with a smile. And he went through every other facet of the business. If ever a man knows the restaurant business from the ground floor up, George

BARTENDER HANK DAVERO pours a drink of Ancient Age for Partner George Marianetti. Only top level brands are featured in the restaurant, a tradition that dates back over the 85 years the Fior d' Italia has been operating. Davero has been with the restaurant for the past 15 years—which, by Fior d' Italia standards, means that "he is coming along very nicely, and might make it all the way."

LEO QUATTRIN, the personable partner-chef at the Fior, is understandably proud of his dishes, and the kitchen in which they are created. His domain of utensils, combined with special recipes accumulated over his 40 years with the restaurant, gives his area the pulse-beat of the Fior.

Marianetti does, and the Fior d' Italia reflects it. George's son, Paul Mantee, is a prominent movie and televison actor.

Equally trained in the business is George's brother, Frank, who pretty much duplicated his older brother's career in the restaurant.

Several years ago, the Fior was moved from its long-time location on Broadway to 621 Union-st., with a spacious dining area and a superb decor that makes being there a special pleasure. Even the "old timers," understandably reluctant to see their favorite restaurant move from its venerable location, agreed that the change was even

for the better, perhaps the greatest compliment they could pay.

The Marianettis and their partners have followed faithfully the principals of their family in operating the restaurant. There are no short cuts to success, is their philosophy. Give people excellent food, drinks, atmosphere, and friendship, and the rest will take care of itself.

That's how the restaurant was founded. And that's how it still functions, 85 years later.

Beverage Industry News, June 1, 1971.

Fior d'Italia
San Francisco ★ California
SINCE 1886

Wednesday, April 26, 1978

APPETIZERS

Crab Cocktail 3.50	Shrimp Cocktail 3.00	Crab Legs 4.25	Olympia Oysters 3.75
Blue Point Oysters 3.50	Cherrystone Clams 3.00	Fresh Artichokes 1.75	Prawn Cocktail 4.25

SALADS

Fior d'Italia Salad 7.25	Chef Special Salad Bowl 4.95	Washington Square Salad 6.95
Prawns, Crabmeat, Avocado	*Tom, Salami, Turkey and Cheese*	*Fresh Artichoke, Crabmeat, Jumbo Prawns, Calif. Shrimp*
Crab Legs Louis, Suprême 7.95	Fresh Crab Louis 6.75	Fresh Fruit Salad with Sherbet 3.75
Cottage Cheese and Fresh Fruit 3.75	Avocado with Chicken 4.25	Shrimps Louis 6.25
Caesar Salad 3.50	Luncheon Salad 1.25	Avocado with Crab 6.25
Avocado with Shrimps 5.75		Avocado and Prawns 6.75

CHOICE OF DRESSING

SOUPS

(BOWL 1.75)

Soupe du Jour .85	Vichyssoise 1.00	Minestrone .85	Onion Soup 1.25
Consommé with Pastina 1.00	Clam Chowder (Friday only) 1.00		Chicken Broth with Rice .85

PASTE

Fettuccine Alfredo 3.75 Cannelloni 3.75 Spaghetti Caruso 4.75 Spaghetti Marinara 3.75 Spaghetti Bolognaise 3.50

OMELETTES & EGGS

Cheese 3.50	Chicken Liver 4.25	Mushrooms 3.75	Ham or Bacon 3.95
Joe's Special 4.25	Fior d'Italia Special 3.95		Frittata Toscana 3.95
Ground Beef, Spinach and Eggs	*Minced Ham, Mushrooms and Spinach*		*Fresh Artichoke South*
Frittata della Casa 4.50	Shirred Eggs and Sausages 3.75		Eggs Bénédict 4.50
Artichokes and Italian Sausage			

FISH

*Rex Sole Pan-Fried, Boned, Meuniere 5.50	Louisiana Prawns, Fried, Tartar Sauce 6.85	*Steamed Clams, Bordelaise 4.25
Steamed Clams, Plain 3.95	Filet of Petrale, Meuniere 6.25	Crab Legs Sauté Meuniere 7.50
	Eastern Scallops, Saute Meuniere 5.95	

ENTREES

Veal Cutlet Parmigiana 7.95	Breaded Veal Cutlet with Spaghetti 7.95	Minute Steak 8.25
Medallions of Tenderloin Fior d'Italia 8.75	Filet or New York Cut 11.75	Chicken Livers Sautés 4.95
Veal Scaloppine Marsala 7.95	Chicken Livers Sauté, Fresh Mushrooms 5.75	Veal Piccata 8.50

TODAY'S SPECIAL

Sirloin Tips Sauté, Fresh Mushrooms 4.35	Italian Sausage with Polenta 4.35
Chopped Sirloin Steak, Fresh Mushroom Sauce 3.95	Veal Genoa with Potato and Peas 4.35

DIET SPECIAL: Chopped Sirloin Steak, Cottage Cheese, Sliced Tomato 3.75

SANDWICHES

Sliced Breast of Turkey 3.75	Monte Cristo 4.50	Ham and Cheese 3.50
Club House 4.25	Deluxe Hamburger 3.75	New York Steak Sandwich 5.75
	With French Fries	

CHEESE

Monterey Jack .95	Danish Blue .95	Fontina .95	Camembert

DESSERTS

French Pastry 1.50	Fresh Fruit in Season 1.25	Cheese Cake .95	Fresh Fruit Cup 1.35
Ice Cream or Sherbet .75	From our Cart Assorted Cheese 1.50		Crème Caramel 1.25

BEVERAGES

Coffee .60	Pot of Tea .60	Sanka .60	Iced Tea .60	Milk .60

*Please allow 15-20 minutes for proper preparation

◀ H. J. CARLE & SONS

1978 Menu.

Larry and Sergio Nibbi reacted with dismay at this possibility. They immediately thought of buying the restaurant – not because they wanted to be in the restaurant business -- but rather to preserve an important piece of their own culture.

Larry Nibbi recounted, "We mentioned it to Bill (Armanino), who mentioned it to Charlie (Ramorino). We sat down with George Marianetti, and asked, 'Are you serious about selling?' "

From his own vantage point, Armanino remembered lunching one day with Ramorino and Sergio Nibbi "as we did every day, at Lorenzo's North Beach restaurant. Somebody came in and said the Fior d'Italia was up for sale." With his companions, he rose and went across the street and cornered George Marianetti about purchasing the business.

"On a handshake, we told them we'd buy it," he said.

But according to Ramorino, the idea to buy the Fior was planted in their minds much earlier in an indirect way. Ramorino recalled that he and Armanino ate at the Fior regularly where longtime waiter Mario Pucci usually served them.

One day Armanino ribbed Pucci: "If you don't serve us well, we'll buy the restaurant."

Ramorino recalls: "I remember very clearly that I looked at Bill and he looked and me and we said, 'Why don't we buy the restaurant?' And it was in the same time period that (a sale) was there in Herb Caen's column. So he says, 'What do you think?' and I said, 'Oh my. I don't have any time to devote to it.' And he said, 'Either do I. Let's just buy it.'

In all, each had his different approach, but all had the same answer.

New Blood and Old

In a gesture of gentility and good business sense, the new management asked Frank Marianetti to stay on as the maitre d' during lunch. He was beloved and an important link with the restaurant's history, they reasoned. George, who had a bad knee and other ailments, retired.

"Frank was so excited about (the restaurant) coming back up again. The fact that there was money that was going to get pumped into it and that people with reputations in San Francisco would bring people in exhilarated him," architect Terry Lofrano recollected.

The Fior had enjoyed an unbroken family ownership of the restaurant from 1886, when Del Monte bought and owned it, to the Marianettis who now had just sold it. Now Leo Quattrin, who had cooked at the Fior for decades, was the link that brought his brother-in-law, Achille Pantaleoni, to a brand new lineage

Pantaleoni

Decades earlier, when Marino Nibbi had started his business, he had hired Achille Pantaleoni as his first carpenter. Born outside of Lucca, Pantaleoni learned his skills from his father and grandfather. He was a consummate craftsman, as capable of fashioning an armoire as erecting a sink and shelves of sheet metal. He worked for the Nibbis

Achille Pantaleoni.
Courtesy Tom Vano

his entire career until the 1970s when he had open-heart surgery and decided to retire. Now the new owners invited him to join them as an owner and be a part of a restaurant he also loved.

When the five owners divided up their responsibilities, Pantaleoni assumed the job of maitre d' during the evenings and weekends when Frank was not working. At first, Frank trained him. But his brother-in-law, Quattrin, did not continue with the Fior after the sale.

While many personalities in the Fior had been treasured over the decades, Achille's spirit shines through until today and so many still remember him with fondness.

"He was the Nibbis' best-dressed carpenter," jokes his son, Tony. He was always impeccably groomed and attired. But even more so, he had fallen completely in love with the Fior and served the restaurant as a faithful suitor.

Pantaleoni would meet customers at the door with a flourish and an enthusiasm about sharing the Fior with them. He was dashing, suave and a charmer. His Italian accent led people to believe he was the sole proprietor or even the founder of the business. He was even nicknamed "Mr. Fior d'Italia."

Besides his gallantry to the customers, he used his artisan's skills at the restaurant. The architects earlier had erected a working fountain between the columns of the main dining room. Pantaleoni puttered and tinkered with it, making sure its water wouldn't splatter the diners. He also built cabinets, fixed chairs, built shelves in the kitchen and tended to any woodworking that the Fior required.

Eventually, photographer Tom Vano captured him in a portrait that now hangs in the main dining room named after him, the Pantaleoni Room.

Mormando Leaves the Casinos

"Larry Nibbi contacted me and said, 'We're looking at a restaurant and want you to come down here.' I said to him, 'You guys are all successful, what do you want with a restaurant?'" "Lenny Mormando recalls his disbelief the time the contractors phoned him. Whether Larry answered his question convincingly didn't matter. Mormando accepted the job of restaurant manager.

Mormando, whose career had until then focused on Lake Tahoe casinos, found a new kind of lifestyle with his latest gig at the Fior. "I was used to people that ate and went to play in casinos. In San Francisco, they dined and dined gorgeously. It gave me warmth to watch people sit there with a bottle of wine and enjoy it. It was important to me to get couples talking," he said. He left the Tahoe life and took his new post at the Fior in late 1977 and stayed almost three years.

One night in April of 1978, Mormando waited on Frank Sinatra and his retinue after the singer had closed his show at the Circle Star Theatre in San Carlos. Armanino led the party into the Tony Bennett Room "where they wined and dined until the wee small hours of the morning," reported the *San Francisco Chronicle* on May 5, 1978.

The New Fior

None of the new owners had run a restaurant before. Except for Armanino, they were not in the food business. None of them had ever served the individual consumer either. They had just served other businesses.

Still they were enthusiastic and unanimous that the first step they should take with the Fior was to redecorate it. It had been over 20 years since the famous architect, Mario Gaidano, had transformed the old Riviera restaurant premises into the award-winning Fior d'Italia. The new owners looked at the Fior as it stood and knew it was dated.

The Nibbis and Armanino already knew architect, Terry Lofrano. Lofrano had been a close friend of Marino Nibbi and considered him a mentor. Armanino and Lofrano knew each other from *Il Cenacolo*. So the owners gave the firm of Neeley/Lofrano the task of transforming the Fior anew. This time it was to be a clubby, dimly lit atmosphere where the main dining room and bar would be snuggled deep within the interior.

Lofrano rendered designs to suggest an Italian garden, with a broken arch as the central theme, dark, heavy textures and stucco. He engaged glass artist, John Lewis, to create hand-blown lampshades that would suggest Murano craftsmanship.

Coincidentally, Achille Pantaleoni's son, architect Tony Pantaleoni, worked for Neeley/Lofrano and was charged with assembling the historic photographs, old menus and other memorabilia that were to be framed and hung in the newly-designed interior.

The Fior had a reputation for being open every day. But, while making the transition from old to new kitchen, they had to shut down for a day. Refurbishing the outside of the building brought even more unanticipated repercussions. The owners and architects had to deal with the delicate problem of the residential hotel upstairs. It was owned and operated by Elmer Gavello, the Fior's landlord. The man who owned 601 Union St. was the same who owned and managed the Lucca restaurant to great acclaim in the 1920s-1930s. He also owned and operated the Gianduja Restaurant and later, the Riviera, which preceded the Fior at 601 Union Street. However, the hotel did not live up to the standards of Gavello's other properties.

It was in every sense of the word a flophouse, inhabited by derelicts, addicts and all manner of low life. While the Marianettis had tolerated the malodorous encroachments from above, the new owners felt compelled to sanitize this presence that was so alien to what they were trying to create. Mormando said he was aghast to see that, while the Fior's workers were stitching a new awning, hotel residents above were throwing cigarettes and ashes down, burning holes in the awning.

"I got so mad with all these burning holes, I went running up the stairs and could not believe my eyes. There was garbage all over. Doors to rooms were broken down. Some of the derelicts in there were unbelievable. We had to work on getting them out," he said.

Transforming the property upstairs became another project for the four new owners. They appealed to Gavello who was unmoved by their problems and uninterested in changing the nature and tenants of the hotel. With no investment in it other than wanting to maintain the Fior's good image, the owners took on the task at their own expense.

"Armanino offered them money to get them out. Some were not happy and asked for more money. (The owners) were shaken down. It took several months of bothering, arguing. We knew if we put a nice place downstairs, we'd have to change the hotel," Mormando said.

The owners at this point in their careers were also involved in bringing honor to North Beach by sponsoring and supporting efforts to celebrate the locale's Italian culture and heritage. They were also concerned about their own elderly parents and Italians of the same generation. They devised a plan to transform the upstairs into a home for the Italian elderly and named it the Casa Costanza, after Father Joseph Costanza, pastor of Sts. Peter and Paul's Church, the Italian church across Washington Square.

Tony Pantaleoni and a principle of MBH Architects, John McNulty, went up to the hotel and did the drawings needed to refurbish it, climbing over rubble and debris to do so.

"We were trying to do something good for the Italian community and Gavello was Italian. But he was not cooperative at all. The Nibbis did a lot of gratis work on it, pro bono. We contributed a reasonable amount ourselves. It was fun at a time when a lot of things were happening in North Beach related to the Italian community and their advancement. People were stepping up to the plate who were making money and were noteworthy San Franciscans," recalls Lofrano.

The owners of the Fior were among many Italian-Americans concerned about the direction North Beach was taking. The area was becoming more Chinese in ownership and less Italian. Partly this change occurred because, as Italians became richer, they left North Beach and bought homes elsewhere, in the Sunset district, in Marin or Alameda Counties. As the Chinese grew richer, they by and large maintained their holdings, expanding into new territories. Chinese property owners by the mid-1970s had crossed Broadway, which had been the dividing line between Chinatown and North Beach until then.

The Fior owners and other Italian-American entrepreneurs, landlords and proprietors formed a coalition to keep North Beach Italian. There was also apparently some cooperation from the Chinese landlords with stakes in North Beach.

Warren Hinckle of the *San Francisco Chronicle* labeled Bill one of "The New Medicis of North Beach":

Armanino has slick graying hair and thick, flying saucer-shaped black eyebrows which hover over his dark eyes. His speech has an epochal quality. He and a group of associates just spent $600,000 buying and refurbishing the Fior D'Italia. That is just the first step in what he plans on "revitalization" (his favorite word) of Italian ethnic pride in North Beach. The exercise could cost upward of $15 million to $10 million dollars. [3]

Hinckle quotes him:

'We bought the Fior because it was going down the drain. It's the oldest Italian restaurant in San Francisco; it had to be saved. It's the anchor, across the square from Sts. Peter and Paul. We're in the process of purchasing other properties along the square to revitalize them in an Italian orientation. Then we're going to bring Italian stores and boutiques into the blocks around the (Washington) square. We're going to build a garage underneath it. We're going to make North Beach an ethnic example to the rest of the city. The tourists will learn a thing or two.'

Talk is cheap, but the Italian investment-leadership block – the 'We' – Armanino is forming is anything but. It includes the Scatena and Nibbi construction interests, major Italian bankers, realtors and investors, Italian priests and social workers, and 'a lot of Chinese friends.'[4]

Hinckle observed that Chinese investors would accept making North Beach an "Italian boutique" because doing so would produce more tourists, benefiting restaurant and commercial property owners, whatever their ethnic background.

There has been some $2.5 million invested just in North Beach restaurants in the last five years – and not a Chinese restaurant in the lot. Armanino's $600,000 in the Fior – with its unforgettable Tony Bennett Room complete with his gold records – is the high card. [5]

Parts of the grand scheme did not materialize, particularly the parking lot under Washington Square, which the neighborhood association blocked.

RAGÙ PER LA PASTA (RAGU FOR PASTA)

Preparation should begin with soaking the dried porcini mushrooms for one hour.

1/2 cup olive oil
2 stalks celery, finely chopped
1 small onion, finely chopped
1 medium carrot, peeled and finely chopped
2 cloves garlic, minced
1/2 pound ground veal
1/2 pound ground pork
1 cup dry marsala or dry red wine
1 ounce dried porcini mushrooms, drained, and coarsely chopped
4 bay leaves
Salt and freshly ground black pepper
1 pound ripe tomatoes, seeded and chopped, or 1 (28-ounce) can peeled,
   chopped tomatoes Freshly grated nutmeg
1/4 cup heavy cream

In a large sauté pan, heat the olive oil over medium-high heat. Add the celery, onion, carrot, and garlic; cook until the onions are translucent, about 2 minutes. Add the veal and pork; cook, using a spatula to break up the meat into small chunks, until any water the meat releases has evaporated. Add the marsala, porcini, and bay leaves, and season with salt and pepper; cook until the wine has evaporated. Add the tomatoes (and a little water if your tomatoes are very thick), lower the heat, and simmer very gently until the tomatoes are disintegrating and the vegetables are very soft, about 1 1/2 hours. (If the ragu seems too thick during cooking, add a little water.) Remove from the heat and season to taste with the nutmeg. Add the heavy cream and stir to combine.

Use immediately or transfer to an airtight container and refrigerate up to three days or freeze up to six months.

Serves four

CHAPTER 15: Singers and Chefs

Armanino brought an unexpected dividend to the new Fior, his friendship with singer Tony Bennett. The new owner rubbed shoulders with many entertainment luminaries from his involvement in fundraising for various charitable and political causes, Vic Damone and Frank Sinatra among them.

The owners wanted to heighten the Fior's profile in its design, menu and publicity. The man who sang "I Left My Heart in San Francisco" was the absolutely spot-on figure to lend fame to the Fior, the owners figured.

"As we progressed with the remodeling job, we wanted to bring excitement in. We called Tony. We told him we found where he left his heart in San Francisco. We asked for his family portraits and told him we'd make it a shrine. Tony was doing San Francisco quite often at that time. Most of his peer entertainers, they'd play the Fairmont and then they'd go to Tony's show," Bill said.

He broached to Bennett the idea of a room named after him, adorned with his family and professional memorabilia. Bennett agreed. San Francisco photographer, Tom Vano, was a childhood friend of Bennett's. They had grown up attending the same high school in Astoria, Queens. Vano had been living in San Francisco for many years and he also knew Bill Armanino through *Il Cenacolo*. At one point, the photographer produced a food magazine to support Armanino's family business.

Vano, highly esteemed in the photographic industry, was acclaimed as an artist. His photograph of the Golden Gate Bridge entitled, "Gateway to the Orient," hangs in the New York Museum of Modern Art as part of its permanent collection. A modest and unassuming man, his subjects have included U.S. Presidents, royalty and diplomats.

When Bennett gave the go-ahead for the Tony Bennett Room, Vano collected photos of Bennett's family and professional shots along with the many he'd taken of the singer throughout their friendship. He had them framed, hung and strikingly presented in the Tony Bennett Room where they hang today.

Also in evidence are Bennett's silver record, presented to the Fior by Columbia Records commemorating the sale of 500,000 copies of "I Left My Heart in San Francisco," and gold record for his sales of a million copies of the Hank Williams tune, "Cold, Cold Heart."

Architect Lofrano designed the structure and concept of the room and worked closely with Bill on color coordination. Tony Bennett inaugurated the room in a soft opening of the Fior a week before the official one. The restaurant was closed and limited tickets were sold. There were cameras, the press and it was a mob scene. Mayor George Moscone and entertainers, such as Clint Eastwood, attended. Bennett's performance that night was electric. Bennett was being feted in the room named after him as the other patrons ate outside.

When he emerged into the main dining room, the patrons spontaneously rose and broke into "I Left My Heart in San Francisco."

"He was overjoyed, he thought it was great," Tony Pantaleoni said. The successful event cheered the owners, giving them great hopes for the eatery's new reincarnation.

In 1989, over a decade later, *San Francisco Examiner* columnist, Noah Griffin, recounted the history of the famous song and Bennett's rendition.

Happy birthday to "I Left My Heart in San Francisco," which by my calculations should be 35 years old this year. Written by Douglass Cross and George Cory back in 1954, it may have languished in local obscurity if it weren't for Tony Bennett's 1962 recording. The circumstances of the recording were prompted by Bennett's piano player. He collected and saved original material that he thought Tony might perform well. During a 1962 appearance in the city, the song was pulled out, dusted off, performed and received enthusiastically. It was then recorded. Many locals didn't warm immediately to the new offering. It seemed a bit hokey first, with its "little cable cars climbing halfway to the stars." But once it became a national hit, we had no choice but to make it unanimously our own, and in 1967 Mayor Joe Alioto declared it San Francisco's official city song. The Tony Bennett room was dedicated at North Beach's Fior d'Italia restaurant in 1978 with Tony present and the gold record adorning the wall. [1]

A Chef's Passion

In preparation for the opening under the new ownership, more than the visual aspect had to be repaired. There was the all-important gustatory side.

Tony Bennett appears at the Fior to celebrate its opening under new management, with a new design and in the room named after him, the Tony Bennett Room.

Photos Courtesy Tom Vano

Armanino knew one of San Francisco's most celebrated chefs of the time, Ruggiero, or Roger as he was often called, Bertola. At the time he was working at the Iron Horse, an eatery with its own colorful history and repute. He had also opened the famed Doro's as chef.

Armanino knew he would bring attention to the Fior. But he didn't guess Bertola would also bring chaos.

Superstitious, Bertola would not open on a Tuesday or a Friday. The opening date was set for a Thursday in November. It was a quiet, uneventful opening. But the first Saturday after, there was a full house. Word was out that Bertola had joined the Fior and he always had a big following.

Unfortunately, the staff had received minimal training but they got it the very night of the opening. "We had a new, extensive menu to go over. There was construction noise outside. He spends about 10 seconds discussing these dishes. Fifteen minutes and boom, we were out of there. We hadn't seen them or tasted them," recalled Rick Marianetti, Frank's son who had been serving that night.

Bertola did not mix well with waiters and acted as the king of the kitchen rather than a leader of a team. Sergio Nibbi observed that the staff was simply not prepared that night for the large crowd. By 7 P.M., 200 people were sitting at table waiting for their orders to arrive. The waiters were not taking them from the kitchen fast enough and the orders were backing up.

Bertola became enraged. He saw all these dinners sitting under the heat lamp, the sauces beginning to separate. In a spasm of fury, he flung the dishes at the waiters, sweeping platters full of food onto the floor and against the wall. He said it was "garbage" and he wasn't going to serve garbage. He shrieked at the waiters. Then he flew out the door. About half an hour later, he returned, went to the bar and started drinking.

Larry Nibbi went up to him to him to inquire what the problem was. Bertola fulminated about the stupid waiters. Fortunately, there were five other cooks who bravely began again to fulfill all those orders. The diners were not happy and the reviews reflected the discord. Rick Marianetti painted a grim picture:

The place was jammed with all the publicity. The screaming started about 5:30 or 6:00 P.M. He's swearing at us in Italian and English. 'You guys pick up the food, you goddamn mother -------s.'

The place started piling up. Everybody's confused trying to get the place numbers set up. There's beef tournedos on the menu and filet mignon. Which is which? And there's brand new china.

Every time you go back there, you hear it nonstop. Red veins on his neck. I thought he was going to have a heart attack. Around 7 P.M. people are getting impatient. They've waited a long time for their food. Suddenly he takes the food, the plates, and starts throwing them at the waiters. I looked around for a door. I thought he was going to kill someone. I thought I'd better get out of here in case he comes after me. He must have thrown down 30 plates of food on the floor, broken china, expensive veal, and goes downstairs and then he goes to the bar to have a drink.

People walked out, mad and angry. The maitre d' Frank Perez asked people, 'Please stay. Please, please stay.' But the evening was a fiasco. Though the place was packed, there was nothing in the paper.

The following Monday, Bertola told the Nibbis it was a good thing he walked out. "I would have killed someone," he said.

Bertola was as exacting of his clientele as he was of himself and the waiters. If people didn't eat their food, he would demand to know why not. Or he'd walk out into the dining room and inspect what people were eating. He might have seen someone eating a steak. Regardless of whether it was cooked as the patron ordered it, if Bertola thought it was improperly done, he'd yank it away and cook them another.

While he was erratic and unpredictable, his cooking was acclaimed far and wide. Rita Paoli, wife of Joe Paoli, deceased owner of Paoli's restaurant, said Bertola had cooking down to a science. "He was the greatest *saucière* I ever knew," she said.

Lenny Mormando recalled his sauces were so "vitally rich" that if they sat under the light any length of time, they'd get a film on top. "You'd have to pick them up right away."

But that evening, while Fior personnel were in agony and many customers were restless, outraged or had walked out, others were having a wonderful time. Architects Neeley and Lofrano were holding a party for partners, associates and employees and they had booked the Tony Bennett Room for the occasion. Their evening started with drinks and copious hors d'oeuvres. They had ordered a full course meal to celebrate their work on the restaurant.

"We were having a gay old time. We sat down after two hours of hors d'oeuvres and salad comes and then nothing....They kept sending us wine. My whole room gets snockered. It must have been about 11 o'clock when we finally got our entrees. We were just carrying on like crazy. A group of us went outside and hung signs in the window for our benefit. One guy got so smashed, he passed out into his dinner," Lofrano said. The party left around 12:30 A.M. after having arrived about 7 P.M.

Bertola had rigid standards of service. Clientele at the Fior have always demanded a lot of conversation at the table, asking the waiter's opinion about this or that item on the menu and delaying them to some degree. It was attention that the Fior's waiters always felt proud to give, sharing with the diners their expert knowledge of the menu. But if they were tardy picking dishes up, Bertola would put a serving fork on the flame and when the waiter or the captain came to pick up an entrée, he'd find his fingers burned.

Bertola's menu was not the family-style restaurant the Marianettis had been known for. He redesigned the menu from the copious meals the Marianettis and Leo Quattrin had been serving for decades to an à la carte menu. It was closer to the continental style for which he had drawn acclaim at Doro's. And it was, according to Rick Marianetti, "spectacular."

Maitre d' Enrico Obert remembered that until this period waiters were tossing the salad and mixing the fettucine at the patron's table – with the result that no two salads nor dishes of fettucine were standard..

"It was impossible. You had no control and you couldn't change because you had waiters here for 30 years. You had customers coming in telling what to do or not do. The employees and the waiters were running the show. Slowly, slowly I could change that and there were some people who were mad and said 'We won't come back.' "

The new owners wanted to put calamari on the menu. They approached Bertola who said, "I don't cook calamari. That's peasant food. I don't cook peasant food." Today, the Fior has three different calamari dishes on the menu, which are among the most popular ones the restaurant serves.

The new owners in a sense were stuck with him until they could find a replacement. Mercifully, a dispute around Valentine's Day brought Bertola's reign of terror to an end definitively. His replacement was Stelvio Storace.

Storace left his own stamp on the menu with a veal dish of mushrooms and white wine. Called Veal Stelvio at the time he introduced it, it remains a favorite under the name Veal Fior

Three years after the opening, Mormando left because he missed the life of Lake Tahoe and its golf courses and Las Vegas and the casinos. The Nibbis tapped Lee Leardini, an experienced restaurant manager to take over. "The first order of business was to get some activity through the restaurant and to develop the front portion," Leardini said.

At that time, the part of the restaurant on the corner of Union and Stockton Streets was partially boarded up and used for storage and for employee dining. Also near the front entrance was the Renaissance Room used for banquets. As was typical of restaurant design of the era, the bar was located in a corner deep in the interior.

From the left: Francesco Borlassi, Frank Marianetti, Enrico Obert, Gianfranco Audieri, Achille Pantaleoni, Gus Rivas and Joe Musso.

Leardini convinced the new owners that they had a million-dollar view overlooking Washington Square Park and should relocate the bar and part of the dining area there. Leardini researched the photographs of the Fior when it was on Broadway.

"We took some of the interior of the photos and tried to emulate the same design. It took me a month and a half looking at different lighting companies and catalogs to find the chandeliers," he said.

He successfully recreated in the bar and bistro area the look of the restaurant from pictures of the early 20th century. Today the bar overlooks Washington Square and the kitchen is behind it. The Renaissance Room, used frequently for banquets, has retreated toward the back.

The owners had a clever idea and made a small private dining room out of what used to be a broom closet. Called the Godfather Room, it sports a peephole in its door -- for humorous effect rather than utility. Some handsome art from the previous Riviera is hung there along with an enlarged reproduction of "Ripley's Believe It or Not" comic strip featuring Luigi Scaglione and his 54-year patronage of the Fior.

The first few years were not easy. Ramorino remembered that comparable restaurants were having challenges at the same time. The Fior owners had to strain at times to service their debt. There were occasional cash calls among them to make ends meet. They wondered if they should close. But they didn't.

They became slowly aware too that the chef, Storace, was taking money from vendors, a fact that was obscured apparently by his brother, who was the restaurant's bookkeeper. When he became aware of Storace's corruption, Pantaleoni was personally wounded since they had worked together trustingly for years.

His second in command, Gianni Audieri, who had joined the staff in 1982, was promoted to chef. He remains the chef today and is a co-owner.

SORBETTO (SHERBET)

Gianni's favorite is fresh pear. If you use a fresh one, sherbet will taste like a fresh pear. If you used canned, it will be somewhat more bland. Experiment with the tiniest bit of Poire William or grappa with raspberry or strawberry.

1 cup dry white wine
1/4 cup granulated sugar
1/4 cup freshly squeezed lemon juice
3 cups pureed fresh mango (about 3 to 5 mangoes, peeled, cubed, and pureed in a blender or food processor until very smooth)
Splash of eau de vie or other liqueur (orange goes well with mango), for drizzling

In a small saucepan, combine the wine and sugar. Bring to a boil over medium-high heat and cook until the sugar has completely dissolved and the mixture has turned from cloudy to crystal clear, about 1 minute. Remove from the heat and set aside until cool.

Ready an ice-cream maker according to the manufacturer's instructions. In a medium bowl, combine the sugar mixture, lemon juice, and mango puree; stir well to combine. Transfer to the prepared ice-cream maker and process according to the manufacturer's instructions. Stop the freezing when the sherbet has reached a semi-soft consistency. (The sherbet can be transferred to an airtight container and frozen at this point, but transfer to the refrigerator to soften for 20 to 30 minutes before serving.)

To serve: Scoop into individual serving dishes and drizzle a splash of eau de vie or your favorite liqueur over the top. Serve immediately.

Makes about 4 cups

CHAPTER 16: Through Rick's Eyes

Rick Marianetti was of a different generation than the owners. A student of philosophy at university, he was a passionate observer of politics, popular culture and the music scene. He recognized patrons of the Fior who exemplified his lifestyle or stimulated his intellect. Many times during the 1970s, he served the then managing editor of the *San Francisco Chronicle*, Scott Newhall, and the great Latin jazz vibraphonist, Cal Tjader. When Rick expressed to his father his delight over serving these figures, Frank told him that they'd been coming in for years already.

He served Dee Anthony, manager of performer Peter Frampton, who dined at the Fior during Frampton's acclaimed concert at the Oakland Coliseum in 1976. This was the tour when Frampton recorded "Frampton Comes Alive," reputed to be the biggest selling LP until that time.

"Every San Francisco mayor from George Christopher to Dianne Feinstein dined at the Fior while I was there. Christopher was serious and liked scotch. Feinstein seemed very straight-laced. Moscone was fun-loving," Rick said, remembering another former mayor, "charismatic" Joseph Alioto.

He recalled serving songwriter and singer Roy Orbison, famed for his poignant, soaring melodies and heartfelt delivery. Al Martino, the actor who played the character of Johnny Fontane in "Godfather I", popped in for a bite from time to time. In one instance, Rick remembered Kyra Nijinsky, the daughter of Vaslav Nijinski, dancer and choreographer of Russian ballet. She dropped into to join eight seated diners, members of the Oakland Ballet.

In Rick's words:

She approached the table wearing a colorful cotton jacket, scarf, and shimmering pillbox hat embroidered with enough purple, green, blue, red and yellow glitter to accommodate a New Year's Eve celebration in downtown Fresno. This outfit would've looked gauche on anybody else but on her it was absolutely stylish. She must've been close to seventy at the time, but radiated an exuberance and independence that was utterly irresistible. I wanted so much to sit down and talk to her about dance and life and whatever.

The Fior had its share of comical goofballs, too, Rick said:

One evening this guy comes in by himself. He's wearing a long black trench coat and carrying a large manila envelope with about 20 stamps and postmarks that indicate it had arrived from overseas. He looks like he hadn't cracked a smile in about three weeks. After being in the business for a while, you get an uncanny knack for identifying a person's origins just by their body language: French, Italian, German, whatever -- there are certain idiosyncratic countenances you can spot 20 yards away. I pegged him as East European. It's the mid 70s, the height of the Cold War, maybe he's a secret agent, I think.

I go up to the guy and ask him if he'd care for a cocktail: 'Give me an order of crepes suzette and a coke!' I tell him we don't have crepes. 'OK. I'll have a cup of coffee and a shrimp cocktail.' I go to the kitchen to put in the order and by the time I get back, I notice he's carefully taking items out of the envelope and placing them on the table against the brick room separator to his right. There's a photo of Joe Alioto with a big smile plastered across his kisser. Then out comes a portrait of Joe DiMaggio. Next, a picture of Karl Marx. Finally, directly across from him where the other place setting would normally be, he's got an eight-inch by 12-inch color portrait of the Pope. Table conversation was understandably subdued.

Rick seemed to be a magnet for the unconventional customer. There can be few patrons of the Fior who were more out of the mainstream than Oscar Zeta Acosta and later John C. Holmes.

Zany, wacky, brilliant and sometimes destructive are words that could apply to Oscar Zeta Acosta. Notable for two works of fiction and for his political activism, Acosta was a Chicano lawyer in an era when the Chicano society was extremely troubled. He excelled in defending the Mexican community and being their advocate against injustices. But he achieved notoriety as much for his antics as for his politics.

His semi-autobiographical novels, *The Autobiography of a Brown Buffalo* and *The Revolt of the Cockroach People*, are as brash and unsettling as they are comical.

In The Revolt of the Brown Buffalo, his protagonist visits the Fior d'Italia. Having risen from the depths of poverty, the main character felt uncomfortable in a milieu where others have known gentler, more secure lives. His comrade, Owl, is a prosperous drug dealer. They are alighting from their car in front of the Fior.

We don't wait for the nod from the parking lot attendant. The Owl merely stops the black machine, leaves the motor running and nods to the guard in front of the restaurant where Mr. Louis Scaglione has eaten twice daily in his pin-stripped suit for fifty-four years.

'How they hanging, Hank?' the Owl says to the man in the long, red coat. The doorman salutes him with a tip of the cap and takes each woman by the hand. I follow behind them. My eyes are giant floodlights, concentric circles of white and red.

'This is real class, Owl,' Maryjane, the gypsy says to him.

'Just another joint,' he shrugs.

I tiptoe into another world of fat-red carpets, violet tablecloths, dazzling chandeliers, white camellias, red roses and purple spider-mums. Young olive trees and casual green elephant ears are potted along the sides. There are pink brick walls to separate the parties and in the center of the dining room is a fountain spouting yellow water from the pelvic bone of a whale. I see huge men in black suits and black glasses; old women with powder blue, short hair; young women with shivering gowns; furs of dead animals, diamonds from the caves of deepest Africa, rubies from the eyes of Asian deities. Soft yellow lights, simple music from Mantovani, big black cigars, champagne, truffles, crepes suzettes, squab, wild rice, sweetbreads, saltimbocca, mushrooms and scampi à la casalinga…yes, sir just another joint….[1]

When the main character indulges in a snort of cocaine, the dinner party degenerates and he ends the evening hallucinating.

In reality, Acosta did patronize the Fior and Rick saw him there twice. Once, when Rick was parking cars for the restaurant, the lawyer-novelist arrived in his decrepit automobile with two attractive women. When Rick returned the car to Acosta, the writer handed him a copy of *Revolt of the Cockroach People* in lieu of a tip.

"I look up from the book and three of them have these goofy grins on their face and drive off into the sunset. I had no idea who this guy was," Rick said.

Later Acosta came with his friend Bob Henry, the man who was the author's model for the Owl. They brought along two store window mannequins whom they propped beside them at the bar. On a busy night, the men ordered four shots of tequila for the four of them.

"They proceeded to carry on a rather animated conversation with their 'dates' as a perplexed group of tourists looked on,' Rick said.

Rick also served one of the most famous pornography stars to date, John C. Holmes, known as Johnny Wadd. This is how he remembered it:

It was sometime in the mid '70s when John first began to frequent the Fior D'Italia in North Beach. I remember he was tall with light brown bouffant hair and a long face like Max von Sydow. He was very friendly, and came in about once a week. He always sat at the same table in my station. He told me he was a graphic artist working for the telephone company. He asked me a lot of questions about my physical stature, everything from my hat size down to whether my Adidas were size 11 bb or 12 cc. He stood up in the middle of the dining room and pressed himself next to me arm to arm like sardines in a can to compare our jacket sizes.

One day he mentioned a print advertising project he was working on. He said it required him to sketch a model dressed up as a pirate, and that I had just the swashbuckling 'look' he wanted….

What I actually wanted to say was 'How in the heck do you plan to work a sketch of me gussied up like Captain Hook into an advertising campaign for the Telephone Company?' He seemed like a nice enough guy and I didn't want to alienate him. While I was flattered, I thought I should drop a hint that I was a flaming heterosexual: I can't help it; I was born that way. So I mentioned something about Barri, my romantic interest at the time. That's when he suggested he and his girlfriend meet up with us later that evening.

Rick declined and it wasn't until years later that he learned this man was the notorious Johnny "Wadd" Holmes and his date was Serena, "one of the biggest porn stars of the Disco era," Rick said.

His Honor

While San Francisco's mayors have frequently patronized the establishment of Angelo Del Monte, George Moscone's custom was remarkable. Even his tragic death had a poignant connection to the restaurant.

Fior staffers saw him as expansive and convivial. They joined in singing "Happy Birthday" to him the last four or five years of his life. "He was a fun-loving guy. You could often find him hanging out at some of the great jazz clubs that used to be on Broadway. I remember seeing him at Basin Street West when Bill Evans was performing there," said Rick.

The mayor of San Francisco from 1975 to 1978, Moscone climbed out of near poverty by his own efforts. His divorced mother acquired church support to send him to the premier boy's Catholic high school,

St. Ignatius. After the navy, he went to University of California Hastings Law School in San Francisco and became involved in city politics early in his career. He served as a state senator for a decade and was on the city's Board of Supervisors under Mayor Joseph Alioto. He was elected mayor in 1975 at age forty-nine.

He signed a gay rights bill into law permitting sexual relations between consenting adults, a spectacular feat in its day. He supported bilingual education and school lunches for needy children. In a city that was predominantly Caucasian at the time, Moscone opened city government to minority employees.

He was, in other words, putting stress on the old guard, easing the way for changes they resisted. As he was a native of the city, one could say he was from the old guard himself. Many people, who cared about him because he had grown up among them, did not necessarily sign on to his political agenda.

Both loved and hated, Moscone may have underestimated those who despised him. He was slow to hire personal protection.

"George thought everyone loved him," observed Ramorino.

Ramorino and Armanino counted themselves among his friends but didn't share his politics. Moscone named Armanino the chairman of San Francisco's sister city relationship with Assisi, Italy. Armanino remembers asking the mayor, "Why? I never voted for you. I don't like your politics. But I like you."

Armanino attributed part of the reasons they got along well to the fact that Moscone's family was Genoese, as was his. And he was certainly pleased to be front man for the sister city link.

"Assisi is probably one of the most symbolic cities around the world," he reckoned.

Armanino and Ramorino ribbed the mayor about his cavalier attitude toward his personal security. One morning late in his mayoral term, Moscone went to the Jack Tar Hotel on Van Ness Avenue to meet Ramorino and Armanino for a breakfast meeting. It was late October 1978.

The two Fior owners stood at the window of the hotel watching as Moscone drove up in his Fiat sports car, the top down. He was late as usual. He parked in front and jumped out. Ramorino asked him about his lack of body guard or a driver.

"George, aren't you concerned with all the *babaos* in town?" he asked. Babao (ba-BOW) is Italian slang for jerk or doofus. Moscone merely laughed.

On November 27, 1978, Leardini instructed Rick to set table three for eight people. There would be the mayor, Armanino, Joe Tarantino of Tarantino's of Fisherman's Wharf and five others.

Rick called it "one of the saddest days I remember. The city was still spooked by the hideous events at the People's Temple, a formerly San Francisco-based religious cult that ended in the mass suicide of over 900 people in Jonestown, Guyana, just a few days before. Table three was set for a party of eight. It's the one in the corner of the bar under the mural by the window…I was truly looking forward to greeting the gentleman who had requested my table that morning, Mayor George Moscone. But another tragedy was unfolding that very moment back at City Hall, and table three was never seated."

The mayor never arrived. That morning, former Supervisor Dan White assassinated the mayor and Supervisor Harvey Milk in City Hall.

Bookkeeper Linda Tomback remembered when the horrible news came to the restaurant. "They brought Tarantino into the office and Bill (Armanino) told him the mayor had been shot. He stood there in shock," she said.

The whole city was devastated by grief, the Fior family no less than others.

Athletes Rule

Athletes bring glitter to a restaurant as surely as actors and politicians. Forty-niner Joe Montana began patronizing the restaurant in the early 1980s, about the time when John Carmazzi came to work as a waiter. Carmazzi, or J.C. to those around him, was a football enthusiast. After Montana won the Super Bowl in 1982, bringing the 49ers from obscurity to new fame, Montana became J.C.'s idol.

Enrico Obert, the maitre d' at the time, made sure J.C. waited on the football great. After Montana helped the team win the Super Bowl, J.C. was prepared for his next visit to the Fior. He bought red and gold flowers at a florist nearby and put them on Montana's table. When Montana came in, they were introduced and they raised a glass of champagne together.

"We've had many other 49er players here -- Fred Dean, Fred Solomon, Dwight Clark, the coach, (George) Siefert, and his wife and then Joe Montana's parents came in here one time and I got to meet his parents from Pennsylvania," said J.C., the fan.

Coach of the Los Angeles Dodgers, Tommy Lasorda, was also a regular on the corner of Union and Stockton Streets. Lasorda would come before three-game sets over Friday, Saturday, and Sunday.

Fridays were night games and he'd bring 10 to 15 team members for lunch, waiter Rudy Velarde recalled. Saturdays, he would bring trainers and administrators.

Lasorda recalled first coming to the Fior about two decades previously when he was addressing a group, not unlikely the *Il Cenacolo*. He so identified with the Fior that he asked for a dish to be named after him. The Fior accommodated him gladly with a pasta dish, Amatriciana Lasorda.

Waiter Velarde remembered that after U.S.S.R.'s debut of its perestroika program of economic and political restructuring, a delegation of Soviet industrialists came to San Francisco on a diplomatic visit and ate at the Fior. Velarde served them in the Tony Bennett Room on a day when Lasorda was also dining at the restaurant.

Velarde ushered the coach into the Tony Bennett Room. "I said, 'Hello everybody, Mr. Tommy Lasorda, manager of the Los

Angeles Dodgers. And they looked at him and clapped and said, 'Ya, oh, Slim Fast guy.' (Tommy) was pitching that product on TV," the waiter said.

Despite Lasorda acting as a spokesman for diet food on June 14, 1989, USA TODAY quoted him praising the Fior's "terrific homemade pasta." [2]

A Tenor's Taste

In 1982, *Il Cenacolo* invited a special guest to speak at one of their luncheons, a guest whose celebrity would make the chefs think hard. Frank Marianetti, whose job it was to plan the menus for the men's club, described the dilemma that the expectation of Luciano Pavarotti posed for the Fior. The maestro was used to being feted with the best but *Il Cenacolo's* longstanding agreement with the Fior did not permit extravagance. Frank said:

> What're we going to do? Come up with filet mignon? They (*Il Cenacolo*) got a bargain deal. Wherever he goes, he's going to get treated royally, like a king. We would do it differently. We would come up with platters of peasant food, inexpensive, like a poorer group of people in Italy would have. We had stuff like tripe, and polenta and sausage and beans, boiled beef, lots of vegetables, pasta.

The whole restaurant and its customers were energized in anticipation of the great artist's arrival. The restaurant staff wondered if they were doing the right thing. The neighborhood found out Pavarotti was expected and that caused a stir. The customers positioned themselves in their seats to see him as he passed through the main dining room to the Renaissance Room where the men's club met. They craned to see him when he entered. Frank reported that the menu "went over big" with the famous guest:

> He raved about it. He knew what it was. It was stuff he hadn't had for years. It went over beautifully…. At the end of the meal he called me over and says, 'Do you have a doggie bag?' 'Yes, I do', said. 'I do not have a dog,' he says. 'It's for me. Give me sausage and beans and polenta.' The chef fixed up a beautiful package for him.

Not many restaurants can say they sent Pavarotti home with a doggie bag.

The Dodgers' Tomy Lasorda salutes Larry Nibbi in this autographed photo after a meal at the Fior.

By this time, Armanino had left abruptly in 1981. The man who inspired the others to buy the restaurant decided other interests were drawing him. The Nibbis, Ramorino and Pantaleoni remained.

Now appointed chef, Gianni Audieri made changes. He had found the Fior at first a little bigger than restaurants he had managed or owned but he was ready for the challenge. He altered his method of cooking, presentation and menu to suit the Fior's tradition and clientele.

He redesigned about 50 percent of the menu and removed the German, French and Portuguese wine entries. Gianni adjusted the wine list to constitute 60 percent Californian and 40 percent Italian labels, with the exception of Dom Perignon for champagne. More about Gianni's cuisine and his philosophy of cooking can be found in the appendices.

The Pacific Club

The Pacific Club moved its regular meeting place from the Leopard Café to the Fior. In the mid-1980s, this network of businessmen became the second men's club to enjoy weekly meetings at the restaurant on the corner of Union and Stockton Streets.

Founded in 1940, the club attracted bankers, insurance men and professionals. Past President Al E. Maggio recalled that during World War II, as men returned to civilian life, they needed help establishing their careers. Founding the Pacific Club gave them reinforcement and a chance to network.

Each Monday, a leading businessman addresses the group about his industry or company. Athletes and clergymen have also been speakers.

"Most of us went to high school and college together, Lowell, St. Ignatius, USF (University of San Francisco), Saint Mary's College and Santa Clara University. We were mostly close friends, many Catholics," he said.

Maggio himself had a connection to the Fior since his maternal grandfather, Zeffiro Marianetti, Armido's brother, was a chef and a part owner in the late 19th and early 20th centuries.

"I remember going there when I was boy after school. I used to visit back in the kitchen, they'd give me fried cream. We had family reunions there through the years, the Marianettis and the Maggios," he said.

Cenf'anni (100 Years)

1886. 1986.

There it was. One hundred years since Angelo Del Monte had bought the Mexican restaurant under the brothel on Broadway and named it the Flower of Italy.

The current owners had the brilliant idea to celebrate the event and to bring attention to their passion, the Fior d'Italia. They decided to recreate the original menu Del Monte had recorded and – this was the kicker – to serve these dishes at their original prices. Today, the restaurant still reproduces this menu in postcard form as souvenirs. Frank Marianetti had done the research to unearth the original menu and prices.

With the help of publicist, Donna Ewald, they began preparing months in advance. Ewald placed an ad in the personals columns of newspapers' classified sections asking if anyone had any memorabilia from the early days of the Fior. Many came forward with mementos, menus from another era, photographs of their family events taken at the restaurant. Everything was displayed on the chosen day.

*Patrons wait for hours to enjoy
the Fior menu at the original prices.*

Courtesy Tom Vano

"We opened the doors at in the morning and the people came in all day long," Sergio Nibbi remembered. The event was covered in the papers and broadcast on television. Channel 7 sent a news crew in a helicopter to show the line of customers that wound its way around the block the whole day long.

Although recreating the original menu, the Fior did not skimp on quality or service. Everyone was served in the style the restaurant is famed for giving and with the same attention. For their part, customers generally left tips that were consistent with modern prices. The management also bought $100 worth of 1886 silver dollars, at the cost of $125, and gave them as change that night as long as the cache lasted.

Waiters John Carmazzi and Rick Marianetti, who worked that day, recalled there was indeed a sprinkling of those who left a dime or a quarter but they were exceptions. And contrary to the owners' fears, street people and derelicts did not take advantage of this opportunity to eat cheaply. Maybe they hadn't been reading the papers.

In 1988, Frank, now ailing, quit the restaurant. According to him, he didn't formally retire, he just stopped coming. His brother George, himself an old man, was also in failing health.

From left: Larry Nibbi, Joe Musso, Herb Caen, Sergio Nibbi,
Achille Pantaleoni, Charles Ramorino
Courtesy Tom Vano

By the late 80s, the remaining partners had actually recouped their original investments in the restaurant and drawing profit. Ramorino and Pantaleoni were still in love with the restaurant and passionate about their connections with it, but the Nibbis' interest was waning. They "had had enough," as Sergio put it.

Another Quake

Then something happened that almost literally pushed them over the edge – the horrifying 1989 Loma Prieta earthquake. This killer was the costliest natural disaster in the country until that time. Crushing buildings and thoroughfares, it toted up damage of almost $6 billion. The Loma Prieta disaster slew 63 people and injured over 3,700.

With the main arteries to San Francisco's downtown destroyed, restaurant traffic ebbed enormously throughout the city, the Fior suffering along with the rest.

At the 100th anniversary party, from left:
Joe Musso, Sergio and Larry Nibbi,
Achille Pantaleoni and then Mayor Dianne Feinstein
Courtesy Tom Vano

PEPERONI ARROSTITI CON BAGNA CAUDA
BAGNA CAUDA WITH ROASTED PEPPERS

Bagna cauda (hot bath) is a typical Piemontese appetizer. It is a dip, served in the middle of the table in a fondue pot over a sterno. Besides peppers, which are noted below, other common vegetables that can be dipped into the bagna cauda are broccoli, carrot sticks and green onions.

Traditionally, the Piemontese dip cardoon into the bagna cauda. A tall plant that resembles a giant stalk of celery, cardoon is actually related to the artichoke. Cardoon requires effort to clean. The leaves must be plucked. The stalk is boiled in acidulated water. It will turn gray since it is high in tannic acid.

3 tablespoons olive oil (Do not use virgin olive oil. Since it contains remnants of vegetable matter, it will burn.)
4 cloves garlic, thinly sliced
3 to 4 anchovy fillets, finely chopped
1/2 cup heavy cream
2 roasted red bell peppers cut into 1-inch-wide strips
2 roasted green bell peppers cut into 1-inch-wide strips
2 roasted yellow bell peppers cut into 1-inch-wide strips

In a small, heavy saucepan, combine the olive oil and garlic; cook over medium-low heat, stirring frequently, until the garlic is hazelnut colored. Using a wooden spoon, stir in the anchovies. Add the cream and bring to a boil. Lower the heat and simmer until reduced by one-third. Transfer to a small warmed bowl and serve immediately with the roasted peppers for dipping.

Serves four

ROASTED BELL PEPPERS

Preheat the broiler. Lightly oil a baking sheet.

Using a sharp knife, cut off the tops and bottoms of the peppers. Halve and remove the cores, ribs, and seeds. Arrange the peppers cut side down on the prepared baking sheet. Broil, about 4 inches from the heat source, until evenly charred. Transfer to a large bowl and cover with plastic wrap. Let rest until cool enough to handle. Using your hands, gently rub off the charred skin and discard. Don't rinse under running water, or you'll lose the lovely smoky flavor. Roasted peppers will keep, refrigerated in an airtight container, up to three days.

CHAPTER 17: The Next Incarnation

The Loma Prieta quake of October 17, 1989, did not touch the Fior, but it ruined business by damaging freeways and the San Francisco-Oakland Bay Bridge that brought traffic into the city from the East Bay. The freeway that connected downtown San Francisco to the cities in the south was also demolished. Along with many other dining and entertainment spots that suffered, the Fior did too. So after years of refashioning the Fior, its look, its clientele, and signing a new lease in the late 1980s, the Nibbis estimated the earthquake slashed sales between 30-50 percent that year.

"We didn't want to go through this all again," said Larry Nibbi.

"So at that point, we decided, let's get out," Sergio recalled.

When he realized the Nibbis wanted to sell, Achille suggested to Charlie Ramorino that they buy them out. Charlie felt his family's trucking business came first, and he couldn't put it at risk once more. Again, the Fior was facing uncertainty.

In the year it took for the economy to settle and for people to find other ways to drive in from outlying cities, the Nibbis did not actively look for a purchaser. However, they mentioned their interest in selling to acquaintances who knew that restaurateurs Bob and Jinx Larive and Hamish Fordwood were looking for a new investment.

In 1990, after about a year of negotiations, the Nibbis sold their interest to Bob, Jinx and Hamish. Charlie and Achille retained small shares. For the first time, the principle shareholders in the Fior were neither Italian nor Italian-American. However, the Larives appreciated the restaurant's history and sought to celebrate it.

Despite the spelling of their surname, Larive, Bob and his family pronounced it LAR-vee. "We either don't know how to spell it or we don't know how to say it," he would quip. As the son of a career officer in the U.S. Air Force, Bob was born in the Black Hills of South Dakota, but spent his childhood in Colorado and other bases around the country as well as Japan. At sixteen, he started working at the Air Force Exchange service cafeteria and was soon made night manager.

After three years at Colorado State University, Bob joined the U.S. Army and graduated from OCS. In the same era, he married Jinx Lindman, who has been his partner in business and in the Fior. From 1967 to 1972 he flew planes in West Germany and Vietnam. After being discharged as a captain, Bob entered Embry Riddle University in Daytona Beach, Florida, where he earned a Bachelor of Science in Aeronautical Science, graduating magna cum laude.

Bob's goal was to become a commercial pilot, and Delta Airlines hired him. However, in the spring of 1973, the Organization of Petroleum Exporting Countries drastically slashed its exports of oil to the United States. Delta was one of several airlines that cancelled classes for new hires. Bob never got the chance to fly for Delta or any other airline. Asked if he was disappointed, Bob recalls, "Well yes, but you can't spend your life looking back at stuff like that. And the food industry has been good to me."

Now returning to civilian life, Bob worked for Burger King and developed the chain in Europe. In the 1980s he became president of Burger Chef. He was later president and chief executive officer of a 160-unit restaurant chain named CALNY, a franchisee of Taco Bell.

When he relocated from Indianapolis, Bob encountered Virgil Dardi, a Taco Bell franchisee. At seventy-two, Dardi was a North Beach treasure and a character. Dardi had been a protégé of A. P. Giannini, one of the Bank of Italy's youngest stars. In the 1940s, Dardi acquired Blair & Co., one of the country's oldest financial houses. Eventually, Dardi became a good friend of the founder of McDonald's, Ray Kroc. At the time Bob met him, Dardi was also owner of Bruno's in the Mission District. As a gesture of hospitality to the newcomer, Dardi took Bob to his favorite restaurant in San Francisco - the Fior.

"That was my introduction to the Fior," said Bob. He didn't recognize the full scope of the coincidence until much later.

When PepsiCo purchased CALNY in 1984, Bob left the company. He soon found an opportunity to be president and CEO of a biotech company named Bio-Care Inc. in Campbell, California. At the same time, Bob, Jinx, and Hamish started looking for new restaurant investment opportunities in the Bay Area under their company name RosiJinx Foods, Inc. They had been looking for several years when a friend told them the Fior was on the market.

"What fascinated me about the Fior was, granted it looked like a good business opportunity, but I loved the history and the fact that it had been around so long," Bob recalls. But before he closed the deal, he had to make sure of one thing -- the chef, Gianni Audieri. They soon sat down for a chat.

"We'd gotten all the business points decided, but the last thing you need to do in a restaurant like this is have a complete change-over of staff, including the chef. We were about to make the deal and I had to interview Gianni. I hadn't spent any time with him. We sat down in the wine room and talked for probably an hour. It was obvious from the beginning we basically had the same philosophy of service and food and how a restaurant should operate. I asked him the really telling question finally."

"I said, 'Well, Gianni, do you like it here at the Fior d'Italia? And he got real quiet. I was worried that the answer was going to be 'no' because if it was 'no' we weren't going to go through with the deal. There was a long pause. And finally he looks up at me and he said, 'No, Bob, I don't like it here, I love it here!' And that was what made the deal. If he hadn't stayed, then we wouldn't have done the deal," Bob said.

There was considerable speculation about what would happen to the Fior under the new ownership. The uncertainty was even recorded by Herb Caen in a column for the *San Francisco Chronicle*:

> The rumors were true after all: the Nibbi brothers have sold their 98 percent chunk of the historic Fior d'Italia restaurant to Robert Larive and Hamish Fordwood, the Hillsborough owners of something called Ms. Rosiejinx Foods. Does this mean no more spaghetti and meatballs? [1]

Left to right: Jinx Larive, chef Gianfranco Audieri and Bob Larive.

Courtesy Tom Vano

Bob tried to assuage fears that he would strip the Fior of its character. "Once the restaurant business is in your blood, it's in your blood," he told the *Nation's Restaurant News* (Sept. 3, 1990) upon his acquisition of the Fior. "Bio-Care is my full-time position; this is kind of a hobby, and it was a good business opportunity. Besides, running something like The Fior, isn't work. It's fun." [2]

Eventually, Bio-Care went out of business, and the Fior took center stage in Bob's professional life, no longer just a hobby. He was already dazzled with the restaurant's history and its traditions and felt a certain sense of stewardship in maintaining both. What previous owners took for granted because the Fior's background was also their own, Bob determined to accentuate and bring to public awareness.

It was this feeling that prompted him to research the Fior's position among other Italian restaurants in the United States. He wanted very much to make the claim that the Fior was the oldest Italian restaurant in the nation. Bob turned to Research On Demand, Inc., part of the Maxwell Group of Companies, to track down other long-respected restaurants, those that served Italian food and those owned by Italian families.

Isabel Maxwell, then senior vice president of Research on Demand, explored the archives of several Eastern daily newspapers, *Gourmet Magazine*, and consulted online search engines. She found that the oldest existing restaurant in the country is the Union Oyster House in Boston, founded in 1826, 60 years earlier than the Fior. The Boston eatery has always been in the same location and has been in the hands of three Italian families. However, it boasts a seafood menu and does not present itself as an Italian restaurant.

The Despigno family has run Ralph's in Philadelphia since 1900, 14 years after Angelo Del Monte started the Fior. Historians may argue with the Fior's claim of being the oldest Italian restaurant in the United States. Unlike the Union Oyster House and Ralph's, the Fior's ownership has not been an uninterrupted family tradition. And unlike the Union Oyster House, the restaurant has changed addresses more than once.

Columnist Stu Bykofsky wrote about the controversy in the *Philadelphia Daily News* (Oct. 23, 1995) after a visit to the Fior: "But since the Fior has been sold twice, it is no longer owned by the original family, which makes Ralph's the OLDEST family-owned (fourth generation of the Dispigno clan) Italian restaurant in America." [3]

Nonetheless, the Fior does predate Ralph's and, in contrast to the Boston establishment, it serves only Italian cuisine. Despite changes of address and ownership, Bob maintained, "we are continuing the same unbroken tradition of Northern Italian cuisine that Angelo Del Monte started in 1886."

However, this difference does not appear to be an issue over which the contenders exhibit any bitterness. The book, *Ralph's Italian Restaurant, 100 Years and 100 Recipes*, by owner Jimmy Rubino, Jr. and Ted Taylor, describes Ralph's of Philadelphia as "the oldest family-owned Italian restaurant in America." [4] The authors presented to the Larives a copy inscribed with the message: "Bob & Jinx, It's an honor to be the second oldest Italian restaurant in the country, especially when you're the first."

The Larives and their other partners have tried to instill a sense of the Fior being a family restaurant again. "We try to have fun with the customers. We try to make it very formal from the service standpoint, but very casual in terms of our relationship with the employees and the employees' relationship with the customer. So, we want to do things right but we don't want to have a lot of pretense and stiffness and stuffiness about it," he says.

While the Larives embraced the Fior, its history, and its world with warmth and enthusiasm, it took some of the staffers a bit of time to accept the new owners at first. During the first year of their ownership, Bob did not go into the Fior on a daily basis since he was still involved with Bio-Care. Instead, Jinx went in every day to support maitre d' Peter Osborne and learn from him how manage the day-to-day operations. Until that time, there had been no women in management at the Fior. There had been waitresses (at that time, Donna Cronin was still waiting on tables) and there had been hatcheck girls and female bookkeepers. But no female managers.

"The waiters didn't like me," Jinx said. "They'd never had a woman at the door before. They acted as though I was going to turn away customers. I'd go back into the kitchen and they didn't talk to me. They'd leave insulting material on the bulletin board. I'd tear it down and walk away. I thought, 'Guys, I'm here for the long run. I'm not going anywhere.' But we never lost any business, and I'm already here." Jinx quickly showed she couldn't be intimidated, and the problem resolved itself.

The new owners also saw that the older customers, who had been the restaurant's mainstay for decades, were dying off. The Larives and their partners increased the Fior's marketing outreach and appealed to a diversity of groups and populations to bring in customers who otherwise would never have experienced the Fior.

Gregarious and hospitable, Bob, through the Fior, donates over $1 million a year to charities and worthy causes. His generosity has

been governed by his conservative politics. "I think conservatives have bigger hearts than liberals do. Conservatives give their own money while liberals like to give purely other people's (in the form of increased taxes)," he has said. "I am active with charities even though I am part of the vast right wing conspiracy," he jokes. In fact, he has been a member of a self-satirizing group that can be found on the Web at www.vastrightwingconspiracy.com

These new owners supported any cause that made an appeal to them by giving them the means to earn money. "As an example, for the Shrine Game, we give them a million dollars worth of certificates to sell with their tickets so they can enhance their value -- and therefore sell more tickets and therefore raise more money. We used to do a big program for KQED during their auctions," Bob said of the local public broadcasting station.

It did not matter if an organization's political tint was at variance with his. "We almost never say no. We just don't say no. The only time we get offended is when they don't ask for enough," he says smiling.

However, in the very liberal Bay Area, Bob Larive did pose a challenge for many, especially when he took steps to protect his authority in running the Fior. His beliefs have come to the fore in dealing with Local Two of the Hotel and Restaurant Workers Union and with the Internal Revenue Service. He wished to avoid as much as possible the influence of government or other institutions in the running of his business. And that influence included organized labor.

Beginning in the mid-1980s, it became the trend for the staffs of better restaurants to cut their ties with the union. When Bob and his partners bought the Fior in 1990, the restaurant staffers were members of Local Two. By 1994, some employees favored decertifying, making the Fior a non-union workplace. Despite the fact that the workers made that decision independently of management, that is when the relationship between the Fior owners and the Local Two executives became adversarial in the extreme.

The union accused the Fior of mistreating its employees. "His agenda is to drive workers rights back to the Stone Age," charged Mike Casey, an executive of Local Two, by decreasing their benefits, being laggard with pay raises and not contributing to a pension fund. He described Larive as "the biggest right-wing asshole I've ever met."

Meanwhile the restaurant felt the union was not a strong advocate for employees when they needed help or jobs, all the while taking their dues. "We are paying more money for our benefits than with (the union). There never was a labor problem because we don't abuse people, so there were few complaints filed. I just didn't like having all this money [union dues] wasted and particularly the retirement fund stolen. To this day we don't know where that money went," says Bob of Local Two's stewardship. He also resented what he felt was the local's intrusion into his kitchen and management practices.

Regardless of the restaurant management's policies, it was not up to the owners to decertify the union. By law, they could not interfere in the employees' decision. Had they done so, the election would have been challenged. The employees eventually voted for de-certification, and today, they are non-union. Their benefits far exceed those they had under the union. They have the same health provider, more dental coverage, and a 401(k) plan for which the Fior matches employee contributions up to $750 a year. Under the union's pension plan, an employee paying $55 a month for 15 years would earn a pension of $100 a month. The Fior also contributes $500 a year to each employee and each of his dependents for advanced education tuition.

SPAGHETTI TUTTO MARE (SEAFOOD SPAGHETTI)

Do not serve cheese with this dish.

To purge sand, place clams in a large bowl of slightly salted water for one hour, or pass them under running water.

16 mussels, scrubbed and debearded
16 Manila clams, scrubbed
3/4 cup white wine
3 tablespoons olive oil
2 shallots, minced
2 cloves garlic, minced
2 pounds tomatoes, seeded and chopped
Pinch of red pepper flakes
8 extra large prawns, shells on, deveined
1 pound calamari, cleaned and cut into rings
Salt and freshly ground black pepper
1 pound spaghetti
Chopped fresh flat-leaf parsley, for garnish

In a large saucepan, combine the mussels, clams, and wine. Cover tightly, bring to a boil, and cook, shaking occasionally, until all the clams and mussels have opened, 5 to 8 minutes (discard any that don't open). Using a slotted spoon, transfer the clams and mussels to a bowl and set aside. Strain the cooking liquid through a fine-mesh strainer lined with a coffee filter or paper towel and set aside.

In a large skillet, heat the olive oil over medium-high heat. Add the shallots and cook until translucent, about 2 minutes. Add the garlic and cook until fragrant, about 1 minute. Add the reserved cooking liquid, tomatoes, and red pepper flakes. Bring to a boil; lower the heat and simmer until the tomatoes begin to break down, about 25 minutes. Add the prawns and calamari; cook until opaque, about 4 minutes. Add the reserved clams and mussels, in their shells, and cook just until heated through. Season to taste with salt and pepper.

In a large pot of lightly salted boiling water, cook the spaghetti until al dente, according to the package directions. Drain. Add the pasta to the sauce and toss well to mix.

To serve: Divide the pasta evenly among four warmed pasta bowls, garnish with the parsley, and serve immediately.

Serves four

CHAPTER 18: In Search of the Perfect Ravioli

During the previous three decades, George's son Paul Mantee, who had been acting in movies and television in Los Angeles, had also become a writer. In 1991, he published his first novel, *In Search of the Perfect Ravioli*. A *roman à clef* in which the fictional characters were thinly disguised representations of real people, the novel was a hilarious homage to his own childhood, his relationship with his father, his father's wives and the importance of cooking in his family. While many episodes were only loosely based on fact, the novel was rooted in the Marianetti family's story and their history with food, all heated into a witty concoction.

The title of the story comes from a recipe for ravioli that was handed down by Paul's great grandmother, Mariuccia Corassa, for her esteemed 22-ingredient ravioli.

In the first chapter, the narrator explains to a friend that he cannot divulge the family recipe.

`I made my father a solemn promise.´

I had to. I swore I wouldn't share the recipe with anyone, unless I purposely left something out. He'd sent it to me ten years ago. Two single-spaced typewritten pages, as he remembered it from watching his mother create the original. My grandmother (altered from his great-grandmother for the book) had ravenous relatives all over northern California, not to mention five brothers and a sister who lived in the Bay area: Nard, Balto, Vic, Dino, Charley, and Clo. Some of them were stevedores, and all of them ate like it, especially Clo. I knew I was going to be stuck with enough ravioli filling to stuff a basketball but I didn't care. The recipe was a goddamned heirloom. [1]

In the novel, the main character, and actor named Peter, sets out to recreate the dish. While shopping for the ingredients and preparing to cook, he calls his father in San Francisco to ask his advice. These phone calls elicit reminiscences of his childhood. The novel's flashbacks center on Peter's youth, his sexual awakening, and his conflicts with his stepmother. Poignant and witty, the novel paints the portrait of an Italian-American Holden Caulfield.

Paul and his then publicist, Susan Shaw, decided to launch *In Search of the Perfect Ravioli* at the Fior, with the enthusiastic cooperation and support of the restaurant's management. The launch took place at the bar where dozens of Paul's friends assembled to buy the novel and to have Paul sign it. Beforehand however, Paul made 300 ravioli from Mariuccia's recipe and brought them up from Los Angeles to serve at the event.

"Gianni supplied the sauce, and the staff enjoyed doing it. They were very, very sweet," Paul remembered.

Even George had his day. Glorying in his son's accomplishment, and maybe taking some of the credit, the elder Marianetti also signed books for patrons. Paul remembered the night fondly, with one reservation. His Uncle Frank did not attend because he wanted to avoid George. He told Paul: "Part of me would love to be there, the other part of me cannot."

In the March 4, 1993, edition of the *Los Angeles Times*, Paul was featured with his recipes for the unique ravioli and other dishes from Mariuccia's kitchen. The reporter recorded Paul's reminiscences.

As a teenager, Mantee worked as a busboy in his family's restaurant, Fior d'Italia, in San Francisco's North Beach ('I spilled a lot of soup on a lot of nice people,' he remembers fondly). There he observed the bustle of the chefs in the kitchen.

'The reason we were so successful was that none of the chefs were very careful, and that's the essence of good cooking,' he says. 'Cooking Italian food is a very sensual experience. I'll never forget the chef, whose name was Leo Quattrin. I can see him now as he would walk by the salt bin and *en passant* toss a handful of salt at the stove and hit the pot. No recipes there.'[1]

Guilt and Calamari

Fiction does seem to love the Fior. In the same era that gave us *Perfect Ravioli*, thriller writer, John T. Lescroart, commemorated the restaurant in two of his novels. In *A Certain Justice*:

Glitsky was sitting with Loretta at a back corner table in La Pantera on the corner of Colombus at Washington Square. Up the street was the much more tony Fior d'Italia. [2]

More elaborately in Lescroart's *Guilt*, a meal at the Fior on page one sets the scene for intrigue that turns into a discussion of the menu:

Mark Dooher couldn't take his eyes off the young woman who had just entered the dining room at Fior D'Italia and was being seated, facing them, at a table ten feet away.

His companion for lunch was, like Dooher, an attorney. His name was Wes Farrell and he generally practiced in a different stratum, lower than Dooher did. The two men had been best friends since they were kids. Farrell glanced up from his calamari, his baleful eyes glinting with humor, trying to be subtle as he took in the goddess across the room.

"Too young," he said.

"My foot, Wes."

"All parts of you, not just your foot. Besides which," Farrell went on, "you're married."

"I am married."

Farrell nodded. "Keep repeating it. It's good for you. I, on the other hand, am getting divorced."

"I can never get divorced. Sheila would never divorce me."

"You could divorce her if you wanted to..."

"Impossible." Then, amending: "Not that I'd ever want to, of course, but impossible."

"Why?"

Dooher went back to his pasta for a moment. "Because, my son, even in our jaded age, when ninety percent of your income derives from your work as counsel to the Archdiocese of San Francisco, when you are in fact a prominent player in the Roman Catholic community as I am, a divorce would play some havoc with your business. Across the board. Not just the Church itself, but all the ancillary."

Farrell broke off a bite-sized piece of Italian bread and dipped it into the little dish of extra virgin olive oil that rested between them.

"I doubt it. People get divorced all the time. Your best friend, for example, is getting divorced right now. Have I mentioned that?"

"Lydia's divorcing you, Wes. You're not divorcing her. It's different. God," he said, "look at her."

Farrell glanced up again. "She looks good."

"Good?" Dooher feasted for another moment on the vision. "That woman is so far beyond 'good' that the light from 'good' is going to take a year to get to her."

"At which time you'll be a year older and forever out of her reach. Pass the butter."

"Butter will kill you, you know."

Farrell nodded. "Either that or something else. This calamari *milleottocentoottantasei*, for example"

"Or pronouncing it." [3]

Farrell was referring to the calamari dish named 1886 (the year of the Fior's founding), or in Italian, *milleottocentoottantasei* (MEELeh-OTto-CHENto-otTAHNta-say)

When asked why he referred to the Fior in two of his novels, Lescroart explained, "I really love the Fior. To me it's a quintessential San Francisco North Beach venue." He remarked that referring to it was a kind of writer's shorthand for setting the atmosphere for the reader: "If you say Fior d'Italia, you know it's a certain level, certain clientele. It's basically cheating."

The author said the restaurant has been "a big part of his life. He first dined there with his father in the 1970s. He celebrated his 50th birthday there."

"It has the best bar in the city," Lescroart said. The physical bar itself is fantastic. The bartenders are always great and the room is a great lively, terrific place. I don't go looking for celebrities. I go to where it's a down-home kind of feel."

With permission from Paul Mantee, his recipe for his great grandmother's 22-ingredient ravioli, as it appears (with minor editing) in his novel In Search of the Perfect Ravioli.

When Paul told his father he was going to write the recipe in his book, George instructed him, "Always leave one ingredient out, so it's good but not as good as we do it." But Paul assured the recipe as it appears below is complete.

MARIUCCIA CORASSA'S 22-INGREDIENT RAVIOLI

1. $1^1/_2$ pounds boneless veal
2. $^3/_4$ pound ground pork
3. 1 pound hamburger or stewing beef
4. eight or ten slices of Italian salami
5. four or five slices of prosciutto. By all means, imported.
6. two Italian sausages, or calabrese (mild). Don't use the hot variety, for chrissake.
7. the skinless meat, white or dark or both, of half a three-pound fryer
8. two whole beef or calf brains. (Boil these in salted water for fifteen minutes.)
9. any leftover meats from your Frigidaire, like some boiled beef, chicken or maybe a piece of hamburger you didn't finish. (Fat chance.)
10. two large or three medium-sized dry onions.
11. four large cloves of garlic
12. several sprigs of fresh parsley
13. two stalks of celery with tops
14. one bunch of Swiss-chard stems and all-not the red chard. Must be green.
15. a pinch of nutmeg
16. rosemary-mixed ITALIAN herbs-I feel rosemary should predominate
17. a little oregano
19. grated parmesan cheese - four cups
19. French bread-five slices
20. imported pignoli-six packets
21. a dozen eggs-maybe more-depends on the wetness of the mixture.
22. salt and pepper.

continued

Boil brains. Saute ingredients #1 through #9 in olive oil. When brown add #10 through #13 chopped. Add Swiss chard (#14) after washing and cutting into four-inch squares. Add #15 through #17 and salt and pepper (#22). When chard has blended into mixture and softened, take whole mixture off fire, let cook and pass through a fine meat grinder.

Take the whole mixture off the fire-let it cool.

Pass it through the meat grinder.

On top of this mixture break a dozen eggs. Add the four cups parmesan cheese and the six packets imported pignoli.

Soak the five slices of French bread in water till soft. Then squeeze dry and crumble it up into the mixture. Then with your big mitts, mix. Mix the whole thing till it becomes one unidentifiable mass. If the consistency of the mixture is too dry, add more eggs. If it's too wet, add more cheese. Then mix thoroughly again.

Pick up two four-foot sheets of dough from a ravioli factory. Also a three-foot rolling pin, a three-foot roller-shaper with one-inch square compartments a quarter of an inch apart, and a cutter. Simply spread the filling an inch and a half thick onto the bottom sheet, then cover it with a second sheet. But don't cover the bottom sheet entirely. Leave a one-inch empty border all around so that too much filling doesn't squish out onto the floor. And for chrissake don't forget to flour the table (the bigger the better) first.

SAUCE

1. several cloves of garlic. The more the merrier.
2. olive oil.
3. 3 very ripe tomatoes
4. 1 can tomato sauce. Not the small size, not the large size-the middle size.
5. plenty of hot red pepper (The flakes are easiest.)

CHAPTER 19: Navy Gravy; Smoking out Joe Camel

Patriotic, Bob and Jinx Larive have used the Fior to demonstrate their respect for the U.S. Armed Forces. Since 1992, the restaurant has hosted the navy, marines and Coast Guard personnel based in the Bay Area or visiting the Bay Area during the navy's annual Fleet Week celebration. That event transpires in every major naval base in the country and aims to promote goodwill between the military and the community. After a decade, the Fior estimates that it has served 6,000 meals (valued at $240,000) to visitors from the armed forces during Fleet Week.

Sailors and officers from all Californian bases and former bases, the Pacific Northwest and the Coast Guard are invited to participate

U.S. Navy and Coast Guard officers and sailors enjoy their meals at the Fior during Fleet Week.
Courtesy of Bob Hanson, Fleet Week Staff

in the week's celebrations that include the aerobatic feats of the navy jets, the Blue Angels, a parade of military vessels, and demonstrations on preparedness and search and rescue operations.

"The Fior has been among the first to step up and volunteer to do some of the hosting for the sailors," said Admiral Ernest Tedeschi, who was Commander of the Naval Base of San Francisco that was headquartered at Treasure Island from 1993-1995. He co-chaired the military-civilian committee that yearly prepared for Fleet Week.

"Many of these have been younger men who didn't have the means to eat in that kind of restaurant frequently" the Admiral explained. "My first impression of eating at the Fior during Fleet Week was the restaurant's incredible hospitality. Bob and Jinx were extending hospitality to everyone who arrived in uniform. I was struck by the way the other patrons caught on to this. All of a sudden everyone in the restaurant was helping them host the navy, buying drinks for the sailors and some even offered to buy them dinner."

During these week-long Fleet Week events, the Fior has typically hosted 600 to 700 navy personnel. "That comes right off the bottom line," Larive said. The Fior has continued its hospitality for every Fleet

U.S. Navy and Coast Guard officers and sailors enjoy Fior d'Italia hospitality during San Francisco Fleet Week, greeted by Bob Larive owner, and Chef Gianfranco Audieri.
Courtesy of Bob Hanson, Fleet Week Staff

Week since 1992 except for 2001 when the celebration was cancelled following the terrorist attack of September 11, 2001, for reasons of security.

Smoking Guns

Bob was active in the National and California Restaurant Associations, the NRA and the CRA, as well as the GGRA, the Bay Area's Golden Gate Restaurant Association. In 1992, when he was on the GGRA board, legislation to ban smoking in California restaurants was being debated in Sacramento, within the industry, and throughout the country as well. Not only was the public divided, but the jurisdictions from municipality to state levels were passing diverse legislation that had anti-competitive consequences. When one restaurateur was operating a non-smoking establishment but was based close to a border of a jurisdiction that allowed smoking, he would lose business to the eatery across the street.

"It was an ugly war," Bob recalled. "Half the restaurateurs were against it. They feared if we banned smoking, everybody was going to stay home and eat meat loaf or something. People would quit going out."

The question among CRA members was whether a statewide ban on smoking in restaurants should be passed or should establishments risk the local governments taking an initiative at some point. "Most of us didn't like the idea of government interfering, but government was already interfering in a way, so there was no level playing field. We decided to get the state government involved with an overriding piece of legislation banning smoking," he said.

The GGRA's executive director, Patricia Breslin, observed that it was a bad business practice to make smoking illegal in restaurants while smoking itself was still legal. She spoke for her members who objected to "consumer protection of unknown dangers" that threatened the livelihood of small business owners.

To avoid the confusion posed by a patchwork of laws, the CRA board decided to support a statewide ban on smoking in restaurants, which eventually succeeded. They reached a consensus about the same time as the CRA's annual autumn lobbying visit to Sacramento. In this era, the Speaker of the California Assembly was Willie Brown, later mayor of San Francisco. Brown was believed to be beholden to the tobacco lobby. The tobacco industry was certainly opposed to banning smoking in restaurants.

In 1993, the *American Journal of Public Health* reported that "Brown (a nonsmoker) received $410,517 in campaign contributions from tobacco companies from 1980 until 1993, with $221,367 in the 1991-92 election cycle alone." This made him the largest single legislative recipient of tobacco industry contributions in the United States, the Journal said. On September 17, 1995, the *San Francisco Examiner* reported that campaign contributions, gifts, and legal fees from tobacco to Brown totaled $750,000.

Part of the CRA delegation's agenda while in the capital was a chat with Speaker Brown. Bob recalled that meeting:

"We were sitting waiting in this conference room. He finally showed up, stormed through the door and just reamed us. Called us every four-letter word in the book. It was grotesque. 'This is the stupidest legislation I've ever seen.' He was just livid, veins sticking out on his neck. There were a half-dozen or eight of us in the room. He unloaded on us for 10-15 minutes telling us how stupid we were. Finally he shuts up and sits down. Being the shy person I am, I asked, 'Speaker Brown, I have a question about this.' "

According to Bob, Brown shouted, "I won't talk about it anymore, I won't discuss it any further." Curiously, they went on to discuss other subjects quite amicably. Later that evening, when Bob joined the 100 or so CRA colleagues for cocktails, he described the scene with Brown. Those who had also been there confirmed his account.

The next day, Bob returned to the Bay Area where he received a call from a CRA official telling him that *Capitol Weekly*, the Sacramento journal that covers the political scene, wanted to speak with him about his meeting with Brown. Apparently, the press had caught wind of the meeting. The CRA cautioned Bob of the repercussions of going public with this tale. He shrugged off the warning and gave an interview to *Capitol Weekly*.

When the issue came out the following week, the front page was emblazoned with a caricature of Joe Camel with Speaker Brown's face superimposed on it, Bob recalls. This picture accompanied a two-page article that described the scene Bob had witnessed with the Speaker. (*Capitol Weekly* no longer keeps that year's issues.)

Brown, incensed, called the CRA and threatened to close every restaurant in California. Since the industry represents the largest employer in the state, the threat was clearly a bluff. Brown never appeared at the Fior again where previously he had been a fairly regular customer. He would not grant an interview for the purposes of this book.

COZZE E VONGOLE ALLA MARINARA (MUSSELS AND CLAMS MARINARA)

Marinara means sailor-style cooking. Anchovy and salt preserved the items on hand for long voyages.

To purge sand, place mussels and clams in a large bowl of slightly salted water for an hour, or pass them under running water.

3 tablespoons olive oil
2 cloves garlic, chopped
2 shallots, chopped
2 anchovy fillets, chopped
1 pound Manila clams, scrubbed
1 pound mussels, scrubbed and debearded
1 sprig thyme
1 bay leaf
1 cup white wine
Freshly ground black pepper
Chopped fresh flat-leaf parsley, for garnish

In a large, heavy sauté pan, heat the olive oil over medium-high heat. Add the garlic, shallots, and anchovies and cook until the shallots are translucent, about 2 minutes. Add the clams, mussels, thyme, bay leaf, and wine; cook, tightly covered, until the mussels and clams have opened, 5 to 8 minutes (discard any that don't open).

To serve: Using a slotted spoon, transfer the clams and mussels to a large serving bowl. Carefully pour the pan juices over the shellfish, taking care to leave the sand in the bottom of the pan. Season with black pepper, garnish with the parsley, and serve immediately with lots of bread to soak up the juices!

Serves four

CHAPTER 20: La Qualità

Over the years, food and travel writers have celebrated the Fior's cookery and the skill of its chefs. Two notable examples appear in the feedback reported from *WHERE Magazine* and the DiRONA Institute that rate restaurants on the basis of popularity and patron acclaim.

WHERE San Francisco, a periodical that informs tourists and hotel guests about local attractions, is placed in 3,500 hotels around the world. Since 1994, it has published a dining guide amplified by a visitor's choice award contest. *WHERE* readers fill out a ballot identifying their favorite restaurant discovery during their visit to San Francisco.

"For the five years between 1994-98, the Fior received honorable mention. Twenty to 25 get honorable mention, exclusive of the top three," explained Associate Editor Rob Bhatt in 2002.

DiRONA, the Distinguished Restaurants of North America, headquartered in New New York, N.Y, honors fine dining establishments. In 1992, DiRONA introduced an award for excellence based on the reports of independent and anonymous "inspectors."

Former Administrative Director, David Armanasco, reported that the Fior was among the first recipients and has received an award every year since 2001.

"This is the only award conferred both anonymously and independently by inspectors and certified by Johnson & Wales University in Rhode Island, the largest U.S. hospitality school. The inspectors are independent in that they are not in food service. They are CEOs, doctors, lawyers, people with a lot of travel and dining experience," Armanasco said.

Sunset Magazine published Gianni's recipe for bread and cabbage soup in its October, 1995, edition. *Bon Appetit's* September, 1992, edition featured his gnocchi called "Potato Dumplings with Gorgonzola Sauce." *Gourmet Magazine* has also offered readers Gianni's recipe for Fior d'Italia duck.

The chef appeared on "Live with Regis Philbin and Kathy Lee" on October 16, 1992, to demonstrate the creation of *cazzuola*, a pork and sausage casserole.

Reviewing the Reviewers

But there have been disparaging reviews too, and from one particular publication, the *San Francisco Chronicle*, the Fior has won only brickbats. The last review the *Chronicle* did up until this printing appeared on April 12, 1992, and it stung. *Chronicle* restaurant critic Patricia Unterman started her piece with the words:

Fior d'Italia, which claims to be America's oldest Italian restaurant, unfortunately serves what tastes like some of San Francisco's most tired food. [1]

It got worse from there. She called the restaurant "a minefield of disasters." Unterman claimed that the food coming out of the kitchen was so aged as to be inedible all three times she ate there. She said the chicken she was served "had gone bad." That "the veal and chicken filling in cannelloni…tasted off to me."

Such a drubbing would have hurt any restaurant. The *Chronicle's* review was published in an era when there were only two daily newspapers in San Francisco and the *Chronicle* was the dominant one.

Bob said the repercussions were felt at once. "We had a lot of cancellations. The (hotel) concierges stopped sending people. Just stopped. We talked to them and asked why. They referred to the review. We said, 'Well, didn't you send us people yesterday and weren't they happy?' (They said,) 'Well yes, but Patty Unterman said…'."

Bob said that upon reading the review he "totally lost it. The regulars were as livid as we were. They were beside themselves. They said it was bullshit."

"It's nothing but lies. There's nothing true in that thing. She said she made three visits here and was served rotten chicken. It is absolutely a lie. Not only a lie, it ended up costing us at least half a million dollars and it was ages before we could repair the damage," he said.

Gianni discredited the review, pointing to statements in it that were errors of fact. He questioned her expertise and he challenged the very tradition of critiquing restaurants as a journalistic form.

"My big complaint about food critics is that, of course they are entitled to their opinions, but it's impossible that somebody can know Italian and Tibetan cuisine (equally well). How could you? It bugged me that she said we served spoiled food. That's hitting below the belt," he said.

Gianni allowed that in rare instances if a chopping surface is not cleaned with the punctilious care, bacteria may linger in a spot and affect the next piece of meat to be cut there.

"But it's nearly impossible because of the amount of food we sell here and the rarity of complaints. It just almost never happens," he said. And the fact that she said it happened the three times she visited the Fior?

"Incredible," he said. According to Gianni, there were no other complaints about tainted food in the months preceding her panning of the restaurant. Nor since.

The internationally known chef of 30 years' experience attributed Unterman's thumbs-down review to differences in taste. She complained that the pumpkin ravioli was too sweet, that the *bagna cauda* had peppers in it. According to Gianni, the Fior's preparation of these dishes is normal in Italian cuisine as he knew it. He reckoned her taste was in more modern combinations of food, adhering to a fashionable trend that the Fior had neither the number of cooks nor size of restaurant to present. Nor did he favor it anyway.

"I don't believe in frou-frou food," he said.

Never one to cringe from a fight, Bob wrote a letter to the editor at the *Chronicle*. It did not appear. He scheduled a meeting with an editor who had authority over the restaurant reviews and asked to see Unterman as well.

"I called them and told them this is absolutely libel. We don't serve rotten food…the editor was scared enough to meet with me. In my experience in the (restaurant) industry, we never get responses (from editors). Not just the Fior d'Italia. They just don't respond."

Bob met with the editor but Unterman did not appear. He referred to the chicken dish the reviewer complained of. He said to her, "We serve thousands and thousands of this dish every year. Nobody complains. It's not rotten. It's fresh all the time. What's going on here?" But she couldn't give him any answers. In fact, he said, she was trembling.

He asked for a retraction. There was none. His attempts to reach Unterman herself were fruitless. He contacted several attorneys who said the chance of winning a libel suit was extremely slim because it would be difficult to prove malicious intent on the paper's part.

Instead, he turned the tables on the newspaper and the restaurant critic. Bob took his cue from a technique seen often in movie advertisements in which a movie publicist has extracted phrases from a review that is tepid or even negative. Taking those phrases out of context, he created an ad that sounds laudatory. For instance, if a critic panned a film and said the lack of acting talent displayed was "breathtaking", the movie ad would display in quotation marks the word "breathtaking" followed by the reviewer's name.

Bob used Unterman's name and phrases from her damaging critique in similar fashion by planting the impression that the review was a rave. But it was cold comfort.

It's hard to understand how the restaurant could have survived 106 years at that point by serving tainted meat, Bob observed. Since the *Chronicle* editor and Unterman did not respond in candor, it will remain a mystery.

The Fior owners felt the press had burned them amply and they didn't want any more powerful journalists eating there. At this time, the most powerful food critic in town was also a *Chronicle* employee, Michael Bauer. Bauer was loved and hated by the restaurant industry in San Francisco. His benediction could bring life to an eatery. His disdain, ruin.

Bob called and wrote Bauer more than once over a period of about five years instructing him to stay away from the Fior or he would have him arrested for trespassing. When the critic disparaged any other restaurant in a way Bob felt was unjust, Bob wrote him and lambasted him for it. The Fior owner went so far as to create a poster entitled 'UN-WANTED." Accompanying a picture of Bauer, the text read:

Michael "Butcher" Bauer and members of his gang of arrogant know nothings…. (including those from other periodicals) are unwanted for ruining jobs and businesses. They are unwanted for being arrogant, not knowing food and not understanding the restaurant business. They have been known to lie to the public and represent their personal tastes and opinions as fact.

PUBLIC NOTICE

Any food writer/critic entering these premises are trespassing and will be arrested and convicted to the fullest extent of the law.

He distributed these placards among other restaurants particularly in North Beach where they were displayed as well as on the street. Bauer declined a request for an interview.

Unfortunately, restaurateurs also declined interviews on the subject of reviewers. It is safe to say they fear them to the same degree they fear tangling with the Internal Revenue Service. But here's where another journal, the monthly *San Francisco*, provided some comfort to the restaurant industry and the dining public. Its August, 2001, edition criticized Bauer's influence over local restaurants, restaurant patrons and his questionable methods of favoring some establishments over others based on whim.

"…many are terrified to say anything negative about him on the record," the magazine found in trying to get chefs to discuss his treatment of them. [2]

The tradition of reviewing the arts or restaurants poses a difficult challenge for both reviewing journalists and the craftspeople and artists who are the subjects of reviews. Journalists ideally remain independent of influence from their sources. But in the case of Unterman, the fact that she was herself a restaurant owner at the same time she was critiquing other establishments turned that standard of professionalism on its head.

Critics may feel their work displays their sense of quality or esthetics, but artisans see them as people who have undue influence on their livelihoods. Unfortunately, in San Francisco where the tourist trade is a dominant sector of the economy, restaurant reviews can make or break a restaurant.

"A bad review can close a restaurant pretty quick. When harm is done, few recover. A restaurant really has to have the resources to buy a PR bandage after an unfavorable review", said Patricia Breslin, executive director of the Golden Gate Restaurant Association.

"The issue has surfaced (among GGRA members) a number of times…I feel sometimes their personal likes and dislikes and favoritisms figure too much in their reviews," she said. But the association was able to do little about it. "We've talked about putting up a Web site where people could post a review of a restaurant and have people give their opinions. Then we decided that would be a disservice to a restaurant that had already received a bad review. The more times people read it, the worse it is," Breslin observed.

RISOTTO AUDIERI (RISOTTO WITH CLAMS AND TOMATOES)

No cheese with fish. To purge sand, place clams in a large bowl of slightly salted water for 1 hour, or pass them under running water.

4 pounds Manila clams, scrubbed
1 cup dry white wine
4 cups fish stock, or 2 cups bottled clam juice plus 2 cups water
2 tablespoons olive oil
1 medium yellow onion, chopped
2 cloves garlic, chopped
1 1/2 cups Arborio rice
2 medium tomatoes, seeded and chopped
2 tablespoons unsalted butter
Salt and freshly ground black pepper
Chopped fresh flat-leaf parsley, for garnish

In a large saucepan, combine the clams and wine. Cover tightly and bring to a boil over medium-high heat. Cook, shaking the pan occasionally, until all the clams have opened, about 5 minutes (discard any clams that don't open). Using a slotted spoon, remove the clams. Set aside 4 clams for the garnish. Remove the meat from the remaining clams and set aside; discard the shells. Carefully pour the remaining pan juices into a small bowl, taking care to leave any sand in the pot; set the pan juices aside.

In a medium saucepan, bring the fish stock to a boil. Lower the heat and maintain at a simmer. In a large, heavy pot, heat the olive oil over medium-high heat. Add the onion and garlic and cook until translucent, about 2 minutes. Add the rice and cook, stirring continuously, until well coated with the oil, about 2 minutes. Add the reserved pan juices and 1/2 cup of the stock and cook, stirring continuously with a wooden spoon, until all of the stock has been absorbed, about 3 minutes. Add another 1 cup of stock and cook, stirring continuously, until all of the stock has again been absorbed. Repeat with the remaining stock, adding it 1 cup at a time, until the rice is tender, but firm to the bite—this will take about 15 to 20 minutes to complete. Remove from the heat and gently stir in the clam meat, tomatoes, and butter. Season to taste with salt and pepper.

To serve: Divide the risotto evenly among 4 warmed serving dishes. Garnish with the parsley and the reserved clams in their shells. Serve immediately.

Serves four

CHAPTER 21: Little Frankie

While Frank Marianetti spent less time at the Fior as he enjoyed a quiet life in Marin County, he had not been forgotten. One day in the early 1990s, maitre d' Jim Bril greeted an ancient man who sat down and asked how "little Frankie" was.

"I couldn't think," Jim said. "I asked, "Little Frankie? Who's that?"

"You know, little Frankie and Georgie," he said.

"Well, Frankie is seventy-five or seventy-eight now," Jim replied.

The elderly gent, whom Jim guessed to be in his nineties, said he remembered Frank "when he could barely look over the table." He said he had been a busboy at the restaurant when Frank was a tot and the old-timer used to work in the kitchen.

"So I brought him in the kitchen to look around. It was all stainless steel, different from when he worked there. He saw the old cheese grinder in the kitchen that he used 60 years ago. Now we've attached a motor onto it and it's electric and it grinds cheese. But at the time he worked on it, it had a hand grinder on it. That's what he did every morning. Grind cheese on that same machine. When he saw it, he broke down in tears," Jim recalled.

POLLO ALLA MANIERA DEL CACCIATORE (CHICKEN CACCIATORE)

This is a regional dish. Venetians use peppers and Tuscans use olives. Northern Italians are likely to add mushrooms, but Southern Italians use bell peppers.

Polenta is a great accompaniment to this dish but it should be a base and should not flavor the dish.

2 tablespoons olive oil
1 (3 1/2-pound) chicken, cut into 8 pieces
Salt and freshly ground black pepper
All-purpose flour, for dusting
4 ounces pancetta, coarsely chopped
1 medium yellow onion, diced
2 cloves garlic, minced
1 pound cremini or button mushrooms, sliced
1 cup red wine
1/2 cup chicken stock
1 (28-ounce) can diced tomatoes
Polenta (page 110), for serving
Chopped fresh flat-leaf parsley, for garnish

Preheat the oven to 350°F.

In a large sauté pan, heat the olive oil over medium-high heat. Generously season the chicken with salt and pepper. Lightly dust the chicken with flour and shake gently to remove any excess. Arrange skin side down in the hot pan in a single layer and cook until golden brown, about 3 minutes. Turn and cook until golden brown, about 3 minutes. Using tongs, transfer to a large plate and set aside.

In the same pan, combine the pancetta, onion, and garlic and cook until the onions are golden, about 4 minutes. Add the mushrooms and cook until the liquid they release has evaporated. Add the wine, bring to a boil, and cook until reduced by half. Add the chicken stock and tomatoes and season with salt and pepper. Return the chicken to the pan, bring to a boil, cover, transfer to the oven, and cook until very tender, about 45 minutes.

To serve: Divide the polenta among four warmed serving plates. Arrange the chicken on the polenta and spoon the sauce over the top. Garnish with the parsley and serve immediately.

Serves four

POLENTA

If you serve polenta alone and not as a side dish, you may use butter and cheese instead of sauce. For leftover polenta, place it in a loaf pan and let it firm in the refrigerator. Then slice, flour and sauté in butter, adding Parmesan cheese.

4 cups water
1 tablespoon salt
1 cup coarse cornmeal
1 tablespoon unsalted butter

In a large, heavy pot, bring the water and salt to a boil over medium-high heat . Lower the heat to a simmer and, stirring continuously with a strong wooden spoon, add the cornmeal in a very thin stream. Continue to cook, stirring continuously, until the polenta begins to pull away from the sides of the pot, 20 to 25 minutes. Remove from the heat. Add the butter and stir until melted.

To serve: Transfer to a warmed platter and serve immediately.

Serves four

CHAPTER 22: George Exits

George Marianetti maintained an apartment in town where he enjoyed a lively social life and a steady female companion, Ellie Mack. During these later years, George lived on and off with Ron Edwards, the Fior's parking attendant of years past, who now owned his own business.

Ron made videotapes of George at his 80th birthday party where the bon vivant danced with the ladies, including his first wife, Olive, Paul's mother. He engaged the belly dancer, mirroring her movements in a pelvic riptide to everyone's glee.

George always liked to entertain friends and drew much younger people to him. One such friend was Linda Tomback, a former Fior bookkeeper. "He used to cook chicken cacciatore and polenta for me. We'd sit around and smoke dope and he had his special drink -- vodka with brandy and something red in it," Linda said.

George invented a concoction he called "Ruffino." The actual recipe was: Equal parts of vodka, sweet and dry vermouths and Campari, a liqueur. Add a twist of lemon peel, pour it over the rocks and top that off with a bourbon float.

It was a killer drink and George drank it by the jug-full, according to his son, Paul. Eventually George began hallucinating and lost his mobility. He accused Ron of being a Mafioso. One day Paul came over to visit. George looked at him accusingly and said, "Oh. You too, huh?"

"It was a hard time for those who loved him" said Paul. He took his Dad to a convalescent home to dry out and managed to convince him that booze was the cause of his pitiful deterioration.

"And I was a hard man to convince," George later admitted. But he quit drinking cold turkey. He took physical therapy to learn how to walk again and regained the ability to sign his name. He was very proud of his signature and would practice over and over his imposing "G. Marianetti." During the stay in the convalescent facility, Frank and Ruth came to visit him and apparently had pleasant moments together. Sober and dry, George returned to his apartment and where he kept alcohol for his friends, but he never drank again.

But something was still not right. Eventually, it was obvious George was seriously ill. Paul took him to San Francisco General Hospital for tests in 1993. At one point "he opened his eyes and this really attractive woman doctor told him he had cancer. 'I guess I'd better start having fun'," Paul said George replied.

George went in and out of consciousness. The doctor told Paul to bring him anything he wanted to eat. Paul reached out to the staff to make friends with them.

"I gave them the osso buco recipe. I had an affair with someone on staff. I did anything to bring them into the family and keep this guy alive," he said.

After less than a week, George was transferred to Laguna Honda Hospital and Rehabilitation Center for hospice care. At one point, Paul found him looking at the ceiling. "So this is the goddamn grand finale," he said. The next day he died.

ZUPPA DI CAVOLO CON FORMAGGIO
(CABBAGE AND BREAD SOUP)

Easily double the recipe for a crowd. This soup is salty, so it's good to use low-sodium beef broth. Italian country-style bread goes well with this dish. Ciabatta is also fine. It's a full meal, with a salad on the side.

1/2-pound loaf Italian country-style bread, cut into 1/4-inch-thick slices
1 pound Savoy or green cabbage, thinly sliced
1/2 pound Fontina cheese, thinly sliced
1/4 cup freshly grated Parmesan cheese, plus extra for garnish
2 ounces pancetta, finely chopped (Consider grinding in a food processor. Do not use bacon which is smoked but salt pork is a good substitute.)
6 cups brown stock (page 24), or 3 (14-ounce) cans low-sodium beef stock plus 2/3 cup water

Preheat the oven to 400°F. Lightly oil the domed lid of a deep 6- to 8-quart ovenproof soup pot, because the soup will puff as it cooks.

Cover the bottom of the soup pot with one-third of the bread. Layer one-third of the cabbage over the bread. Top with one-third of the Fontina and one-third of the Parmesan. Repeat the layering two more times. Using the palms of your hands, press down firmly on the ingredients to compress and level.

Heat a large saucepan over medium-high heat. Add the pancetta and cook until slightly crisp, about 5 minutes. Using a slotted spoon, remove the pancetta and sprinkle evenly over the top of the soup. Discard the rendered fat.

In the same large saucepan, bring the stock to a boil over high heat. Remove from the heat and pour evenly over the soup.

Place the soup pot on a sturdy rimmed baking sheet, cover tightly, and bake until a crispy brown crown forms, about 1 hour and 15 minutes.

To serve: Scoop down through all the layers and spoon into warmed individual serving bowls. Serve immediately with extra grated Parmesan.

Serves four

CHAPTER 23: Club Pork

George's departure was a rupture with history. Still, life at the Fior did not stop. Bob recalled 1995, the Year of the Pig in the Chinese zodiac, he and Jinx were palavering with frequent patrons, Jeff and Suzanne Varacalli.

"We were sitting here one night after probably way too many scotches. One of us said we had to figure out something to do to celebrate the Chinese Year of the Boar. So we decided the most appropriate thing to do was to eat pig every day for a year. A bunch of us did that. If we missed a couple days, it was purely by accident. It was just for a lark. Lark or not, the group spread to include about 10 people, including Fior staffers, partners, and friends. "We had big dinners at people's houses where we had pork for every course including dessert. It was fun," recalls Bob. The group of friends continued the practice as they traveled together that year to Mexico, Scotland and England.

Today, many of the artifacts and decorative elements in the Fior celebrate swine-hood, from the guestbook stand at the entrance to the running hog figure over the bar.

The executive director of the North Beach Chamber of Commerce, Marsha Garland, described Club Pork in her column, titled, "And the Beach Goes On" in the September, 1996, issue of *North Beach Magazine*:

> The zaniest restaurant in North Beach has to be Fior D'Italia. Last year, during the Year of the Boar, proprietors Bob and Jinx Larive, maitre d Jim Bril, waitress Donna Cronin, and North Beach residents Jeff and Suzanne Varacalli, found themselves boared one slow winter's eve. They agreed they ought to celebrate the Chinese New Year and decided there and then to eat pork every day for the entire year.
>
> Oink, oink, Club Pork was born. At one dinner, they even had the audacity to purloin (porkloin) a video of "Babe." (After watching "Babe," how could anyone eat pork again? They did.)

Bob is now VP of Promotions and Marketing, Jinx is President, Donna is Treasurer, Jim is VP of Travel and Entertainment. Suzanne and Jeff Varacalli are VPs of Special Events and Special Projects. Stop by Club Pork's world headquarters at 601 Union and check out the pig paraphernalia.

All the fun stopped at the onset of the Year of the Rat. "We really couldn't get into the other animals of the Chinese calendar," Bob said.

Patrons Become Partners

Silly and bizarre though it was, Club Pork brought these devoted customers, the Varacallis, even closer to the Fior. Jeff had started frequenting the restaurant some years earlier as a member of the Friday Lunch Bunch, a group of professionals connected to the construction trades that eats monthly at the Fior. Jeff was a New Jersey native transplanted to the Bay Area and an executive in the trucking, moving and storage trade. He began hanging out in North Beach and, through the Friday Lunch Bunch, became enamored of the Fior, where he met his wife-to-be, Suzanne.

"The place was always magic," he said and spoke warmly of his admiration for Achille Pantaleoni, whose elegance and humanity commanded Jeff's respect. He struck up a friendship with maitre d' Jim Bril and they started golfing together. Eventually, Jeff married Suzanne and moved to North Beach.

One day, they sauntered into the Fior, still only slightly acquainted with the Larives. Bob pointed out an advertisement in the paper offering a round-trip fare, San Francisco to London, for $300.

"But we had to sign up that day," Jeff remembered. And they did. The four of them, along with waitress Donna Cronin and Jim, took off together. The Varacallis returned much better friends with the Fior community.

A couple of years later, the couple joined Bob, partner Hamish Fordwood, and other Fior denizens on Bob's yearly trip to Scotland to play the course at St. Andrews Links and enjoy the pleasures of Scottish distilleries.

Jeff felt more and more drawn to the restaurant and wanted to become even more a part of it. When Bob and the other partners invited him to become a partner, he wasn't ready at first. Because of his impending retirement, it seemed prudent to him to keep the status quo until then. But in 1999, after suffering through the deaths of his father and some close friends, he decided that enjoying the present was the greater wisdom. He resigned from NorCal Moving, an agent of

Allied Van Lines. His colleagues wished him farewell in the Tony Bennett Room.

Jeff came on as a maitre d' expecting to learn the restaurant business in a methodical way. He trusted the knowledge and professionalism of Gianni, Bob, Jim and the others who kept a steady course at the restaurant. However, a week after he started, the unexpected happened. Bob and Jinx went on holiday to Hawaii as Jim sought his vacation in Singapore. While Gianni was quite capable of taking charge, he fell ill. The first morning Jeff put the key in the door of 601 Union Street with managers Gina Daler and Arlene Wrobleski waiting for him to let them in, he realized how little he knew about what he was doing.

"I was scared to death," he said.

While every day brought a new lesson, Varacalli came with his own basic and excellent management experience that he simply now transferred to the Fior. It's important to keep the staff pumped up," he said. "When it gets really going in the kitchen, you say, 'Thanks. You guys did great.' It gets wild in there. You can't just think it's going to happen; you have to walk around and make sure you are part of the team. They know you are there for support."

GAMBERI IMPANATI ALL'ARANCIO (PRAWNS WITH ORANGE BREADING)

This recipe delivers a zesty experience. If you use a peeler on the lemons and oranges, then chop the zest very fine. Otherwise, use a fine grater.

Serve with a spring, mixed salad and a light vinaigrette dressing.

2 oranges
2 lemons
2 tablespoons extra virgin olive oil, plus extra for drizzling
24 extra large prawns, peeled and deveined
1 1/2 cups fine dried breadcrumbs or panko (Japanese breadcrumbs)
1 teaspoon salt
1/4 teaspoon ground white pepper
Lemon wedges, for garnish

Zest the oranges and lemons, taking care not to grate into the white pith beneath the colored portion of the peel. Transfer the zests to a medium bowl; set aside.

In a shallow dish or sealable plastic bag, combine the juice of 1 of the oranges, 1 of the lemons, the oil, and the prawns; toss to coat. Let marinate for 10 minutes.

Add the breadcrumbs, salt, and white pepper to the bowl of zests; toss to mix.

Preheat the oven to 450 F. Generously oil a large baking sheet.

Remove the prawns from the marinade and coat with the breadcrumb mixture, using your hands to press the crumbs on firmly. Transfer to the prepared baking sheet, drizzle very lightly with olive oil, and bake until the prawns are opaque throughout, about 10 minutes.

To serve: Arrange the prawns on a warmed serving platter. Drizzle with the juice of half of the remaining lemon. Garnish with the lemon wedges and serve immediately.

Serves four

CHAPTER 24: Arrivederci, Achille

On September 12, 1995, Herb Caen's column in the *San Francisco Chronicle* read:

> Farewell to yet another old friend: Achille Pantaleoni, elegant maitre d' at Fior d'Italia, who died last week at 72 of a lung problem. [1]

The Fior community of owners, staff and patrons were crushed when the beloved Achille left them. His portrait by photographer Tom Vano was hung in the main dining room, which was renamed the Pantaleoni Room. His funeral reception was held at the restaurant.

POLLO ALLA LIGURE (LIGURIAN CHICKEN)

1 ounce small sun-dried tomatoes
4 tablespoons olive oil
4 (6-ounce) boneless, skinless chicken breasts
Salt and freshly ground black pepper
All-purpose flour, for dusting
4 small zucchini, cut into 1-inch slices
4 cooked artichoke hearts, quartered
4 shallots, chopped
2 cloves garlic, minced
2 cups chicken stock
1 pound linguine, cooked, buttered, and kept warm, to serve

In a small bowl, combine the tomatoes with just enough water to cover. Soak until soft and pliable, about 20 minutes. Drain well, thinly slice, and set aside.

Preheat the oven to 400°F.

In a large ovenproof sauté pan, heat 2 tablespoons of the olive oil over medium-high heat. Generously season the chicken with salt and pepper. Dust lightly with flour and shake gently to remove any excess. Arrange in a single layer in the hot pan and cook until golden, about 5 minutes per side. Using tongs, transfer the chicken to a plate and keep warm.

In the same pan, heat the remaining 2 tablespoons olive oil. Add the zucchini, artichokes, shallots, and garlic; cook until just tender, about 5 minutes. Add the stock and sun-dried tomatoes and bring to a boil. Season to taste with salt and pepper.

Return the chicken to the pan, along with any juices that have accumulated, and transfer to the oven. Bake until the juices run clear when the chicken is pierced with the tip of a knife (or until an instant-read thermometer registers 160°F), about 10 minutes.

To serve: Divide the pasta evenly among four warmed serving plates. Arrange the chicken over the pasta and spoon the sauce over the top. Serve immediately.

Serves four

CHAPTER 25: The Unsung Little Guys

The Fior, under the leadership of the Larives, Gianni and their partners, honors those it feels society hasn't sufficiently acknowledged. In February of 1992, a Superior Court jury ordered cab driver, Chuck Hollom, to pay $24,595 to a mugger. It was an award that irked many citizens in San Francisco, both on his side and against him. The Fior came out for the cabbie.

In 1989, while driving, Hollom witnessed Ocie James McClure knock down a Japanese tourist, Chihiro Saka, near the Civic Center, grab her purse and run off. Instinctively, Hollom, with a passenger in his cab, sped after the robber as did another cab driver. The two drivers pursued McClure for several blocks shouting at him to stop. *The Los Angeles Times* February 17, 1992 reported the story:

> Finally, Hollom made a sharp turn, driving onto a sidewalk to block the mugger's path. The mugger ran into the path of the cab, and Hollom, sensing that the man was about to get away, drove forward, pinning a panting McClure against a building wall. The mugger, according to his attorney, suffered two severe leg fractures, a severed artery, and a torn calf muscle.
>
> Police arrived, and McClure was arrested. But in 1990, McClure brought a civil personal injury suit against Hollom and the Luxor Cab Co., seeking damages for assault and battery, negligence, and intentional infliction of emotional distress, an allegation later dropped. The taxi firm was dismissed from the suit. [1]

The jury on February 6 ordered the cab driver to pay McClure $24,595 to cover most of the assailant's $32,000 bill at San Francisco General Hospital. The case caused considerable controversy. As McClure's lawyer argued, many accused Hollom of excessive force and held that he should have

called the police and continued to follow the robber until the police arrived. Hollom's lawyers countered that his extreme measures were reasonable at the time and under the circumstances.

The Fior owners, as did many people, felt a citizen was being punished for stopping crime. They hosted a fund-raising dinner for Hollom to launch an appeal. Participants in the fund-raiser praised his actions and lambasted the jury for exacting $25,000 from him. According to the *Associated Press*, at the fund-raiser Hollom responded to someone who asked whether he felt like a hero: "Salami between two pieces of bread? You really have a low opinion of me. Yes, I feel like a hero, but I'll have some spaghetti first," he quipped.

The Fior contributed $1,500 to the fund set up by San Francisco radio station KGO.

Associated Press

Cabbie Chuck Hollom greets restaurant patrons.

Hungry hero cabbie feted at fund-raiser

SAN FRANCISCO (AP) — Irate citizens put money and pasta where their mouths were, digging into their wallets and plates of linguine to support a cabbie who captured a mugger but then was himself caught by a $25,000 jury award to the injured crook.

Patrons of an Italian restaurant burst into cheers Wednesday night when hungry hero Chuck Hollom attended a fund-raiser to help pay the award.

Hollom, surrounded by reporters and cameras, affably shook hands with well-wishers at Fior d'Italia. But he made his way over to a corner table with one thing on his mind: dinner.

"I feel a little rambunctious and hungry," Hollom said when asked how he felt. Didn't he feel like a hero?

"Salami between two pieces of bread? You really have a low opinion of me. Yes, I feel like a hero — but I'll have some spaghetti first," he quipped.

Despite Hollom's focus on food, patrons insisted on praising him for his intervention in a 1989 mugging, in which he pinned the crook to a wall with a cab.

And they blasted a Superior Court jury that decided last week that Hollom acted with excessive force and ordered him to pay $24,595, after the mugger suffered a broken leg and sued. Hollom says the injury occurred as the mugger, who later got a 10-year sentence, tried to wrench himself free from the cab.

After Wednesday's benefit, the restaurant expected to contribute up to $1,500 to the fund, set up by San Francisco radio station KGO.

The fund topped $25,000 by Wednesday afternoon, said Ronn Owens, a station talk show host who organized the drive to help Hollom.

Reprinted with the permission of Associated Press.

A Bad Welcome

In another well-publicized incident, the Fior was featured in Herb Caen's popular column in *the Chronicle* on October 19, 1995:

An unfortunate and shocking incident that received shockingly little coverage occurred early last Thursday at Columbus and Green in North Beach, where two visitors from England were savagely beaten by three ruffians, swinging fists and bottles. One of the victims, Jerry Reynolds, 38, of Chessington (Surrey), was released from S.F. General with "minor" injuries (cuts and a broken nose,) but 30-yr-old Noel Miller, also of Chessington, is still there, having lost the vision in his fractured right eye (S.F. General's eye surgeon, Dr. Michael Jumper, patched it with 18 stitches but much more treatment is necessary.)

Noel's mother and sister flew over immediately from London and were warmly welcomed to North Beach. Hotel Boheme has been housing them free, and Fior d'Italia has dined them nightly. Hanna Suleiman of Caffe Greco and Marsha Garland of the North Beach Chamber took gifts to Noel, and provided transportation for the visitors. The point to all this is that not a single city official visited young Miller or offered apologies, even though the story of his beating was printed all over Britain.

Noel's mother and sister returned to England Tuesday, and Noel leaves today. Having shown signs of life at last, the mayor's office is providing a car to drive him to the airport. (Will the mayor proclaim this "Noel Miller Day"?) Immediately after landing, Miller will go to a London hospital for further treatment of the eye, not the heart, he almost left in San Francisco. [2]

Watching over Us

Then there are the strange stories that never reach the papers. Like the one about the homeless, taciturn Seymour who lived across the street in Washington Square Park.

As he became a fixture in front of the restaurant, the Fior gave him a few bucks for sweeping the pavement and hosing out the garbage receptacles periodically. Seymour was dependable to that degree, and Bob offered to pay for a room for him in the residence over the restaurant. But Seymour wouldn't consider it.

One day he disappeared. Eventually his body was found in the park. The Fior had his remains cremated. They rest today in a white cardboard box on a bookshelf over a window in the bistro section. Somehow the restaurant personnel seem to enjoy the fact that, "Seymour's watching over us," according to Bob.

And every day, patrons sit under that box with little awareness of the old soul above them.

PANNA COTTA (COOKED CREAM PUDDING)

Dissolve gelatin thoroughly or it may settle and form a gummy layer.

3 cups heavy cream
1 (1/4-ounce) envelope plain gelatin
1/3 cup granulated sugar
1 large egg yolk
1 tablespoon vanilla extract

Sauce
1 pint strawberries, hulled and quartered
2 tablespoons granulated sugar
1 teaspoon freshly squeezed lemon juice

Whole strawberries, for garnish

To make the cream pudding: Place 1/2 cup of the cream in a small bowl. Sprinkle the gelatin over the cream and let sit until thickened, 5 minutes. In a medium bowl, whisk together another 1/2 cup of the cream, the sugar, egg yolk, and vanilla; set aside.

In a medium saucepan, bring the remaining 2 cups cream to a boil over medium-high heat. Add the thickened gelatin, lower the heat to a simmer, and whisk until completely dissolved, about 2 minutes.

Slowly pour the hot cream mixture over the egg yolk mixture, whisking continuously. Whisk until smooth.

Divide the mixture evenly among four 6-ounce ramekins. Cover and refrigerate until set, at least 4 hours or overnight.

To make the sauce: In a blender or food processor, combine the strawberries, sugar, and lemon juice; puree until smooth. Pass the mixture through a fine-mesh strainer and set aside and keep refrigerated.

To serve: Run the tip of a thin-bladed knife around the top edge of each pudding. Dip the bottom half of the ramekins in boiling water for 30 seconds. Cover each ramekin with a serving plate and invert. Shake gently to release the pudding, then remove the ramekin. Garnish with the sauce and fresh berries.

Serves four

CHAPTER 26: The 110ᵗʰ Anniversary

The year 1996 marked the Fior's 110ᵗʰ year of operation and the owners decided to offer a reprise of the original menu and prices that the previous owners had pulled off with great success at the centennial in 1986.

Waiter Rudy Velarde was delighted to don the 1890s Victorian duds – voluminous aprons, sleeve garters and a huge, fake handlebar moustache -- mimicking what waiters wore at the Fior's founding. A picture of him and similarly attired staff hangs in the outside dining room.

On April 18, 1996, the *Marin Independent Journal* announced the upcoming anniversary celebration:

Guests who brave the expected two-hour line to get into the famous corner restaurant at Stockton and Union streets will enjoy four-course meals at prices ranging from $.05 to $.30 per person….

People are begging but Larive is not accepting reservations for the 11:30 to 9 p.m. affair. 'One lady called and said she wanted to order take-out for 25 for her husband's birthday that day,' laughed Bob. 'I've heard every story in the book.'[1]

Waiter John Carmazzi remembered the event as running more smoothly than the 100ᵗʰ anniversary for the waiters. "Bob let us keep all the money. We didn't take any money (for the management). So if it was a 30-cent lunch we kept that and the tip, Bob didn't make a single penny that day," he said.

Magic Penne

Besides the many performers and politicos who have hung their hats at the Fior, so have athletes. Some like then San Francisco Giants pitcher Shawn Estes came to see the restaurant as a safe haven before big games where he could stock up on carbohydrates and good luck.

A young man of twenty-four in the 1997-98 season, Estes moved to Telegraph Hill overlooking the Fior.

One of the Fior's publicists, Dave Craig, who had previously worked for the Giants, introduced Estes to the restaurant. As he became familiar with it, the pitcher began taking family and friends of family there when they visited him.

110th anniversary crowds line up around the block.

Courtesy Tom Vano

Opera singer Geraldine Reicher and concert violinist John Creighton Murray entertain the crowds waiting for a meal at the original prices.

Courtesy Tom Vano

"In 1997 I started eating there for lunch on night games. It was right down from the street where I lived. My diet on the day I pitched consisted of pasta and sometimes chicken, carbohydrates for good energy," he said. While he didn't think he was as superstitious as many other baseball players are said to be, he recognized he'd developed a ritual on the days he was pitching.

At one point, Shawn discovered a dish he liked at another Italian restaurant, penne with spicy marinara sauce. So the next time he went to the Fior, he asked Gianni to make it for him even though it was not on the menu. Gianni was happy to oblige and that became his standard lunch from thereon after.

Shawn could tell the Fior staff began to expect him on the days he was playing and looked forward to his arrival. "Sometimes if I came later than usual, they'd say, 'Oh, we were expecting you.'"

Shawn became a fixture with the staff. Jinx said that it had always been the Fior's policy to let celebrities dine in peace. But when the ballplayer came in, he was treated as one of the family.

"When he would come in, if I wasn't busy, I'd just sit down and chat about anything and everything. He'd ask me advice about his girlfriend, 'What do you think I should do about this? How should I handle that?' He'd always give me a big hug and a big kiss," she said.

Jinx felt particularly close to Shawn because he was within two years of the age of her son, Ian. She and Bob let him know they could be counted on as his family away from home.

"I'm very close to my mother and Jinx has that motherly nature about her," said the ballplayer, who went on to develop golfing friendships with Bob, Ian and Jeff.

In October of 1997, the Giants went to Florida to play the Marlins in the first round of playoffs. Gianni sent a fax to Shawn at his hotel, the Bal Harbor Sheraton, with a steaming bowl of pasta drawn on it. He wrote on it: "I know you can't be there so hopefully this will do the trick."

But it didn't, apparently. Shawn said, "I didn't pitch well that night. So it started to be a joke that he would send pasta to me on the road by Federal Express." Shawn had had the best season of his professional career until he left San Francisco for Florida: He won 19 and lost five games with the Giants.

But then there is always a spoilsport. Fior restaurant manager Gina Daler spoke of a regular patron who hated the Giants and in particular complained about Estes.

"He bitches about Estes whom Jinx loves. Every time I walked by his table, he complained about Shawn. I have to put the customer in table 15 (away from the television in the bistro part of the Fior) so he doesn't have to watch the Giants. He gets upset watching them and then his wife gets upset," Gina said.

Since most of the restaurant staff today is Latin American with the majority from Mexico, it was not surprising that the soccer great Pele drew so much attention when he dined at the restaurant.

"He comes late but he always likes to be in the middle so people can approach him. The last time he was here, I don't know how (the news of his presence) got out because it was late. A lot of Mexicans work around this neighborhood. All of a sudden all the dining room was packed. All his soccer fans. He took pictures left and right. He talked to everybody and signed everything," Daler remembered.

RISOTTO AL LIMONE (LEMON RISOTTO)

This is not a traditional risotto. Liquid should be added one cup at a time. Adding the extra two tablespoons of butter makes a very rich dish. If your lemon is not very juicy, you might want to add more to taste.

2 cups long-grain rice
2 large egg yolks
2 teaspoons grated lemon zest
2 tablespoons freshly squeezed lemon juice
1/2 cup freshly grated Parmesan cheese, plus extra for garnish
2 to 4 tablespoons butter
Salt and freshly ground black pepper

Bring a large pot of lightly salted water to a boil over high heat. Add the rice and cook until just tender, 12 to 15 minutes. Drain and transfer to a warmed large serving bowl. Add the egg yolks, lemon zest and juice, Parmesan, and butter; mix well. Season to taste with salt and pepper.

Serve immediately with additional Parmesan.

Serves four

CHAPTER 27: Another Break with the Past

On February 6, 1997, Frank Marianetti passed away. The restaurant had now lost the last thread that connected it to its founders. His nephew Paul recalled him sorrowfully:

The year before my uncle Frank passed away, he couldn't see me because I reminded him of my father. It broke my heart. My uncle Frank was the one when I was working as a busboy would drive me home and we would sit in his car all night and talk until sunup about things that teenagers need to know from older men. I didn't do that with my father, I did it with my Uncle Frank. And then he couldn't see me anymore. It was devastating.

TIRAMISÙ MOUSSE (TIRAMISU MOUSSE)

This is not the traditional tiramisu but a mousse variation.

Mascarpone is an Italian cream cheese and can be found in any Italian delicatessen

4 Italian-brand ladyfinger cookies or sponge cake
1 cup brewed espresso coffee
2 tablespoons coffee liqueur or rum

Mousse
4 large eggs, separated
1/2 cup granulated sugar
8 ounces mascarpone cheese
Pinch of cream of tartar
1/4 cup chocolate chips

In a shallow dish, arrange the ladyfingers in a single layer. Drizzle the espresso and liqueur evenly over the ladyfingers. Tuck a towel under one side of the dish to allow the extra liquid that has not been absorbed to run off.

To make the mousse: In a medium bowl, combine the egg yolks and 2 tablespoons of the sugar; whisk until pale yellow. Add the mascarpone and whisk until fluffy—do not overbeat or your mascarpone will become butter! Set aside.

In a dry large bowl, combine the egg whites, the remaining 6 tablespoons sugar, and the tiniest amount of cream of tartar—no more than what fits on the very tip of a paring knife! Whisk the egg whites until they form stiff peaks. Using a large rubber spatula, carefully fold the egg whites into the mascarpone mixture.

To assemble: Spoon 1/2 cup of the mousse into the bottom of each of 4 individual glass dessert bowls or parfait glasses. Sprinkle a few chocolate chips over the mousse and cover with a ladyfinger, torn into pieces. Sprinkle a few more chocolate chips over the ladyfinger and top with another 1/2 cup of the mousse. Refrigerate, covered, until chilled, about 1 hour or overnight.

To serve: Garnish with a few more chocolate chips and serve chilled.

Serves four

CHAPTER 28: Cadets and Lasagne

In 1998, the newsletter of the Minnesota Parents' Club of the U.S. Air Force Academy reported :

The parents of C1C Ian Larive own Fior d'Italia, an Italian restaurant in San Francisco. They sent their chef Gianni Audieri to the Academy to work with the Mitchell Hall staff for six days. With the combined effort of the chef, Lt. Col Kramer and the Mitchell nutritionists, a meal of Pomodoro mozzarella, 880 pounds of tortellini in cream sauce, 62 pans of lasagna, Osso Buco, 2,100 services of veal and Panna Cotta for dessert was prepared.

When Ian was a cadet, Bob and Jinx visited him from time to time and, on one occasion, they offered to produce a real Italian meal for the mess hall. Those in authority accepted and worked right along with Gianni to present this tremendous production, perhaps the culinary equivalent of the staging of Verdi's *Aida*.

Mitchell Hall at the U.S. Air Force Academy in Colorado Springs covers two acres and is one of the largest mass dining facilities in the world, according to the Academy. It serves all 4,000 cadets at midday and serves breakfast and supper as well with a staff of 600. But when the Larives got it in their head to serve a real Italian dinner for the cadets who were colleagues of their son Ian, the size of the challenge did not faze them.

Bob recalled it took about six months to prepare. "We sent Gianni out there and we had ordered the bits and pieces we needed to make a Fior d'Italia meal. It was mostly products that they don't normally use."

Cadets mob Mitchell Hall to tuck into the Fior d'Italia's lasagne. At the lower right, Chef Gianni demonstrates for a kitchen staff member how to prepare a dish.

While the Academy was able to source the cream and the tortellini and the grated cheese, it couldn't find osso buco. So the Fior had to order 4,000 veal shanks be sent to Colorado Springs. Gianni recalled some cultural cross-pollination with the kitchen staff at Mitchell Hall:

They use lemon only for iced tea. I had to use it for the osso buco. They were surprised I needed lemon to make a sauce. Tiramisu and the Caesar salad were the biggest things for them. They didn't want to serve them because they are made with raw eggs… I said, 'We've been serving these dishes here for the last 50 years and nobody ever got sick. If it's made fresh, there's no problem.' But they didn't want to take the chance. So we settled. I told them to order me pasteurized eggs. They taste slightly different but not that much. They look like fresh eggs, but they've been steamed to a degree so they don't actually solidify.

The day of the event, Gianni worked along with the kitchen staff. "Ten people started around noon to cook osso buco. About 10 griddles, each guy tending one griddle, sautéing osso buco," he said.

While all 4,000 cadets eat every midday meal at Mitchell Hall, they have the option to eat dinner elsewhere. On average about 2,000-2,500 dine there in the evening. But the Larives and Gianni had been promoting the upcoming event as a night not to miss. So they expected maybe 3,000 would show up. That morning Gianni addressed them at breakfast and said, "I'm not going to cook for just a few people." The full complement of 4,000 young people appeared.

Bob recalled the vivid reactions of the cadets: "One kid comes up to us, and we're standing there all in our tuxedos and having fun with it, and he says, 'This is the first time Mitchell Hall ever smelled good.' Another girl comes up to Jinx, and she says, 'This is the first good meal that I've had since I left home.' They are both standing there, crying, really boo-hooing. Cadets got together and they tried to hire Gianni. They were all excited saying, 'We'll pay you whatever you want, you stay. We're gonna pay you. We'll raise the money.' "

GAMBERI FIOR (PRAWNS FIOR)

The flour adds just enough thickening. Pour off all but a little butter to perfect the recipe.

1/2 cup clarified butter (see page 69)
20 colossal prawns, peeled and deveined
All-purpose flour, for dusting
3 cloves garlic, chopped
2 shallots, chopped
1/2 cup fish stock, or 1/4 cup bottled clam juice plus 1/4 cup water
1/2 cup dry white wine
1/2 cup chopped fresh tomato
Salt and freshly ground black pepper
Chopped fresh flat-leaf parsley, for garnish

In a large sauté pan, heat the butter over medium-high heat. Lightly dust the prawns with flour and shake gently to remove any excess. Arrange the prawns in a single layer in the pan and cook until just pink and opaque throughout, 1 to 2 minutes per side. Using a slotted spoon, transfer the prawns to a plate and set aside. Pour off all but 2 tablespoons of the butter. Add the garlic and shallots and cook until translucent and fragrant, about 3 minutes. Add the fish stock and wine; bring to a boil and cook 2 minutes. Add the tomato and cook, stirring occasionally, until slightly reduced, about 3 minutes. Return the prawns to the pan, season to taste with salt and pepper, and cook until heated through.

To serve: Divide the prawns and sauce among 4 warmed serving plates. Garnish with the parsley and serve immediately.

Serves four

CHAPTER 29: A Premature Millennium and the Real One

Many people, like the Fior, celebrated the end of the first 2,000 years after Christ was born a year in advance. While the beginning of the second 1,000 started on January 1, 2001, the Fior welcomed the new era on December 31, 1999, unable to resist the attraction of the magic number, 2000.

The Fior put on a remarkable New Year's Eve party with a set menu and entertainment. Clara Dayton, manager of the Talent Bank, a company of singers training for grand opera and an offshoot of the San Francisco Opera Guild, produced an evening of song. Bob had retained Clara and the Talent Bank in late 1998 just to make sure they would be committed to be at the Fior on the important night.

The singers began preparing over a year ahead of time. Clara thought long and hard about the program. "I went to the music store. I bought Gershwin and Irving Berlin. I wanted American composers who were very well known and had really contributed to the American scene," she said. Selections from *Die Fledermaus* and Broadway tunes filled out the night's agenda.

"That one New Year's Eve was most memorable. The audience was pleasant. They stopped eating to listen. That's a gift from heaven, it doesn't always happen," she said.

Fior staffers thought Clara Dayton herself was a gift. The diminutive, elderly artist was always elegantly dressed and coiffed and carried herself regally.

"She always says to me, 'Do not hold my arm. I can walk by myself,' " said manager, Gina Daler.

A special menu designed and overseen by Gianni, copious gifts, paper hats and noise-makers completed the evening.

On the following New Year's Eve celebration on December 31, 2000, to welcome January 1, 2001, the evening had just begun for many of the staffers when the clock struck midnight.

The waiters and kitchen staff, many of whom are Hispanic and Spanish-speaking, stayed to raise a glass or two in the wee hours. But waiter Martin Flores decided to head home shortly after midnight. His path took him in front of Moose's, a restaurant a block away on Stockton Street. Two young men were standing outside smoking.

"I recognized them from seeing them in the news," Martin said. They turned out to be the sons of outgoing Mexican President Ernesto Ponce de Leon Zedillo (1994-2000).

President Zedillo remembers it was the first night he and his family could celebrate together after his term in office ended. The rest of the family was within Moose's waiting for a limousine to be summoned. Martin, when he understood their situation, wasted no time.

"I said we can call you a limo from the Fior, if you want to come over and have a drink with us. They did stop by. The whole family was there. I was so thrilled because everybody in the kitchen staff was from Mexico, waiters too," he said.

President Zedillo remembers the restaurant was closed when he and his family, First Lady Patrizia, the two sons and a daughter, were invited inside. "The manager was there. The Mexican workers called him *el patron*. They said he wants to have a drink with you and your family and they started opening bottles of champagne," he recalled.

"I started to drink nice champagne, and my kids and the workers started to sing mariachi songs with the mariachis. We stayed till 4 or so in the morning," Zedillo recounted.

Waiter Martin stepped in and introduced the dignitaries to everyone. "We were all so excited. We showed them the restaurant, the kitchen. We told them about the history of the restaurant. We sang some traditional songs from Mexico. The restaurant stayed open just for the employees and the President," he said.

Zedillo was struck by the fact that the Latino workers at the Fior were not all recent immigrants. "Some workers were there from the third generation. Their grandfathers and their fathers worked there. It was unusual to see. There must be something nice about working there other than getting free champagne," he said.

MEDAGLIONI DI VITELLO INVOLTI IN PANCETTA
(MEDALLIONS OF VEAL WRAPPED IN PANCETTA)

8 (2 1/2-ounce) medallions of veal loin
Salt and freshly ground black pepper
1 cup olive oil
4 sprigs rosemary
4 sprigs sage
4 cloves garlic, crushed
16 thin slices pancetta
1 pound Blue Lake green beans, trimmed and cooked al dente

Generously season the veal with salt and pepper. In a sealable bag, combine the olive oil, rosemary, sage, and garlic   Add the veal and seal, pressing out as much air as you can . Gently shake the bag to coat the veal with the marinade. Let rest in the refrigerator for at least 2 hours and up to one day.

Preheat the oven to 400°F.

Remove the veal from the bag; reserve the marinade. Wrap each medallion in 2 slices of the pancetta and secure with a toothpick or two.

In a large ovenproof sauté pan, heat 2 tablespoons of the reserved marinade over medium-high heat. Add the veal and cook until golden brown, 2 to 3 minutes per side. Transfer the pan to the oven and continue cooking until medium or until an instant-read thermometer registers 130°F, about 5 minutes. Using tongs, transfer the veal to a serving platter and keep warm.

To serve: In the same sauté pan, heat another 2 tablespoons of the reserved marinade over medium-high heat. Add the green beans and cook until just heated through, about 3 minutes. Arrange around the veal medallions and serve immediately.

Serves four

CHAPTER 30: Head-to-Head with the IRS

The Fior owners have taken uncomfortable, often unpopular, stands when they believed they were right. Perhaps the most publicized stand was against the Internal Revenue Service. Restaurant owners typically shy away from confronting the IRS but this time, the Fior went out on a limb.

Under the law, employees have to report their tips to pay the FICA tax for Social Security. This tax applies to all service workers, not just waiters, but also taxi drivers, hairstylists and the like. By reporting tips, the employee increases his Social Security benefits.

In 1987, Congress decided to tax the employer as well for that portion of employee tips that fund Social Security benefits. For about a decade, the IRS let it be known that 8.5 percent of the customer's tab was an acceptable percentage to report for tax purposes.

Then in the early 1980s and 1990s, in a zealous campaign to keep an eye on tipping, the IRS began to audit restaurants, including servers, busboys and employers' books. As this audit became more onerous, the service changed its tactics. It looked at the employee's reported tips and the restaurateur's sales records, especially credit card receipts, and determined what the owner owed based on this evidence.

Across the country, restaurant owners through the National Restaurant Association and their state restaurant associations have battled the IRS for injustices they perceive exist in this system. As Bob and his associates have argued, "The percentage the IRS takes out is arbitrary. The employer doesn't know what the waiters are making. All employees are different. Then when the IRS does collect money from the employer, the money doesn't get allocated back to the Social Security fund where the employee will eventually get the benefit of it. Instead it goes into a general fund."

He and other restaurateurs resented the position the IRS put them in. "There's a lever over the restaurateur to act as a tax collector for the IRS. If they don't, the IRS threatens to audit them."

In fact, the agency can audit restaurants on tips from years as far back as 1988. That is still true today. The IRS audited the Fior for the years 1992 and 1993. The agency sent the restaurant a bill for $23,262 in 1997, claiming the Fior had underreported employee gratuities. The IRS based the bill on an "aggregate estimate." In other words, the agency estimated that employees tips, when taken all together, totaled 14 percent of the restaurant's gross receipts. The Fior's position was that a waiter doesn't collect the entire amount of a tip, and many customers do not tip anyway.

The *San Francisco Chronicle* quoted Fior waiter Matt Herman on the subject:

> Do I take home 15 percent (of customers' tabs) in tips? Are you crazy? Let's say I get $15 (as a tip) on a $100 bill. I give $1.50 to the door (the maitre d'), $1.50 to the bar and $3 to the busboy. That leaves me with $9. [1]

Additionally, tips added to credit card tabs are almost always lower than tips left as cash.

Four restaurants, with the help of their local and national associations, stepped up to the plate to challenge the IRS. Besides the Fior, the restaurants included the Coco Pazzo in Chicago (330 West Hubbard Restaurant Corp.), the Bubble Room in Florida and the Morrison Restaurant, Inc. of Alabama.

While restaurateurs felt unjustly pressured by the demands of the country's tax collector almost universally, when the Fior and the other restaurants wanted to take on the IRS, the restaurant industry was ambivalent. During this period, Patricia Breslin was Executive Director of the Golden Gate Restaurant Association that represents the interests of restaurateurs in the nine counties of the San Francisco Bay Area.

"The reaction (of members) was mixed. Nobody likes to tackle the IRS. There was trepidation. Are we knocking on a door that is going to slam in our faces? Or are we going to succeed and finally get a victory of being acknowledged that we have no control over tips at all?" Breslin said.

The Fior filed suit in U.S. District Court for the Northern District of California. It was an issue of national attention for 200,000 restaurants and their employees and patrons, and the press covered it every step of the way.

Bob told the *Wall Street Journal*, "We're held to a standard that's completely absurd." [2]

The Fior won the suit in district court.

"We won in every court at the district level in the initial cases," said Bob of the Fior and the three other establishments. Three other cases were reversed on appeal, but the Fior's case was not. The Fior won at the Appellate Court level, a victory considered a tremendous one. The IRS then pressed for an en banc ruling, requiring the judges of the U.S. Court of Appeals in the Ninth District to rule on the Fior's case. The government's case was rejected.

Judges Alex Kozinksi and Andrew Kleinfeld wrote in a majority opinion: "While each employee knows how much he receives in tips, the restaurant does not. Employees, moreover, have an obligation to maintain records of their tip income. Forcing the employer to pay the price for its employees' dereliction is simply not the only nor the best way the IRS may proceed."

However, the IRS pressed further, and its lawyers petitioned the U.S. Supreme Court to take up the case, claiming the agency had the right to levy taxes on employers for an amount for Social Security that the IRS had estimated.

Bob and his partners were irate at this move and what they perceived as an injustice, but they were also confident of the Fior's position, based on its success in court to that point. The restaurant engaged the services of Tracy J. Power, of Power and Power, a Washington D.C. attorney who had 16 years' experience in going head to head with the IRS over issues of tipping. This argument would be her first before the Supreme Court.

By this time, the three other cases had failed, so the NRA (National Restaurant Association), the CRA and the local GGRA put their support behind the Fior. Despite the GGRA's original hesitancy, Breslin said, "We weighed the pros and cons of it and we felt the victory would be so important for our industry that we at the GGRA determined that we would contribute in our limited ways toward funding this. We were only able to give $10,000 from the Association, but many of our members contributed independently."

The NRA complained that by making employers liable for workers who failed to report tips to the IRS's satisfaction, the service "pits the restaurateurs against their own employees, putting restaurants in an untenable position." At the appeals level, the NRA had filed an amicus curiae brief, donated $25,000 to the Fior's legal expenses and assisted the Fior's attorney. For the Supreme Court battle, the NRA filed another amicus brief, acted as co-counsel along with Tracy Power and supported the Fior to the tune of $90,000.

Besides the NRA and the GGRA, the CRA and numerous independent restaurants supported the Fior's expenses for the case. By the third quarter of 2002, Bob estimated the case had cost about $500,000 of which the Fior had paid by itself about a fifth. All this effort and these resources were to protest the unjust levying of a $23,000 tax and even more important, however, to object to the IRS's seemingly limitless power over the industry.

After having won the previous decisions and feeling right was on their side, the Fior partners and their supporters felt confident that the Supreme Court Justices would rule in their favor. The court heard the case in April of 2002. The hearing brought to light conundrums and dilemmas posed by the law and by the IRS that the justices did nothing to resolve.

Justice Sandra Day O'Connor repeatedly asked Assistant Attorney General Eileen O'Connor (no relation) how an employer could challenge the IRS's assessments of tips that employees had not reported.

This would seem patently reasonable -- that the employer had every right to challenge an assessment of tips that was based on questionable estimate practices.

Attorney O'Connor did not answer the question directly other than by reading a section that she said defines "what is a tax," and assuming a professorial manner honed at Georgetown and George Mason Laws Schools. [3]

The Fior's lawyer, Power reasoned that it was not logical to enforce a tax on tips when there is no record the tips were ever given. When Justice Anthony M. Kennedy asked if she knew of any precedent for her position in case law, she conceded she did not.

Later, Powers elaborated that "Congress passed a law (referring to Social Security taxes) on individual employees based on what we know those individuals made." However, she observed, this is a far different situation when the IRS wants to assess the employer for all the employees collectively and estimating what no one knows they earned.

The Washington Times captured a telling moment in the hearing:

Justice Kennedy said the IRS seemed to be shifting the burden onto restaurants that are not in as good a position as the employee or the IRS to know the facts. Miss O'Connor (the Government's attorney) responded that restaurants could subpoena workers who do not file required reports.

IRS SERVES HEAPING BILL

Based on tip percentages from credit card sales, the IRS concluded that tip income was roughly 14.5 percent of the restaurant's total gross receipts — cash and credit — for the two years in question.

That equaled an estimated $156,545 and $147,529 of unreported tip income, respectively, for 1991 and 1992, the IRS concluded.

At a 7.65 percent rate, the IRS billed the restaurant an additional $11,976 for 1991 and $11,286 for 1992 to cover Federal Insurance Contribution Act taxes for the restaurant's 30 tip earners.

The government made no effort to collect the unpaid taxes from the tip earners, nor did it credit the taxes to the individual workers' credit histories.

Bob Larive, co-owner of the Italian restaurant in the heart of The City's bustling North Beach neighborhood, said he and others spent about $500,000 battling the IRS, an agency he said was practicing "thuggery."

"We're not fighting over $23,000," he said. "We're fighting something that is wrong."

Larive and his supporters said the taxes should be based on individual audits of the employees, not speculation.

"Such folly circumvents the wisdom of Congress that determinations about tip income be made on an individual basis," said Peter Kilgore, an attorney for the National Restaurant Association.

Federal officials declined comment. But in briefs to the high court, the federal government said the IRS was authorized to estimate the amount of Social Security taxes.

Solicitor General Theodore Olson also told justices that, if the IRS were to audit individual tip earners from an eating establishment, its audits would be based on assumptions as well.

To claim or not claim: Bob Larive, one of the owners of Fior d'Italia, stands in the bar near the entrance to his eatery in North Beach. Fior d'Italia, one of the nation's 170,000 restaurants with tipped employees, is challenging an extra $23,000 Social Security tax that was calculated on estimates.

ERIC RISBERG/AP

Fior d'Italia leads battle on tip tax

By David Kravets
Associated Press

SAN FRANCISCO — Fior d'Italia, one of the nation's oldest Italian restaurants and a veteran of California's Gold Rush, has survived devastating earthquakes and a fire. It has even operated out of a tent.

Now the 115-year-old establishment is fighting perhaps a larger force: the Internal Revenue Service.

In a dispute closely followed by the restaurant industry, the U.S. Supreme Court on Monday heard arguments in a case expected to resolve how the nation's restaurants pay Social Security taxes on their employees' tips — which the IRS said totaled $14.31 billion in 1999.

Fior d'Italia, one of the country's 170,000 restaurants with tipped employees, is challenging an extra $23,000 Social Security tax that was calculated on estimates.

The intricate case hinges on an IRS policy in which the agency levied Social Security taxes on audited restaurants based on assumptions of the tips workers earn, rather than the actual amount.

Restaurants must pay 7.65 percent Social Security taxes on the amount of tips their employees generate. The employee also must pay 7.65 percent of the total.

In Fior d'Italia's case, a San Francisco-based federal appeals court ruled last year the IRS cannot estimate how much a restaurant owes in Social Security taxes.

The 9th U.S. Circuit Court of Appeals ruled the IRS must audit the tip earners and not "slap the employer with assessments based on ... estimates." But other circuits have sanctioned the practice of estimating, forcing the nation's highest court to resolve the conflict.

During an audit, the IRS found a 14.49 percent tip rate on Fior d'Italia's 1991 credit card sales and a tip rate of 14.29 percent for the following year.

Tips shown on credit card sales alone totaled $364,786 in 1991 and $338,161 for 1992.

But the restaurant reported its employees showed tips from credit cards and cash of $247,181 for 1991 and $220,845 for 1992.

'You're suggesting he should fire the employee, so he can be sued for wrongful discharge, so he can subpoena information and give it to you?' Justice Kennedy asked. [4]

This ludicrous suggestion did not sway the Justices. The Court rendered its decision June 17, 2001. It ruled in favor of the IRS. In a six-to-three decision, the Justices said that the IRS had the right to make an estimate of what workers owe and a right to penalize the employer if the employees underreport their tips. That the employees might be penalized was never entertained in the arguments.

Justices Breyer, Rehnquist, Stevens, O'Connor, Kennedy and Ginsburg deemed :

The fact that the employer is placed in an awkward position by the requirement that it pay taxes only on tips reported by its employees, even when it knows those reports are inaccurate, does not make aggregate estimation unlawful. [5]

Despite the fact that the agency's method of estimating taxes will probably result in an overstatement of the entrepreneur's tax responsibility, this does not show "that the IRS's aggregate estimating method falls outside the bounds of what is reasonable," they decided. Neither, they said, is this an abuse of the agency's power.

Justices Souter, Scalia and Thomas filed a dissenting opinion, saying the ruling "saddles the employer with a burden unintended by Congress." They wrote: "It seems clear that Congress did not mean to solve (the problem of underreporting tips) by allowing the IRS to use its assessment power to shift the problem to employers." [6]

Dumbstruck and Dumfounded

The majority ruling might leave philosophers scratching their heads about the nature of reality. The justices said in effect that what the IRS says goes regardless of its accuracy, reasonableness, or justice. The Fior, its patrons and fellow entrepreneurs in the industry were amazed almost to the point of speechlessness. They thought the decision was anything but fair and accurate and in no way minimized the burden on employers. Quite the opposite was true. The decision left all employers of establishments where tips are customary in the position of having to pressure their workers or else face an IRS audit.

NRA general counsel Peter Kilgore said of the decision, "The threat against the industry is hanging low and heavy. (The decision) has caused great concern."

Unfortunately, the IRS doesn't worry about burden or concern.

Bob told the *Washington Post*, that "We hoped a decision in our favor would force the IRS to do their job the right way and not resort to threats and guesses to coerce taxes out of restaurants and employees, but now we will probably have to go to Congress for clarification of their original intent and for relief from the IRS's draconian methods."

Breslin said of the GGRA and its members, "We were completely shocked at the outcome. The dissenting argument made so much sense. We felt all we can do is educate the legislators and proceed to Capitol Hill."

Not long after the decision was announced, Bob and the NRA approached Congressmen Wally Herger (R-Cal) and John Tanner (D-Tenn.) to clarify Congress's intent on the subject of gratuities. Kathleen O'Leary, the NRA's Director of Tax Policy, reported that the lawmakers had drafted the Tips Tax Fairness Act for this purpose. It was introduced to Congress in September 2002.

All the months leading up to and months after the decision, the Fior was flooded with wishes of support from patrons and from the hospitality and food industries. The restaurant received letters of support, enhanced by donations.

The following letter, dated July 19, 2002, included a check for $100. It is typical of the many that the Fior received leading up to and long after the Supreme Court decision.

I have followed with great interest your resolve to receive fairness and justice from the IRS. It's truly scary what they, in this case, and others are doing to our freedoms. It was Winston Churchill that said "All that's needed for evil to triumph is for good men to do nothing."

My brother Mike died in a foxhole on Okinawa, fighting to keep our freedom. Once in a while, unfortunately not often enough, along comes a person like you that seems to understand to be free is a never-ending fight.

Please accept our modest contribution to your (our cause).

Albert Del Masso, President
Bay Cities Produce Co., Inc.
Oakland, California

Attorney Power also received a flood of queries. "Restaurant companies have called to discuss their practices," she said.

NRA chief counsel Kilgore congratulated the Fior for fighting the good fight: "Hats off to the Fior. They carried the fight from the local level to the Supreme Court." He said the decision would be a particular hardship for the smaller restaurants and might even put some out of business. But Power thought that in the long run, the restaurant industry as a whole would survive.

"We're going to have to see what the IRS does. I think the restaurant industry position is very strong. The IRS needs the restaurant industry to get tip reporting up...The end result is employers will be more involved in the employees' tip reporting processes, and employers should become more aware of tipping practices in their restaurants to protect themselves," he said.

While the IRS had its way, the case was a great benefit to the Fior. The restaurant's name became known nationwide, splashed across the headlines of the best newspapers and journals of the country. Surely Angelo Del Monte and Armido Marianetti would have been horrified at the conflict that created the Fior's notoriety, but they would have approved of the result.

GNOCCHI

For light, tender gnocchi, use freshly baked russet potatoes, because their low moisture content requires less flour. Alternatively, you can boil the potatoes until very tender in lightly salted water. Forming the gnocchi takes a bit of practice, but it's fun, especially if you have the traditional wooden paddle used to make the grooves. If you don't, simply use the tines of a fork. It's a good idea to test-cook one gnocchi to see if you have added enough flour to your dough so that they hold together.

4 russet potatoes (about 2 pounds)
1 egg, lightly beaten
1/2 cup freshly grated Parmesan cheese
1 1/4 to 2 cups all-purpose flour
1/2 teaspoon kosher salt

Preheat the oven to 350F. Line a large baking sheet with parchment paper.

Prick the potatoes with a fork a few times. Place on the oven rack and bake until completely tender, 40 minutes to 1 hour, depending on their size. Halve the potatoes and, using a small spoon, scoop out the hot potato flesh. Press through a potato ricer into a large bowl, or place in a bowl and mash until smooth with a potato masher.

Make a well in the center of the potatoes and add the egg, Parmesan, 1 1/4 cups of the flour, and salt. Using a fork, gradually stir the potatoes into the contents of the well, pulling them in from the sides, until all the ingredients are combined. Knead the mixture until it forms a soft, smooth dough. Continue adding flour 1/4 cup at a time until the dough is no longer sticky and holds together. Turn out onto a lightly floured work surface. Divide the dough into 8 to 10 portions; roll each portion into ropes 1/2 inch thick. Cut each rope into 1-inch pieces.

To make the traditional grooves on your gnocchi, gently press the tines of a fork into the top of a dumpling – as if trying to squash a pea – and with very gentle pressure, push the gnocchi away from you, rolling the gnocchi about a half turn and lifting the pressure on the fork as you finish. The fork will leave little grooves. Transfer to the prepared

baking sheet. (It may take a few tries to get the pressure and rolling technique down; be patient while you get the hang of it, and re-roll the gnocchi for another attempt if necessary.) Repeat with the remaining gnocchi. Let dry at room temperature for about 1 hour.

Bring a large pot of salted water to a boil; reduce the heat to maintain a simmer. Add a handful of the gnocchi and cook until they float back up to the surface. Using a slotted spoon, immediately transfer to a bowl. Repeat to cook the remaining gnocchi.

For sauce, refer to Ragu for pasta on (P. 97).

Serves four.

Epilogue
They're Just Not Going to Let Go.

Founder Angelo Del Monte and his daughter, Eva Del Monte Biagini, still live on near the Fior d'Italia.

Angelo's grandchildren sponsored the casting of a bronze plaque commemorating him and his legendary restaurant. The plaque is embedded in the pavement on Stockton Street half a block from the current Fior. It is one of the Barbary Coast Trail series of medallions, a program of the San Francisco Museum & Historical Society.

Meanwhile, two blocks away at 700 Vallejo Street near Powell Street stands a public parking structure, the Chinatown/North Beach Garage. As part of a public art program of the San Francisco Arts Commission unveiled in 2002, local artists Harrel Fletcher and Jon Rubin scouted out portraits of neighborhood ancestors. They borrowed photographs of North Beach and Chinatown ancestors, scanned them onto ceramic steel and emblazoned them onto the façade of the building.

One of those is the face of Angelo,s daughter, Eva. It is a detail from her family photograph that hangs in the Fior.

Angelo and Eva are just not going to let go of the Fior.

INSALATA DI CAPESANTE (SCALLOP SALAD)

Use a hot, hot heavy iron pan to sear the scallops most effectively.

Vinaigrette
1/4 cup extra virgin olive oil
2 to 3 tablespoons freshly squeezed lemon juice
1 1/2 teaspoons chopped fresh tarragon
Salt and freshly ground black pepper

4 cups frisée, torn into bite-size pieces
24 kalamata olives, pitted
1 pint cherry tomatoes, halved, or 4 heirloom tomatoes, coarsely chopped
12 large scallops
2 tablespoons olive oil
Salt and freshly ground black pepper
Lemon wedges, for garnish

To make the vinaigrette: In a small bowl, whisk together the olive oil and lemon juice. Stir in the tarragon; season to taste with salt and pepper.

In a large bowl, combine the frisée, olives, and tomatoes with 1 to 2 tablespoons of the vinaigrette; toss to mix. Set aside.

Using paper towels, dry the scallops and season with salt and pepper. In a large, cast-iron sauté pan, heat the olive oil over medium-high heat until very hot. Arrange the scallops in a single layer in the hot pan and cook until the insides are opaque and the outsides are golden brown, about 2 minutes per side.

To serve: Divide the salad evenly among 4 serving plates. Place 3 of the scallops on each of the salads and drizzle with the remaining vinaigrette. Garnish with the lemon wedges and serve immediately.

Serves four

The World according to Chef Gianni

Gianfranco Audieri was born in Milan in 1937. At the age of fourteen – as was common at the time – he decided to pursue a trade rather than to continue his studies. Through a family connection, he ended up working at the Savini, one of the premier restaurants and the oldest one in Milan. It was located in its chic and historic plaza, the Galleria.

Starting at the very bottom, Gianni spent over a year cleaning string beans, potatoes, carrots and celery to the point of exasperation. Fortunately, his employer saw a spark in him and sent him to hotel school for 12 months in the Piedmont city of Stresa.

A few months back from school, the Savini management sent Gianni to Lausanne, Switzerland to learn French and French cooking. Thus began his travels. Gianni then worked in the Channel Islands and London before jumping into a cruise ship's kitchen where he spent almost two years sailing between New York, the Caribbean and South America.

Since that time, private clubs and upscale restaurants have formed the bulk of Gianni's career. For several years, Gianni worked for Holiday Inn Resorts, sometimes a food and beverage manager and sometimes charged with opening new restaurants in hotels under construction in the U.S. and Latin America. Eventually, he moved to Southern California where he invested in and managed several dining spots.

In the early 1980s, Gianni received an invitation to work at the Fior as a chef, when the Fior was under the ownership of Armanino, the Nibbis, Ramorino and Pantaleoni.

San Francisco had been suffering through a drought. "The day I arrived, it was raining like crazy," he recalled, reasoning it was a good omen. Chef Stelvio Storace put Gianni in charge of the kitchen and purchases. A year later, Stelvio left. Achille Pantaleoni, who spent a lot of time in the kitchen and had seen Gianni's work, suggested to the Nibbis that they promote Gianni to the position of head chef. They did and Gianni proceeded to make changes.

He had found the Fior at first a little bigger than restaurants of his experience but he was ready for the challenge. He readjusted his method of cooking, presentation and menu to suit the Fior's tradition and clientele. He altered about 50 percent of the menu and removed the German, French and Portuguese wine entries. He adjusted the wine list so it presented 60 percent Californian and 40 percent Italian labels, with the exception of Dom Perignon champagne.

The new chef also developed a philosophy about the type of cuisine the Fior was offering and the market it was targeting. The Fior's fare "is made to be good but not excellent." He said, "I don't have enough personnel to make it excellent. We do not have a kitchen large enough to make it excellent. If we served 100 and below, we could do it; but I can't and we don't charge that type of price. I make a very good cuisine for the price," he said proudly.

While Gianni strove to keep Fior offerings authentically Italian, he also took advantage of native products. "I would never allow garlic bead or meatballs in this place because it is not Italian. But I would allow avocado because we are in California, and salmon, because we have a lot of salmon in California," he said.

Chef Gianfranco Audieri stirs the cauldrons that hold the Fior's aromatic sauces.

Courtesy Tom Vano

159

The Fior menu presents about 20 varieties of pasta and eight veal dishes. Gianni always makes rabbit, quail, and venison choices available because they are low in fat. "When we cook the venison, it is fast-cooked in olive oil; the olive oil is thrown away. The meat is put in a pepper sauce, no fat, and a drop of cream. This is to appeal to Americans who want to lose weight," he said.

Although he felt he had to appeal to local tastes as well as the availability of local food products, Gianni also felt he'd made the modern Fior menu more truly Italian than before. "When I came the menus were really based on American Italian cuisine versus now when the menu is as close to Italian as possible," he said. "Olive oil for bread, I just didn't want to put it on the table. In Italy, we never use it except at harvest season; that's the only time we use it. But the people say, 'Where is the olive oil?' it became very hard for the waiters from a service point of view. So finally I said, 'All right, put it on the table.' Now only 5 percent of the people ask for butter."

He also pondered how, in recent years, the more educated, better-traveled public has become exposed to foods in Italy that heretofore were unknown to any except Italian-Americans here. For instance, the liqueur grappa, is distilled from the leavings of grapes pressed for wine. Foccaccia, a fried bread, and polenta or corn meal, were and still are in Italy the foods of the poor. When the Larives and their partners bought the Fior, they encouraged Gianni to continue his approach. A year later, they invited him to become a partner and he accepted.

The History of Italian Food

The cuisines of Italy and Europe changed with the discovery of the Americas. The process took about 300 years, starting around 1750. A lot of the products we think of as European did not exist in Europe at all, such as the potato. Gianni explained:

Without the potato, we would never have heard of the Irish famine of 1800. We would not have gnocchi. Corn too took a big foothold in Italy, though nowhere else in Europe. We wouldn't have polenta without it. Peppers did not exist in Europe. Can you imagine Italian salad or peperonata or caponata without peppers?

String beans, in fact, all beans period ,with the exception of ceci (garbanzo beans) or favas or lentils emerged with the discovery of

the New World. All the rest of the beans did not exist. Imagine minestrone without beans. Pumpkin and squash did not exist in Europe either. No zucchini either.

Take tomatoes. The first physical evidence that Italians used tomatoes came from a recipe around 1798 or '99…. It took that long for people to appreciate the tomato. First, they thought it was a poisonous plant because it belonged to the belladonna family, which is very poisonous. It took botanical people that long to finally make people realize it was a very good fruit and good tasting with vitamins. Originally it was yellow and became red through hybridization.

Cooking in Italy before the New World consisted of cabbage as a vegetable, root, rutabaga, celery, onion, and garlic, a lot of pine nuts for sauces, raisins, olives and olive oil.

Italian cookery for the general population has emphasized pork, rabbit, squab and pigeon, animals that require no pasture and inexpensive fodder. Gianni remarked:

Beef is very difficult to grow because there is little pasture in Italy and only the really rich people had the pasture…Chickens were raised more for the eggs than for meat, until the hen was too old to have any more eggs, then it was put in the pot.

Gianni's early life in Northern Italy gave a context to his later research about the history of food and cuisine. He remembered his summers on a rustic farm and the co-operative organization of Italian agriculture.

All my summer times from the age of nine till sixteen, just before I went to hotel school, I spent on my grandmother's and grandfather's farm, which was about 200 km from Milan toward the border near the Dolomites. Their cuisine was pre-Colombian because that's how they were living, although they had a Vespa. There was no electricity, no water. You had to go pick it up. Water was used for drinking and cooking but not for personal washing . If you wanted to bathe, you had to go down to the spring.

I saw a lot of what it must have been like in the 17th century. There was no asphalt anywhere, no tractors. Everything was horse- or mule- or donkey-driven. Cows were for producing milk, not to be slaughtered for the meat. Chickens were there for the purpose of producing eggs. With the eggs, they got money. I remember my grandmother picking up the eggs in the morning, and in the afternoon, taking them to the co-op to sell or to keep (the proceeds) on account for her. My grandfather had six cows. He would milk in the morning, put a big jug out and somebody from the co-op would come with a cart to pick up the jug, which held about 50 liters. That's where their money came from. I remember somebody coming to the small hamlet. It was not even a village. He would come on Friday on a bike and he had fish in a box with some ice in it. Most of the fish were sardines. My grandparents followed a strict religious diet on Friday: Fish at nighttime and, during the day, salad with boiled eggs.

My grandmother used to take care of the garden, which consisted of all the vegetables you could need. Of course, tomatoes now, celery, lettuces, a gigantic beautiful fig tree right next to the outhouse. There was no paper to clean your rear end. So you used a fig leaf. One side was smooth, the other was rough. Whatever you were doing, you were using figs at the same time. It showed me the respect for fresh fruit and fresh vegetables. I always like a fresh tomato, just a tomato with a little salt. It's a great afternoon snack instead of scones or pizza or whatever.

There were two pigs, in the springtime two little piglets. By November, they were about 200 pounds. They slaughtered them and used the meat for prosciutto, salami and the blood was kept for blood pudding. The belly was kept for pancetta. That would last them through the winter. All the fat was rendered to use for cooking. Up north there is no olive oil, because it was to be sold, not to be consumed. To my grandparents, it was money, a luxury item. We didn't use that. So we used the fat of the pig.

My grandmother had pigeons in a pigeon coop and she had rabbits. I remember my grandpa before leaving for the field around 5:30 in the morning. He would say, 'What will we eat tonight? How about a rabbit?' So she would go in the cage, pick a rabbit, skin it, cut him and cook it. She would prepare chicken in the same way, but chicken was for Sunday only.

Is Pasta Really Chinese?

Many people believe that Italy's pasta was an import from China, thanks to the 13th century adventurer Marco Polo. But Gianni disagrees. He referred to the records of pasta's existence before Polo's

voyage and reasoned: "There is an instrument in Italy called *chitarra*, which is two pieces of board with string attached to it which are very tight. A housewife would make water and flour mixture and put it on this chitarra and pass it through and you get something similar to spaghetti. So my feeling is pasta is from Italy," he said.

Noodles are a richer version of pasta; they are flour and eggs versus flour and water. What Marco Polo brought back was noodles, or fettuccini, to a public already using pasta, he maintains.

"The difference between pasta and fettuccine is nutrition. Noodles showed that you were richer. In Italy, it was very important to show you were well off up to the 16th century. Why was saffron such a popular item in Italy? Because whoever used it would just think it is the most expensive spice in the world and it still is. But they used it because it made the food look gold. You used saffron to impress people," he said.

Florence is the demarcation point between the pasta-eaters and the fettuccine-eaters. "The north could afford (noodles), the south couldn't afford them," he said.

Rice too was subject to this division of classes. Rice has always been common in Northern Italy. But the south didn't have the tremendous water resources needed to grow the grain so they didn't use rice.

"Another thing Italians decided to do was to introduce carp into the rice fields. Rats are in the rice fields (which the carp feed on). By the time the harvest is in, you have a lot of very big fat carps with the rice. One of the dishes we have in Lombardy we call *carpa in carpione*. Make a sauce with onions, anchovy, sage, vinegar and water. Sauté these until you are left with onion. Put this on top of the carp. It makes a good appetizer. Eels are the same. We have used every single animal because of Italy's historic poverty," the chef explained.

Gianni attributed the poverty during the Renaissance to the stranglehold on the economy held by royalty, the aristocracy and the church. The upper classes controlled trade and commerce and the church supported the upper classes. Peasants had little room to be choosy. They "had to learn to eat anything and everything," he commented, including tripe, salted cod (baccalà), snail and eel.

NOTES

Chapter One

(1) Deanna Paoli Gumina, *The Italians of San Francisco 1850-1930* (New York: Center for Migration Studies, 1999), p. 1.

(2) Graceann Walden, *Bay Food*, (April 1990).

Chapter Two

(1) Colonel Albert S. Evans, *À La California: Sketch of Life in the Golden State.* Database online at the Virtual Museum of the City of San Francisco

(2) The Virtual Museum of the City of San Francisco, http://www.sfmuseum.org.

Chapter Three

1. Malcolm E. Barker, *Three Fearful Days: San Francisco Memoirs of the 1906 Earthquake and Fire* (San Francisco: Londonborn Publications, 1998), p. 38.
2. Ibidem, p. 49
3. Ibid, pp. 114-115
4. Virtual Museum of the City of San Francisco, http://www.sfmuseum.org.
5. Ibid.
6. Barker, Op. cit. p. 49.
7. Ibid, pp. 304-305.

Chapter Four

1. Virgilio Luciani, *Un Italiano in America,* (Pescia: A. Benedetti, 1956), pp. 39-40.
2. Ibid, p. 41.
3. Ibid, pp. 41-42.
4. Doris Muscatine, *A Cook's Tour of San Francisco* (New York: Chas. Scribners Sons, 1963), pp. 256-257.
5. Ibid., pp. 257-258.

Chapter Five

1. Clifford James Walker, *One Eye Closed, the Other Red, the California Bootlegging Years* (Barstow, CA: Back Door Publishing, 1999), p. xiv.
2. Loc. cit.
3. Loc. cit.
4. Op. cit., p. 28.
5. *San Francisco Chronicle*, October 26, 1967.
6. Clifford J. Walker, Op. cit., p. 56.
7. Virtual Museum of the City of San Francisco, http://www.sfmuseum.org.
8. Walker, Op. cit., p. 145.

Chapter Six

1. John Ardoin, *Opera by the Bay,* http://www.pbs.org/wnet/gperf.html/writermaincredit.f4.html.
2. Philip Nobile, "Una Vita Piu Nobile," *I-AM*, vol. I, No. 5; March 1977.

Chapter Seven

1. Marquis James and Bessie R. James, *Biography of a Bank* (San Francisco: Bank of America N.T.& S.A., 1982) p. 285.
2. William H. Mullins, *The Depression and the Urban West Coast 1929-1933: Los Angeles, San Francisco, Seattle and Portland* (Bloomington: Indiana University Press, 1991) p. 11.
3. Doris Muscatine, Op. cit., p. 258.
4. Ibid.
5. Ruth Thompson and Louis Hanges, *Eating around San Francisco* (San Francisco: Suttonhouse Ltd., 1937), p. 51.
6. Mullins, Op. cit., p. 9.
7. Ibid.
8. Kenneth Starr, *Endangered Dreams* (New York: Oxford University Press, 1995), pp. 110-111.

Chapter Eight

1. Muscatine, Op. cit., p. 256.
2. Edith Shelton and Elizabeth Field, *Let's Have Fun in San Francisco*, A Handbook to the City (San Francisco, self-published by Shelton, 1939), p. 23.
3. Thompson and Hanges, loc. cit.
4. Jerry Flamm, *Good Life in Hard Times, San Francisco in the 20s and 30s,* (San Francisco: Chronicle Books, 1999), p. 30.
4. Op cit., p. 51.
5. Op cit., p. 55.

Chapter Nine

1. Virtual Museum of the City of San Francisco, http://www.sfmuseum.org.
2. Ibid.
3. Ibid.
4. Ibid.
5. James O. Clifford, "Italian Americans persecuted during WWII," Associated Press, Dec 18, 1999.
6. John Mariani, *America Eats out* (New York: William Morrow and Company, 1991) p. 157.
7. Virtual Museum of the City of San Francisco, Op. cit.

Chapter Eleven

1. *Pacific Coast Review*, May 1956, pp. 134, 136 and 181.
2. Angelo M. Pellegrini, *Americans by Choice,* (New York, The Macmillan Company, 1956), pp. 33-34.
3. Op. cit., p.34.
4. Ibid.
5. Op. cit., p.35.

Chapter Twelve

1. *San Francisco Call Bulletin*, "Fior D'Italia One of City's Oldest Cafes," February 16, 1952.
2. *Pacific Coast Review*, November 1959, pp. 28-30.
3. J. L. Pimsleur, "The Oldest Italian Restaurant Sports a Handsome New Face," *San Francisco Chronicle*, August 9, 1959; p.16.

Chapter Thirteen

1. Stanton Delaplane, *The San Francisco Chronicle*, October 16, 1967.
2. Pimsleur, op. cit.

Chapter Sixteen

1. Oscar Zeta Acosta, *The Autobiography of a Brown Buffalo* and *The Revolt of the Cockroach People* (New York: Vintage, 1989), p. 59-60.
2. Patricia Brooks, "Pasta? Can't manage without it; on the road to a good meal," *USA TODAY, June*, 14, 1989.

Chapter Seventeen

1. Herb Caen, "The Galloping Gamut," *San Francisco Chronicle*, October 19, 1995, p. B1.
2. Alan Liddle, "Fast-food veteran buys Fog City landmark," *Nation's Restaurant News,* September 3, 1990, pp. 3 and 47.
3. Stu Bykofsky, "Stu prowls San Francisco," *Philadelphia Daily News,* Oct. 23, 1995.
4. Jimmy Rubino, Jr. and Ted Taylor, *Ralph's Italian Restaurant, 100 Years and 100 Recipes*, XLibris, 2000.

Chapter Eighteen

1. Paul Mantee, *In Search of the Perfect Ravioli*, (New York: Ballantine Books, 1991), p 5.
2. Dan Berger, "I Spilled a Lot of Soup on a Lot of Nice People," *Los Angeles Times,* March 4, 1993, pp. H26-27.
3. John T. Lescroart, *A Certain Justice* (New York: David I. Fine. 1995), P.244.
4. Lescroart, *Guilt* (New York: Delacorte Press, 1997), pp.1-2.

Chapter Twenty

1. Patricia Unterman, "S. F. Institution Needs Fresh Approach," *San Francisco Chronicle*, April 12, 1992.
2. "Eating in Michael Bauer's Town," *San Francisco*, August 2001.

Chapter Twenty-four

1. Herb Caen, *San Francisco Chronicle*, September 12, 1995.

Chapter Twenty-six

1) *San Mateo Times,* Feb. 13, 1992.

Chapter 30

1. The *San Francisco Chronicle,* "High Court Hears Case over Taxes on Tips," April 23, 2002.
2. The *Wall Street Journal*, "Justices Hand IRS a Victory on Unreported Tips," June 18, 2001.
3. *The Washington Times*, Supreme court pops 'question' to top IRS lawyer," April 28, 2002.
4. Ibid.
5. Docket 01-463, as reported in Facsnet.org on August 20, 2002. http:// facsnet.org
6. Ibid.

About the author

Courtesy Tom Vano

Francine Brevetti, a native of San Francisco, grew up in the city's Cow Hollow district. She remembers listening to her mother's stories of her father, Alberto Puccetti, who had worked at the finest Italian restaurant in San Francisco, the Fior d'Italia.

Brevetti is a long-time journalist who started her writing career in New York in the late 1970s with America's oldest daily, *The Journal of Commerce*. In 1985 she moved to Hong Kong, where she freelanced for almost 13 years. During that time she contributed to American, British, Australian and Asian English-language dailies, magazines and trade journals, mostly on matters of finance and foreign trade but also on travel. During that time she wrote a guidebook to China. She traveled often to the mainland and throughout Southeast Asia.

Brevetti stayed to see Hong Kong's reversion to China's sovereignty and came back to San Francisco at the end of 1997. She has been working for the *Oakland Tribune* since 1998 as a regional business writer.